D1601328

Globalization and Networked Societies

GLOBALIZATION
and Networked Societies

Urban-Regional Change in Pacific Asia

Yue-man Yeung

 University of Hawai'i Press ■ Honolulu

Library of Congress Cataloging-in-Publication Data

Yeung, Yue-man.

  Globalization and networked societies : urban-
regional change in Pacific Asia / Yue-man Yeung.

      p.   cm.

  Includes bibliographical references and index.

  ISBN 0–8248–2237–4 (cloth : alk. paper) —
ISBN 0–8248–2326–5 (pbk. : alk. paper)

      1. Urbanization—East Asia.   2. Regional
development—East Asia.   I. Title.

HT147.E18 Y48 2000

307.76´0954—dc21   00–020267

Printed by The Maple-Vail Book
Manufacturing Group.

To Ameda, Tao-ming, and Sze-mei,
who went and shared with me

Contents

Illustrations

TABLES

Preface

After a stint of over four years as university registrar, I returned to full-time academic pursuits in 1990. Fortuitously, this coincided with a coalescing global concern on urban issues in developing countries, as manifested in a number of global research projects and action programs. My previous professional involvement in and work on the subject allowed me to plunge right back into the midst of some of these landmark initiatives and respond to many requests for commissioned papers and conference presentations.

For several years after 1991, I was on the panel of advisers in two global initiatives. One was an ambitious and unprecedented research project known as the Global Urban Research Initiative (GURI), with the participation of twelve teams in all major developing regions involving fifty-five countries. It was a project funded by the Ford Foundation and coordinated by Richard Stren of the Centre for Urban and Community Studies at the University of Toronto. I was an adviser to the project and to the Asian components, a role that has enriched chapter 2 of this book, which focuses on globalization and world cities. This research network has completed its third phase.

Until 1996, I was also on the panel of advisers for the Urban Management Program (UMP) during its second phase, with funding provided by the United Nations Development Program (UNDP) and bilateral donors and the involvement of the World Bank and Habitat (United Nations Center for Human Settlements [UNCHS]) as executing agencies. My association with this global research and action program began after my appointment in 1991 by UNDP as one of its consultants to explore modalities to mount the second phase. Since the City Summit (Habitat II) held in Istanbul in June 1996, UMP has entered its third phase.

In addition, in 1991 the United Nations University (UNU) mounted a project that explored the interplay of globalization and the urban system along the western Pacific rim. The project focused on most world cities in that subregion of Asia, with the participation of some of the leading researchers and universities or research institutes to which they belonged. I coordinated this multicountry project with Fu-chen Lo of UNU. This association has resulted in two weighty volumes on the subject of world cities and globalization (Lo and Yeung, 1996, 1998).

My privilege as party to these global or regional research networks not only has taken me to many cities in the world and provided an updated understanding of their problems and policies but has also, through friendships and the exchange of information, greatly deepened my knowledge of cross-cultural urban research. It is hoped that some of that understanding is reflected in the pages that follow.

During the past several years, I had the singular good fortune of being invited by a large number of international agencies and research institutes to contribute to explicating and analyzing the emerging and evolving urban-regional change that has become a central part of socioeconomic life in Asia. While I have selected some pieces for inclusion in this publication, a companion volume, *Urban Development in Asia* (1998), encompasses other essays. For some of the chapters adapted in this book, I wish to register my thanks to the following national or international organizations for extending their invitations and for their support: the United Nations Educational, Scientific, and Cultural Organization (UNESCO), UNU, the Institute of East and West Studies (Yonsei University), the Sejong Institute (Korea), the Asian Development Bank, UNCHS, the University of Toronto, and *Cities*.

Although many of my works found here have been published, some of them appear in places that are more difficult to access than others. Thus, their assembly in a convenient form will facilitate easy reference to an important subject that is strongly impacting our lives at the dawn of the twenty-first century. In consolidating previously published materials into the same book, I have updated some of the earlier published pieces, redrawn maps, and redone tables. In addition, references to all the chapters are consolidated at the end of the book to eliminate redundancies and improve presentation.

My evolving interest in Asian cities and globalization has been shaped and nurtured by my association and collaboration with many friends. I wish to thank, in particular, Richard Stren, Fu-chen Lo, and Shabbir Cheema, whose research projects provided opportunities for me to learn and interact with leading scholars, such as Akin Mabogunje, Terry McGee, Lisa Peattie, Peter Rimmer, and the late Jorge Hardoy. I have benefited by working with Fu-chen Lo in the UNU research project. My understanding of globalization processes gradually assumed a much firmer economic foundation as the project progressed. It is my hope that this collection will contribute to an understanding of the dynamics and patterns of urban-regional change in the fastest growth region of the world.

Many friends and institutions have helped toward the realization of this book project. First, I am indebted to the Lippo Group in Hong Kong, which, since 1993, has been supporting the Urban and Regional Development in Pacific Asia Program of the Hong Kong Institute of Asia-Pacific Studies, The Chinese University of Hong Kong, with an annual grant. This enabled a Lippo Urban Fund to be established that supported some of the activities that are partly reflected in the pieces selected for this volume. J. P. Lee's continual enthusiasm and unflagging support in the program have been critical to its success and achievements. I also wish to express my deep appreciation to Janet Wong, who aided in my frequent communication with friends, international agencies, and research institutes and who typed the original research manuscripts. In addition, she was largely responsible for putting this volume together. Over the years, able and cheerful research assistance has been provided by the program through Irene Lai, Lui Siu-yun, Joanna Lee, Polly Chui, and Connie Tang. Chau Po-kok prepared the index. Too

See-lou of the Department of Geography drew all the maps and deserves full credit for their professional presentation.

This book in its present form represents a much improved and more coherent formatting of an earlier version. I wish to thank the helpful and constructive comments by two anonymous referees. Needless to say, I alone am responsible for any remaining inadequacies and shortcomings.

Above all, I dedicate this book to my family, who, over the years, have been most supportive and encouraging in a variety of ways to enable my undivided attention to be devoted to my academic pursuits. From Singapore to Hong Kong via Ottawa, our love for Asian cities has grown together.

Acknowledgments

I wish to thank the editors of several journals and the publishers of books in which earlier versions of some of these chapters first appeared for permission to make use of the material in this volume. Specific acknowledgment credit is made to the copyright holder for their permission to reprint the following materials.

Chapter 2 has drawn material, duly expanded and updated, from several of my essays on the subject that have been published as "Introduction," with Fu-chen Lo, in *Emerging World Cities in Pacific Asia,* ed. Fu-chen Lo and Yue-man Yeung (Tokyo: United Nations University Press, 1996), 1–13; "Globalization and World Cities in Developing Countries," in *Perspective on the City,* ed. Richard Stren and Judith K. Bell (Toronto: Centre for Urban and Community Studies, University of Toronto, 1995), 189–226; "An Asian Perspective on the Global City," *International Social Science Journal,* no. 147 (March 1996):25–31; and "Geography in the Age of Mega-Cities," *International Social Science Journal,* no. 151 (March 1997):91–104.

Chapter 3 builds on "Growth Triangles in Pacific Asia: A Comparative Perspective," in *Tumen River Area Development Project: The Political Economy of Cooperation in Northeast Asia, comp.* Lew Seok-Jin (Seoul: Sejong Institute, 1995), 57–80.

Chapter 4 is a further revised reproduction from my chapter of the same title in Myo Thant, Min Tang, and Hiroshi Kakazu, eds., *Growth Triangles in Asia: A New Approach to Regional Economic Cooperation,* 2nd ed. (Hong Kong: Oxford University Press, 1998), 123–162 (first edition published in 1994).

Chapter 5 is reproduced, with revisions, from my introductory essay in *Metropolitan Planning and Management in the Developing World: Shanghai and Guangzhou, China* (Nairobi: United Nations Center for Human Settlements, 1995), 3–25.

Chapters 6 and 7 are drawn, with updating and minor rewriting, from my introduction to two books: Y. M. Yeung and David K. Y. Chu, eds., *Guangdong: Survey of a Province Undergoing Rapid Change,* 2nd ed. (Hong Kong: The Chinese University Press, 1998), 1–21, and Y. M. Yeung and Sung Yun-wing, eds., *Shanghai: Transformation and Modernization Under China's Open Policy* (Hong Kong: The Chinese University Press, 1996), 1–23.

Chapter 8 is an updated and revised version of a chapter on "China and Hong Kong," in *Sustainable Cities: Urbanization and the Environment in International Perspective,* ed. Richard Stren, Rodney White, and Joseph Whitney (Boulder, Colo.: Westview Press, 1992), 259–280.

Chapter 9 is a slightly revised version of an article titled "Planning for Pearl City: Hong Kong's Future, 1997 and Beyond," *Cities* 14, no. 5 (October 1997):249–256.

Chapter 10 is an extensively revised, enlarged, and updated version based on a coauthored piece: T. G. McGee and Yue-man Yeung, "Urban Futures for Pacific Asia: Towards the 21st Century" in *Pacific Asia in the 21st Century,* ed. Yue-man Yeung (Hong Kong: The Chinese University Press, 1993), 47–67.

1 Overview

1   Pacific Asia in the Context of Globalization

The word "global" is not new, going back, in fact, several hundred years, in the sense that the world is being homogenized. The dialectics of this process is that the world is also being differentiated. The earliest global exchange revolved around a number of interlocking subsystems in the Old World from Europe to the Orient in the thirteenth century (Abu-Lughod, 1987). However, people's understanding of the world was limited and partial. It was not until Christopher Columbus, who discovered the New World, and Vasco da Gama, who circumnavigated the world in the fifteenth century, that we began to appreciate the true nature of the world. Since then, with scientific advances and technological progress, humankind has progressively reduced the friction of distance and telescoped time to such an extent that the world has, as a result, grown smaller. Time and distance have now essentially collapsed. The world in the last two decades of the twentieth century fundamentally and radically changed at such speed and on such scope never before witnessed. The challenge posed at the threshold of the third millennium is indeed enormous for governments and people all over the world.

Globalization, along with globalism, continues with its unrelenting and accelerating march as it draws more countries, cities, and people closer into interdependent relationships. It also draws them together into growing competition, increasing tension, and creative cooperation. In the process, contradictions emerge and abound as competition results in some nations and cities being winners or losers, a widening gap between the North and the South, and a potential conflict between sovereign nations and transnational corporations (TNCs).

This book attempts to tease out some of the salient elements of globalization, especially as it affects urban centers. This introductory overview goes beyond the globalization of economic production. Globalization and regionalization go hand in hand, and implications for regional development are addressed. As Asia has turned out to be the region that has visibly benefited the most from globalization, this chapter outlines some of the important changes that Asia has experienced, although subsequent chapters focus more specifically on China. China is a late developer on the Asian scene because its pace of development quickened only in the mid-1980s, when processes of globalization gathered momentum worldwide. The organization of this chapter is intentionally sketched on a wider canvas within which individual chapters of the volume can be situated.

GLOBALIZATION WRIT LARGE

Globalization is a multifaceted process that can be defined as the interconnectedness of capital, production, services, ideas, and culture on a worldwide scale. It is characterized by the hypermobility of some of these elements and in large volumes. The cross-border flows of capital, goods, labor, knowledge, and information are mediated primarily by multinational corporations (MNCs), which operate on the principles of comparative advantage and the maximization of varied factor endowments. Consequently, sovereign states are losing control over their domestic economies. Globalizing patterns add new complexity to international relations: They transcend, blur, and even redefine territorial boundaries (Mittelman, 1996:129). A borderless economy has emerged in many parts of the world (Ohmae, 1990). However, some would contend that this condition exists only in folklore, not in reality (H. Yeung,

1998a), and that the international economy is not global *yet* (Castells, 1996:97). Robert Boyer and Daniel Drache (1996) venture further by maintaining that

> the Fordist era opened the door of globalization, but a fully integrated world economy remained a distant reality and will not happen even during the next century. International forces will continue to influence national decisions more than ever, but they will not form a fully fledged alternative system. (13–14)

Many factors have facilitated the currency of globalization during the past two decades, but three may be mentioned here. One is the breathtaking technological change that has run the gamut of computers, electronics, robotics, telecommunications, information technology, biotechnology, and new materials. This has favored flexible production, with its emphasis on "just-in-time" requirements and resource saving. The former Fordist mode of production, typified by large-scale production and heavy capital outlay, has decreased in importance. The new technoeconomic paradigm has created a new geography of space, in particular, one of electronic space in which place and distance are gradually neutralized. It has also given rise to new centers of centrality and importance (Sassen, 1996). More important, technology, including organizational and managerial technology, is the major productivity-inducing factor. Productivity and competition are the actual determinants of technological innovation and productivity growth (Castells, 1996:80–81). In short, the world has experienced an information technology revolution prompting the emergence of informationalism as the material foundation of a new society (Castells, 1998:336).

The second factor is the propitious international political climate in which a general détente between the communist and Western camps in the late 1970s was followed by the sudden demise of communism in Eastern Europe and the Soviet Union in the late 1980s. The post–Cold War era has been conducive to the development of market economies, in which geoeconomics has taken precedence over geopolitics. However, in the Information Age successful governance has become enormously difficult in whatever political system. Three broad political forces, namely, communalism, nationalism, and internationalism, conjoin and collide simultaneously, with much of the developing world in transition from ideological to technocratic leadership (Scalapino, 1998).

The third factor, as a consequence of the previous two, is the general preference for regionalism and multilateralism, with an accent on free trade and open competition. The recent establishment of the North American Free Trade Agreement (NAFTA), a reenergized and united European Union, and the Asia-Pacific Economic Cooperation (APEC) and Pacific Economic Cooperation Council (PECC) movements in Asia are testimony to the realization of the goals of closer cooperation among countries.

Many dimensions of globalization touch on our lives in diverse ways. James Mittelman (1996) has summed this up well:

> The manifestations of globalization include the spatial reorganization of production, the interpenetration of industries across borders, the spread of financial markets, the diffusion of identical consumer goods to distant countries, massive transfers of population within the South as well as from the South and the East to the West, resultant conflicts between immigrant and established communities in formerly tight-knit neighborhoods, and an emerging worldwide preference for democracy. (2)

It has been submitted that globalization as currently experienced is a linear extension of what began in the fifteenth and sixteenth centuries. It is associated with modernization and the European model (Waters, 1995:4–5).

At this juncture, it is apposite to illustrate the nature of globalization in some quantitative measures to press home the magnitude of change that has been witnessed. The increasing interdependence among nations has been reflected in a steadily growing percentage of exports and imports in relation to gross domestic product (GDP) in almost every country. Between 1979 and 1989, international financial markets and international currency trading rapidly expanded, increasing six times during the period (Fardoust and Dhareshwar, 1990). Growing international integration of markets for goods, services, and capital is reflected by the fact that over the past two decades, world merchandise exports have doubled as a percentage of world output, from 10 to

20 percent. Services transacted internationally have risen from 15 to 22 percent. One in seven equity trades in today's world involves a foreigner as a counterparty. Sales by foreign affiliates of TNCs may now well exceed total world exports (Qureshi, 1996:30). The magnitude of change can equally be appreciated by reference to statistics at the country level. Between 1972 and 1992, twenty-five nations either exceeded $40 billion in exports or experienced a tenfold increase in their exports. The average industrial nation increased its exports more than ninefold in just 20 years. Among members of the Organization for Economic Cooperation and Development (OECD), Germany and France increased exports eight times, whereas Spain's exports exploded more than fifteen times. The gains were even more spectacular in East Asia, especially the newly industrializing economies (NIEs) of Hong Kong, Singapore, Taiwan and South Korea, and China, which saw average annual growth at more than 110 percent in exports (Savitch, 1996:43). However, the biggest challenge is just emerging. The move to market-oriented production in Latin America, Indonesia, India, and more parts of China and Southeast Asia is proceeding apace. This will likely put another 1.2 billion workers in developing countries into the worldwide product and labor markets over the next generation (Kennedy, 1996).

These statistics do fully convey the sense of rapidity and profoundness of change that has swept the world since the 1980s (Lo and Yeung, 1998). In this era of globalization, which melts national boundaries and intensifies competition, cities assume new roles and importance. The next chapter largely elucidates the expanding functions and centrality of cities in different geographical and regional settings. As Savitch (1996:55) has highlighted, cities become progressively delocalized and take up a place at the leading edge of the new social paradigm that preaches global action, market awareness, and entrepreneurship. However, cities in both developed and developing countries have come out differently in how globalization has affected them. Some have adjusted well and prospered as they meet new challenges and opportunities successfully. For example, prosperous cities in developed economies have restructured their economies from an earlier industrial base to finance, services, and information processing, otherwise known as "postindustrial employment" (Savitch, 1996:47). Saskia Sassen (1994a:55) emphasizes the role and expansion of producer services that cover diverse dimensions related to economic production with mixed business and consumer markets. In developing countries, the impact of globalization has been even more dramatic. By and large, countries and cities in Africa and, to a lesser extent, in Latin America have been adversely affected by rapid economic and technological changes that have not brought them into play as equal partners and competitors in the new global economy. In a network society, populations and territories deprived of value and interest for the dynamics of global capitalism are "switched off." This has resulted in the social exclusion and economic irrelevance of segments of societies, of areas of cities, of regions, and of entire countries, constituting what has been called "the Fourth World" (Castells, 1998:337).

It is clear from the foregoing that globalization is at once a process, an ideology, and a phenomenon that have brought uneven development with unprecedented prosperity as well as marginalizing consequences. In fact, the pros and cons of globalization and modernization have been debated strenuously in the past—in the 1890s, 1900s, and 1930s (Kennedy, 1996). The late twentieth century has been compared with the late nineteenth century in that both were characterized by overall fast growth, globalization, and convergence. By contrast, the years between 1914 and 1950 were typified by overall slow growth, deglobalization, and divergence. This is especially applicable to the OECD countries, where the gap in the living standard between rich and poor countries narrowed or converged in the two said periods (Williamson, 1996). This conclusion is paralleled by another study of the inequality of nations in which stages of uneven development are marked by divergence followed by convergence. The world economy must first achieve a certain critical level of integration before equalizing effects begin to be felt (Krugman and Venables, 1995).

The globalizing world is one that is as turbulent as it is full of promise. It has thrown up many contradictions and conflicts. One of the foremost contradictions is the conflict between zones of humanity integrated in the global division of labor and those excluded from it (Mittelman, 1996:18). This is underscored by the fact that some 80 percent of the more than five billion people in the world live outside global consumer networks (McMichael, 1996:27). Thus, globalization is "a process of uneven development that fragments as it coordinates" (Giddens, 1990:175). On the positive side, Mittelman (1996:231) depicts it as an ideology extolling the efficiency of free markets and offers the prospect of an open world economy in which actors compete in a positive-sum game in which all players are supposed to be able to win (also Svetlicic and Singer, 1996:vii). In this way, globalization is about opportunities arising from reorganizing governance, the economy, ideology, and culture throughout the world. Indeed, these are the main points of entry in any analysis of the contemporary world. The currency and financial crisis that has rocked much of the Asian economies since mid-1997 has dramatically and painfully demonstrated the perils of globalization (Y. Yeung, 1998a). Although signs of recovery were seen in early 1998, it is now more likely that Asian countries will take at least a few years before steady economic growth resumes (Y. Yeung, 1998b). Skeptics of globalization are even openly emphatic of its more gloomy aspects by asserting that

> globalization is essentially a negative phenomenon, destroying the sovereignty and cohesion of nation-states, and thereby depriving markets of the social and political guidance. . . . Globalization is not inevitable or irreversible; the global élite cannot look forward to steady improvement in its quality of life; a globalized economy will not remain stable or dynamic; training will not rescue the marginalized majorities from decline; and the restoration of national controls would not inevitably lead to disasters, even though, by now, substantial adjustment costs will have to be borne. (Bienefeld, 1996: 434–435)

GLOBALIZATION AND REGIONALIZATION

Because of the interpenetrative nature of globalization processes, a new regime of relationship between power and the division of labor, between nation-states and MNCs, and between national and international governance is being forged. Forces of globalization on the one hand complement and contradict forces of regionalization and localization on the other. Some students would contrast globalization of the world economy and economic integration with political disintegration. Globalization, being driven by centrifugal forces, and regionalization, being driven by centripetal forces, are thus mutually antagonistic (Svetlicic and Singer, 1996:20).

If globalization and regionalization are viewed as opposed processes, regionalization is often seen as a defensive strategy for the protection of local industries. At the same time, limited globalization (in the region) can also be achieved. Others regard regional trading blocs as a stepping-stone to a multilateral trading system (Svetlicic and Singer, 1996:23). Indeed,

> a peculiar paradox of the growing internationalization of the world-economy has been the stimulus it has provided to the destruction of regional-sectoral economies and the decentralization/localization of production facilities. New information and transportation technologies have made it possible to decentralize production operations to "cheaper" locations. (Knox and Agnew, 1991:368)

The emergence of trading blocs in the past two decades has been described as minilateralism, where multilateralism, insists Miriam Campanella (1993), has been deteriorating. Whatever the case, turbulence has been generated externally by transnational actors in monetary and financial volatility and internally, in OECD countries, in economic recession through maladaptations to new challenges of the global economy.

At the center of the debate on political power and governance is the role of the nation-state versus the global economy. The crux of the debate is whether present political forms, embodied in the nation-state, are adequate to cope with a global economy that has outgrown or is outgrowing national boundaries. After many struggles, the nation-state emerged to replace the feudal estate in the eighteenth century in Europe as the accepted and dominant political form (Tyler, 1993:32). For centuries, nation-states have been powerful engines of wealth creation, but recently they have been viewed as having become vehicles of wealth destruction. In their place, Kenichi Ohmae (1995a:xv) has advanced the notion of "region-states," which represent discrete, coherent participants in the global economy. As a rule, region-states center not on countries but on certain geographic areas or parts of a nation, such as the Tokyo area in Japan and the Bangalore area in India, or on contiguous areas of several nations or territories, such as Hong Kong, Taiwan, and the adjacent coastal area of China.

Some would argue that the world is drifting into one in which power and territory no longer coincide and in which the state can no longer hold the two together. In this situation, governance cannot function effectively unless there is a minimally coherent architecture of institutions and a division of labor between them that avoids significant gaps in governance. For example, how can international agencies be held accountable where world cities can manage their own affairs? The nation-state has not declined or become functionless but has changed its role radically and become a key part of a division of labor in governance (Hirst, 1998).

In a recent book on the Information Age, Manuel Castells (1997) reviews the power of the capitalist state and notes the increasing difficulty of government control over its economy. Moreover, computer-mediated communication, escaping the control of the nation-state and its management structure, is territorially differentiated. Even the question of legitimacy is raised, with strengthened allegiance to the nation's symbol (the flag) and growing disobedience to the state's institutions. Castells (1997) summarizes as follows:

> Bypassed by global networks of wealth, power, and information, the modern nation-state has lost much of its sovereignty. By trying to intervene strategically in this global scene, the state loses capacity to represent its territorially rooted constituency. In a world where multilateralism is the rule, the separation between nations and states, between the politics of representation and the politics of intervention, disorganizes the political accounting unit on which liberal democracy was built and came to be exercised in the past two centuries. (354)

Carried to its logical extreme, it can be argued that where the borders fall in a borderless world, regional economies sound the death knell for the nation-state (Ohmae, 1995b). However, Yue-man Yeung

(1995; also H. Yeung, 1998a) has countered by arguing that utility still exists in the nation-state polity and that the promotion of region-states should not preclude nation-states as functional entities, at least in the foreseeable future. Similarly, it has also been argued that the very process of internationalization reveals the persistence of national systems of innovations that are embedded in a web of interrelated political, educational, and financial institutions that are still effective in their ways and that cannot easily be copied or adapted (Boyer and Drache, 1996: 14). International corporate economic production may also have its pitfalls, as Gus Tyler (1993) reminds us:

> The natural inclination of any such [transnational] corporation is to do its work where wages and taxes are lowest, where tariff walls and subsidies are highest, and where governments disallow unions and allow child, or even slave, labour. . . . Viewed globally, the ultimate effect . . . is to convert the globe into a Dickensian England—a world of underpaid and unemployed people unable to buy what they produce. (30)

This is probably the worst scenario of a world dominated by TNCs. In reality, most of them are not heartless exploiters of labor in helpless distant lands. For example, what has taken place in Asia have been many forms of mutually beneficial economic cooperation between TNCs and host countries. The proliferation of export-processing zones in the region is evidence of how TNCs have helped propel national and regional economies.

Even more striking is the emergence of subregional zones of economic cooperation in Asia over the past two decades, where participating economies possess varied factor endowments and resource strengths. The two chapters in part 2 address some of the issues, challenges, and opportunities in what have been called growth triangles in the Asia-Pacific region. The triangular ties and manufacturing within the Southern China Growth Triangle of Hong Kong, Taiwan, and the southern provinces of Guangdong and Fujian are given special attention. In addition, the JSR Growth Triangle, involving Johor, Singapore, and the Riau Islands of Indonesia, mirrors a similar kind of symbiotic relationship. Singapore's development strategy of regionalization has been described as "inner globalization"; inner and outer globalization are seen to benefit each other, whereas outer globalization improves inner globalization (Mittelman, 1996:12).

Carried one step further, conflicts at the regional level can be manifested at the local level. In a study of the Islamic cities of Cairo, Istanbul, and Tehran, it has been shown that local responses have found expression in different ways toward global economic restructuring. Little doubt exists that globalization has sharpened the basic contradictions between the old and the new, secularism and religion, the West and the East, the haves and the have-nots. The outcome, unfortunately, has been rising inequities in which the rich and the poor are not coming closer but rather live in their own worlds, with the potential of future confrontation growing ever more real (El-Shakhs and Shoshkes, 1998).

THE RISE OF ASIAN ECONOMIES

The massive transformation that has been unleashed by globalization has been so speedy and fundamental that worldwide economic change has been described by some authors in the strongest possible terms—revolution, tectonic change, upheavals, and turbulence. Perhaps one of the most spectacular components of the current revolution is the shift of the center of gravity of the world economy toward Asia. This process, which quietly began in the late 1960s, is becoming obvious and is gathering pace. In 1960, East Asia accounted for only 4 percent of world economic output, compared with 25 percent in 1995. Between 1992 and 2000, 40 percent of all the new purchasing power created in the world will be in East Asia, and the region will absorb between 35 and 40 percent of the global increase in imports. Whereas industrially advanced countries are increasingly burdened with foreign debt, Japan, Taiwan, Singapore, and Hong Kong are in an enviable position of having none (Schwab and Smadja, 1995:100).

Many reasons can be advanced for the rise of Asian economies and the shift of economic power toward Asia. National or regional barriers restricting financial flows no longer exist; similarly, technology, management, and marketing techniques do not observe any boundaries. Furthermore, the key prerequisites of economic success are increasingly transferable from one country to another. The result has been a world-wide delocalization of industrial production. For example, Japan and then the Asian NIEs have been relocating their industrial production offshore. Since 1980, Japan has tripled its offshore industrial production to East Asia (Schwab and Smadja, 1995:101–102). For historical and geographic reasons, the countries in East Asia, or the western Pacific rim, are at different stages of economic development, a fact that has worked to their mutual advantage. Their staged development, with Japan and the Asian NIEs leading the countries of the Association of Southeast Asian Nations (ASEAN) and China, has resulted in such a sequence of developmental spurts over time that it has been described as a "flying geese" pattern. Reference to these countries along the western Pacific rim in this book is made in the term "Pacific Asia," which encompasses, geographically, East and Southeast Asia.

Asian economies have been restructured for survival, marked not only by sectoral or regional shifts of industry but also by underlying changes in the organization and technology of production, in labor relations, and in relations among firms (Le Heron and Park, 1995:8). In fact, business networks are so dominant that a distinctive Asia-Pacific form of capitalism is viewed to have emerged and is likely to spur economic integration of the region (Stubbs, 1995; also H. Yeung, 1998b). By now, the countries along the western Pacific rim are so well integrated economically and so highly stratified in division of labor that a de facto regional grouping has formed. An indicator of the success of East Asia has been its ability to attract foreign direct investment (FDI). From the mid-1980s to 1994, the share of world FDI in developing countries soared from 23 to 40 percent, much of which was accounted for by East Asia, which has become the fastest growth region (Qureshi, 1996).

In carrying forward the national economies of Pacific Asia, FDI has played a vital role. Within the region, the process was accelerated by Japan in the late l970s, when the Japanese economy went through industrial adjustment and restructuring and began to relocate some of its "sunset" labor-intensive and resource-processing industries to developing Asian countries. The process was necessitated by shifting comparative advantage and facilitated by what may be called concerns about the greenhouse environment. It included investment in export processing zones and other specially designed locations to accommodate inward FDI. By the mid-1970s, Japan had already built up the largest FDI stock in Asia. Japan's FDI in Asia reached a peak of $8.2 billion in 1989, after which it declined and increased again. By 1995, Japan's investment in Asia reached a record high of $12.3 billion, exceeding $10 billion for the first time. In fact, if FDI is limited to manufacturing industries, the proportion of investment in Asia increased by 19.5 percent in five years, from 23.8 percent in 1991 to 43.3 percent in 1995, ranking as the largest investment destination and replacing North America in 1994 and 1995. Within Asia, China emerged, after shifting from countries in ASEAN, as Japan's most important country for investment in the 1990s, and by 1995 China exceeded Japanese investment in NIEs and ASEAN for the first time (Nakashima, 1998). From a modest start as an exporter of capital in 1970, Japan became the world leader by 1989 (Boyer and Drache, 1996:183).

Pacific Asia remained almost the exclusive locus of Japanese FDI in Asia, and the globalization of the Japanese manufacturing industry, with 80 percent of Japanese employment overseas in the manufacturing sector, has occurred on the strength of the yen. This has led to the deindustrialization, or "hollowing out," of some industrial regions in Japan (Edgington, 1997). A recent study shows that the rise and fall of the yen has, since 1982, been positively correlated with the waxing and waning of economic growth in Asia outside Japan. Not surprisingly, the weakening yen in mid-1998 further deepened Asia's financial turmoil (Kwan, 1998). Through its sustained and substantial FDI flows in the countries in Pacific Asia, Japan has developed extensive, broad-based vertical and horizontal linkages and thus has become increasingly intertwined with the region through trade and investment (Lo and Yeung, 1996). Its continuing impact on the region will continue to be felt, for despite its economic bubble having burst in 1991, Japan's economy is still twice the size of that of the rest of Asia (Rimmer, 1997:129).

Following the same logic of shifting comparative advantage—a cornerstone underlying the essence of economic globalization—the "second generation" of currently industrializing economies (Hong

Kong, Singapore, Taiwan, and South Korea) have lost a large part of their location-specific advantage in labor-intensive and, subsequently, light manufacturing exports to the "third generation" countries, such as China, Indonesia, Malaysia, the Philippines, and Thailand. They all enter actively into the early stages of industrialization. Owing to Asian Pacific countries' record of high and stable economic growth, they continued to remain attractive and major destinations of FDI. In 1985, all the Asian Pacific countries under review accounted for 81 percent of all such investment in the whole of Asia (United Nations, 1988:80–106). Much the same pattern persisted in the 1990s, and between 1991 and 1994 Asia received 60 percent of total FDI flows to developing countries, with China emerging as the leading developing-country recipient of FDI flows (Dunning, 1997:45). Clearly, these patterns of development demonstrate increasing global interdependence and complementarities at work for the mutual benefit of host/home country economies. It is part of the global process of surplus accumulation, in which the Pacific Asia theater happens to be especially active (Armstrong and McGee, 1985). Within Asia, the flows of inward FDI exhibited three marked characteristics: a heavy degree of geographical concentration in Pacific Asia, a wide range of country sources, and the increasing importance of services-related FDI.

Asian countries, being late developers, have the advantage of choosing cost-effective global sourcing and the latest technology, coupled with their competitive labor. Thus, it is possible to have "high technology, high productivity, high quality, and *low* wages" (Schwab and Smadja, 1995:102). One success story is the transformation of Malaysia from a commodity producer to the world's leading producer of semiconductors in the past 20 years.

In fact, many Asian countries have adopted export-oriented manufacturing strategies with notable success. In 1993, Hong Kong and China topped the list of developing-country exporters with $135 billion and $92 billion in overseas sales, respectively, followed by Taiwan ($85 billion), South Korea ($82 billion), and Singapore ($74 billion). Malaysia, Thailand, and Indonesia constituted the second tier together with Brazil and Mexico (Gereffi, 1996:57). The textile and apparel complex is still important to some countries, but many have moved up the technological and value-added ladder with a penchant for export niches. It is a globalizing age in which megacompetition yields super-profits for some countries and cities. The similar and yet contrasting case studies of Hong Kong and Singapore are fascinating. Both city-states increasingly look to their immediate geographic region for economic interaction and sustenance (Chiu et al., 1997).

Against the background of robust economic growth and trade in East Asia, it is noteworthy that intraregional trade now constitutes about 43 percent of the region's total, compared with 33 percent in 1980. For this region, intraregional investment and financial flows represent the fastest-growing share of the region's exchanges. Between 1986 and 1992, some 70 percent of all investment in East Asia was derived from the region. However, this orientation toward more intraregional trade has not diminished the tensions that low-wage economies have posed in their successful competition with developed countries. Industrial nations in Europe and the United States have launched an offensive against so-called social dumping. It is a concerted effort to link trade issues with human rights, social conditions, and environmental standards (Schwab and Smadja, 1995:106).

Urban centers have always played critical roles in the creation of national wealth, and in the present global era, cities, especially global or world cities, are destined to even greater importance. Cities are the workhorses of the world. In the period 1970–1990, many cities registered their GDP increases by more than 1,000 percent, including Seoul and Tokyo, which recorded an increase of 2,127 percent and 2,894 percent, respectively. Indeed, Seoul, Hong Kong, and Singapore are glittering examples of Asia's growth machines. During the same period, Hong Kong's GDP rose fifteenfold, and exports rocketed twenty-seven-fold (Savitch, 1996:46–47, 49–50).

Although Hong Kong's postwar economic transformation has been impressive, its period of most rapid growth began in the mid-1980s, when China's open policy and economic reforms since 1978 matured and yielded astonishing dividends. The chapters in part 3 are designed to sample some of the breathtaking physical and economic changes that have swept the coastal region and the cities of China. It may be submitted that the timing of China's openness could not have occurred at a more opportune juncture. Notwithstanding a historic decision by the central government to experiment with open policy in 1978, the various policy reforms did not really unfold until the early 1980s, coinciding with a period of globalization and rapid growth that had been occurring in many parts of the world. At least in the early period of China's reform period, Hong Kong played a catalytic role through bold investment and cooperation by setting up factories in southern China, especially the Pearl River delta, and facilitated in marketing the finished manufactured goods in the world market. With Hong Kong's return to Chinese sovereignty in 1997, the symbiotic relationship between Hong Kong and China appeared to have consolidated and grown further. Barring any unforeseen political change, China is poised to continue its policy of steady and sustained economic growth and modernization in the years ahead.

For most countries in Pacific Asia, the immediate problem is to confront the near future and to reengineer for survival, restructuring, and growth. Many are still reeling from the shocks and dislocations triggered by the financial crisis of mid-1997. Countries that until recently had been upheld as models of economic transition, such as South Korea, Malaysia, and Indonesia, have been severely set back. Even Japan—the apogee of the Asian economic miracle and the world's second-largest economy—has been hit by endless financial scandals, a foundering banking system, and a weakening yen, which has recently strengthened. Only China appeared to have weathered the financial storm relatively unscathed, largely because of its only partially open economy and partial integration with the world economy. However, the basic strengths of the region—its people, their strong savings habits, the strong family system, the high value placed on education, plentiful resources, and so on—have not changed. All that has been accounted for earlier has not changed, and although the economic prognosis for the next few years is not all encouraging, the twenty-first century promises much with the maturing of the global informational economy. Given the scintillating start that Pacific Asia has made in capitalizing on globalization since the 1980s, no reason exists to doubt the capacity of most countries in the region to resume growth and contribute to the Information Age.

2   Globalization and World Cities

Pacific Asia having been situated in the globalization context, this chapter focuses on the interrelationships between globalization and a special class of large cities—world cities—in the region. It is divided into five sections, beginning with a review of the growing roles of cities in the informational/global economy. The second section concentrates on the interconnections between globalization and world cities. The third section discusses the nature of their interactions and the impact on the region. The fourth section shifts attention to world cities in Pacific Asia at closer range, specifically using actual examples to examine the changing socioeconomic milieu and daily life. The fifth section profiles, by way of summary, what have been the salient trends of urban-regional growth in the region in recent decades.

CITIES IN THE NEW GLOBAL ECONOMY

The international economic order that had governed much of the post–World War II period was thrown into disarray in the early 1970s, and a new global economy has since been created in which a new international division of labor (NIDL) has favored the newly industrializing countries as centers of productive activities and, consequently, as theaters of capital accumulation. The forces driving NIDL essentially stemmed from four sources. First, firms had a strong desire to utilize less expensive sources of labor and more profitable situations for production. Second, firms responded to the growing bargaining power of certain developing countries in stimulating and developing industrialization. Third, firms went abroad from developed countries to respond to the challenge of growing international competition. Finally, firms moved overseas to counterbalance the challenge of well-organized labor and government regulations. These forces, as part of NIDL, have reshaped the spatial hierarchy of economic activities and the relationship and relative importance of industrially advanced and newly industrializing economies. The new global economy is characterized by the international spread of productive facilities, the international spread of corporate-related services, and the rise of a system of international capital markets (Cohen, 1981).

As Peter Dicken (1998) has highlighted, economic activity is becoming not only more *internationalized* but increasingly *globalized*. The relatively simple trade flow of past decades has become far more complex. Economic production has become highly complex and fragmented, involving many production processes and geographical relocation on a global scale in ways that slice through national boundaries. Robert Reich has illustrated this global shift vividly:

> Consider some examples. Precision ice hockey equipment is designed in Sweden, financed in Canada, and assembled in Cleveland and Denmark for distribution in North America and Europe, out of alloys whose molecular structure was researched and patented in Delaware and fabricated in Japan. . . . A microprocessor is designed in California and financed in America and West Germany, containing dynamic random-access memories fabricated in South Korea.[1]

Given these kinds of fine-tuned production processes, one may easily anticipate that, in a decade or two, it will be difficult to identify who

---

[1] This quotation is taken from an address by Professor M. I. Logan at the OECD-Australia Conference on Cities and the New Global Economy held in Melbourne, November 20 to 23, 1994.

does what and which part of the network is related to that segment or that production center of a given firm (Boyer and Drache, 1996:73). Consequently, changes have occurred in the international "competitiveness" of a number of industries and the reshaping of the urban hierarchy throughout the world. Indeed, a new class of cities—world cities—has emerged, or reemerged from old forms, to drive the new global economy. The greatest impact has been felt in the urban centers of developed nations and the larger cities of developing countries (Cohen, 1981:303).

To be more explicit, Saskia Sassen (1991) has identified four key functions for world cities, namely, as command posts in the organization of the global economy, as key locations for finance and specialized service firms replacing manufacturing as the leading economic sector, as sites of production and innovation in leading industries, and as markets for products and innovations produced. These multiple functions of world cities will enable their articulation with other world cities, regionally and globally, so that they can be effectively and functionally networked. World cities are part of the global economy, one where capital flows, labor markets, commodity markets, information, raw materials, management, and organization are internationalized and fully interdependent throughout the world, even on a daily basis (Castells, 1992:5).

The new global economy has affected cities in developed and developing nations in different ways. In industrially advanced economies, previously thriving cities in manufacturing production have lost many factory jobs and restructured their economy, as the experience of Detroit, Chicago, New York, Manchester, and Osaka shows. Some cities have risen to meet new challenges, notably Los Angeles, Miami, Berlin, and Vienna. Cities bordering Eastern Europe, such as Vienna and Berlin, are likely to assume new roles or recapture old ones, as international business centers for the central European region (Sassen, 1994b). However, by far the dominant financial centers of the world are New York, Tokyo, and London. In 1994, their stock markets were the largest, in that order, in the world by capitalization. New York has more Fortune 500 corporate headquarters than any other city, and yet it is struggling to maintain its leading position globally and nationally. London is similar to New York in its absolute population decline, absolute losses in manufacturing employment, and slow overall job growth (Markusen and Gwiasda, 1994). London's claim to leadership in world finance has been greatly strengthened by deregulation of the financial markets in the United Kingdom in the 1980s. In fact, the general climate in the world is for less regulation, more diversification, and more competition, which has also benefited some Asian markets, notably Hong Kong, Bangkok, and Taipei. Compared with New York and London, Tokyo's dominance on the Japanese economy is unrivaled, serving as a center for finance and innovation and for the international trade of a rapidly growing national economy. Japan accounts for nearly half the total value of the global top 1,000 companies, and of total foreign companies (1,251), 84.6 percent have headquarters in Tokyo (Fujita, 1991).

Sassen (1994b) emphasizes that under the new global economy, a limited number of cities emerge as transnational locations for investment for firms, for the production of services and financial investments, and for various international markets. A new type of urbanization and a new type of city—the world city—have emerged. Thus, in the 1980s, New York, London, Tokyo, Paris, Frankfurt, Amsterdam, Zurich, Los Angeles, Hong Kong, Singapore, São Paulo, and Sydney, among others, have discovered new roles and importance in the emergent global economy. They are the points at which the processes of economic globalization, international migration, and new producer services and finance will be played out.

In an examination of the control and coordination of the international exchange of capital and commodities by business intermediaries (financiers, wholesalers, and corporate head offices) as to their influence on change in the world system of cities, David Meyer (1991) has concluded that the reactions of these bodies to competition—altering transaction costs, differentiation and dedifferentiation to control markets, and an appeal to force—offer insights into long-run change. In an earlier, similar study, Meyer (1986) explored the relations between international financial metropolises and South American cities and revealed that the world system of cities is organized independently of national and world regional boundaries. His latest study showed that the keenest competition among financial centers was focused on the acquisition of regional and branch offices of global intermediaries against a background of rapid expansion of international finance (Meyer, 1998).

For world cities to discharge their functions well, they need to be engaged in the process that can be briefly described as world city formation (Yeung and Lo, 1998). They need a strong physical and social infrastructure. For example, office buildings of distinct architectural design convey images of power and prestige, and major international airports, superfast trains, and information highways sustain the global reach of a world city. The social networks are nourished by a large variety of cultural and entertainment facilities (Dieleman and Hamnett, 1994: 358). For example, the Los Angeles metropolitan area expanded its land area by over eight times from a base of 4,070 square miles in 1985. Many new and massive airports in Asia, such as Osaka, Seoul, and Hong Kong, are being or have been constructed on reclaimed land. Expansion of land area into the sea by reclamation and by building intensively and vertically constitute two major methods for Asian global cities to create new space to fulfill their functional needs.

LINKS BETWEEN WORLD CITIES AND GLOBALIZATION

Although many factors have drawn nations and cities together since 1945, it is generally agreed that the global economy has evolved, during the past two decades, as an entity and a system at a speed and in fundamentally different ways never witnessed in human history. So dramatic have been some of the forces that underlie the change in the global economy that Ian Hamilton (1991) described the early 1970s as the watershed years. Specifically, microprocessors were invented in 1969, the Bretton Woods agreement broke down in 1971, the first oil crisis shook the world in 1973, and a "new international economic order" was called for in 1974.

As the new global economy began to unfold, scholars and planners were attracted to its ramifications and meanings. Literature began to accumulate on subjects such as economic restructuring (Cooke, 1986; Gondolf et al., 1986; Kolko, 1988), global capitalism (Peet, 1991; Castells, 1998), the new international division of labor (Frobel et al., 1980; H. Yeung, 1998b), territorial development (Henderson and Castells,

1987), global production (Grunwald and Flamm, 1985; Dicken, 1998), global services (Thrift, 1986), transnational corporations (Kumar, 1980; Dunning, 1997), and global culture (Robertson, 1989; Kim et al., 1997).

At the same time, increasing recognition was given to the links between globalization and cities. Notwithstanding the fact that cities have been traditionally associated with economic development in every part of the world from the dawn of history to the present (the subject of an impressive treatise by Bairoch, 1988), the application of the modern world system (Wallerstein, 1974, 1976) to understanding worldwide urbanization began essentially in the last decade. This approach has been facilitated by the earlier influential studies linking city-forming processes to the broader movement of industrial capitalism (Harvey, 1973; Castells, 1977). However, the recognition of a special class of cities—world cities—began with seminal articles by John Friedmann and his colleagues in the 1980s (Friedmann and Wolff, 1982; Friedmann, 1986; Korff, 1987). Since then, world cities, or the world system of metropolises (or variations thereof), have been studied by Christopher Chase-Dunn (1984), Michael Timberlake (1985), David Drakakis-Smith (1986), David Meyer (1986, 1991), Peter Rimmer (1986), Richard Knight and Gary Gappert (1989), and Anthony King (1990). Underlying many of these studies is the notion that certain key cities in the world play vital roles in the global economy. Indeed, they contribute to the internationalization of capital, production, services, and culture, and in turn the benefits derived augment their wealth, centrality, and importance.

Among the most astounding facets of postwar development are rapid urbanization in developing countries and the concentration of urban population in large cities. The United Nations defined large cities having a population exceeding eight million as megacities, which have gravitated toward Pacific Asia. Of the world's twenty-three largest cities in 1995, Asia had thirteen.

However, population size alone is only a general indicator of the importance of a city and does not reflect its economic and social significance in the global economy. Certainly, world city status cannot be measured only by population size; rather, such factors as the strength of the economy to which the city belongs, its location in relation to zones of growth or stagnation in the international economy, its attraction as a potential base for international capital, and its political stability must be taken into account (King, 1990:37). A broad consensus exists that the operation of NIDL is spatially articulated through a global network of cities (Friedmann and Wolff, 1982; Timberlake, 1985; Henderson and Castells, 1987). David Heenan (1977) emphasized the network of contacts. Friedmann (1986) suggested that the processes of urban change had become increasingly oblivious to national boundaries. Similarly, Toru Nakakita (1988) submitted that the very concept of national boundaries had been altered, owing first to dramatically reduced prices in transportation, information, and communications because of technological innovations and second to the abundance of business opportunities for transferring managerial resources.

Rather than population size by itself, Yue-man Yeung and Fu-chen Lo (1996) have argued that it is the functions of a world city that determine its centrality and importance in the world city system. In the global network society, the functional relationships among countries have become more complex and no longer necessarily stem from the previously linear, core-periphery or dependency paradigms. These functions relate in particular to the economic productive capacity and service infrastructure of the city, such that the administrative, developmental, and financial functions necessary to participation in global capitalism can be effectively carried out. An illustration is that Beijing and Shanghai, despite their huge population size and importance within China, are not world cities simply because they are not yet functionally integrated into the global economy, nor do they perform key functions in a world network of cities.

IMPACT ON PACIFIC ASIA

The rise of Pacific Asia has become one of the salient features of the global economy. Between 1965 and 1985, the Pacific Asian economies increased their share of world gross domestic product (GDP) from 5 to

20 percent and of world manufactured exports from 10 to 23 percent. Japan has emerged as the second-largest economy in the world and a pacesetter in Asia. By the end of the 1980s, the four Asian newly industrializing economies (NIEs) accounted for half the manufactured exports of all developing countries. The region's financial power had grown in tandem. In fact, countries along the western Pacific rim have achieved a substantial degree of integration, and an informal economic bloc is being formed (World Bank, 1991:21).

A detailed assessment of the impact of global restructuring has been undertaken in a different study by Yeung and Lo (1996). For the purposes of this chapter, the spatial transformation of Pacific Asia in response to global restructuring can be examined at three levels.

At the individual city level, because of the primacy of finance in the new world economy, a tendency exists for capital to be centralized in fewer cities. The importance of any city is directly related to the range of key functions that it can attract and provide for in the global division of labor. Briefly, three groups of functions can be identified: goods and commercial transactions, movement of people, and information flows. For example, Seoul has continued to be important as a center for many key functions. It is home to 61 percent of South Korea's managerial professionals in business and 96 percent of the top fifty corporation headquarters. It is also the center of research; about 64 percent of the scientists associated with public and private research in the country are in Seoul. Likewise, the city attracts the majority of international organizations, such as communications media, banks, investment consultants, and the diplomatic corps (Hong, 1996). Similarly, globalization has enhanced the economic and cultural significance of Tokyo, Taipei, Hong Kong, Bangkok, Kuala Lumpur, and Singapore, which are covered in the same study. For manufacturing functions within large cities, such as Bangkok and Jabotabek, the plants are more likely to be located in the suburban regions because of relatively cheap land costs and more stringent pollution controls in the urban areas.

At another level, several economic hubs have emerged in the Asia-Pacific region that have taken advantage of certain complementarities, especially labor supply, across national boundaries. Four growth triangles, on a modest spatial scale, have been identified that have combined local resources to profitable use for all countries and cities concerned:

- Johor, Singapore, Riau Islands
- Southern China, Hong Kong, Taiwan
- Penang, Southern Thailand, Sumatra
- South Korea, North Korea, Russian Far East (Wallace, 1991)

The four growth triangles are examples of NIDL over different territorial space. As these cross-border economic agglomerations prove successful, more such growth hubs have emerged in Pacific Asia. The next chapter focuses on this new spatial form.

At still another level is the formation of urban corridors in many parts of the western Pacific rim; these tend to spread over a wider territory and to connect with a number of megacities (Figure 2.1). Each epitomizes the highest level of interconnections among the cities they encompass. The corridors are identified as follows:

- Circum-Japan Sea Zone
- Circum-Bohai Zone
- South China Zone
- Indo-China Peninsula Zone
- Johor-Singapore-Riau (JSR) Growth Triangle
- Jabotabek

It should be recognized that these urban corridors are at varying stages of formation, some exhibiting incipient development and others quite advanced in form and connectivity among the cities. The best illustration of a mature urban corridor is provided by Sang-chuel Choe (1996): an inverted S-shaped urban belt—the BESETO (Beijing, Seoul, and Tokyo) ecumenopolis—which extends 1,500 kilometers from Beijing to Tokyo by way of Pyongyang and Seoul, connecting seventy-seven cities of over 200,000 inhabitants each. More than ninety-seven million urban dwellers live in this urban corridor, which links four separate megalopolises in four countries (Figure 2.2). With diplomatic ties between China and South Korea established in 1992 and further infrastructure development plans being proposed in this subregion, it is

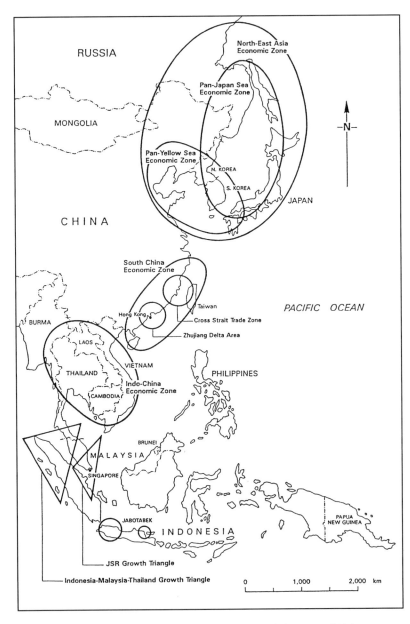

■ Figure 2.1 Emerging Subregional Economic Linkage and Urban
Corridor in Pacific Asia

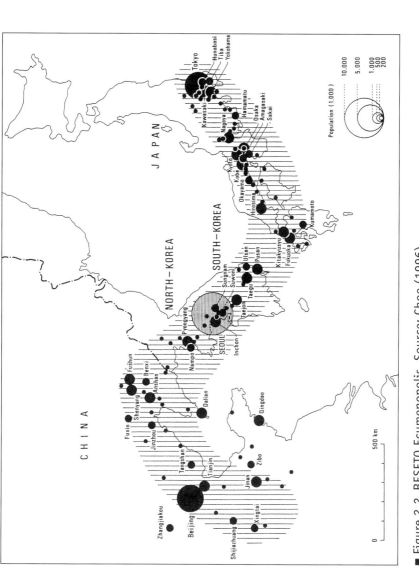

■ Figure 2.2 BESETO Ecumenopolis. Source: Choe (1996).

anticipated that the already well-connected urban corridor will be intensified in contact and convenience.

A number of economic zones have been identified in Pacific Asia that, for geographic and other reasons, have been viewed as sharing an interest in more rapid economic development. These are also the regions where future urban corridors are likely to develop. If all these zones are to witness rapid development as advocated, a scenario is not far-fetched in which the coastal region of Pacific Asia will be a continuous urban corridor stretching from Japan/North Korea to West Java, focused on Jabotabek. The coastal cities of China have effectively linked to form an almost continuous corridor of rapidly developing regions from north to south, with the cities playing catalytic modernization and development roles and with tentacles of positive growth trends reaching far into the inland provinces (Yeung and Hu, 1992).

PACIFIC ASIA'S WORLD CITIES

In a recent study mounted by the United Nations University, the world cities in Asia included Tokyo, Seoul, Taipei, Hong Kong, Manila, Bangkok, Kuala Lumpur, Singapore, and Jakarta (Lo and Yeung, 1996). Obviously, other world cities exist in Asia, notably Osaka, Nagoya, and possibly others. The central thesis of the study is that the world cities in Pacific Asia are networked in a functional system built around transportation, telecommunications, finance, production services, and so on. They are the linchpins of the global network society or the informational economy (Castells, 1998). They fulfill at least four roles for the global economy, namely, personal services, goods and commodity transactions, information flows, and financial services. As world cities, their importance is gauged by the functions they perform as control and management centers in the global economy, headquarters of transnational corporations (TNCs), and providers of advanced services, such as banking, finance, insurance, management consulting, engineering, advertising services, and accounting.

In Asia, the preeminent world city is Tokyo, whose metropolitan area is home to some 27 million inhabitants. Tokyo has seventy-nine of the Fortune 500's private firms concentrated in it, representing the first-ranking city in the world (Rimmer, 1986:131). One-tenth of Japan's manufacturing plants are located in metropolitan Tokyo, most of them in small plants with four to nineteen workers. Tokyo has also become a center of manufacturing innovation, a special type of global city, because of needs arising from the globalization of Japanese production. It has the highest concentration of small pilot production plants, venture businesses, research-and-development (R&D) centers, corporate headquarters, banks, information industries, foreign residents, and institutions of higher education (Fujita, 1991). Indeed, Takashi Machimura (1992) has argued that Tokyo is primarily a world city distinguished by its economic importance. This is attributable to the rapid transnationalization of Japanese capital in the wake of the Plaza Accord in 1985. The mobility of capital and the fluidity of capitalist relations of production have brought an entirely new dimension to the world economy in which Japan notably has become expert at the science of *zai-tech* (financial engineering) and the art of flexible specialization. The advent of telematics and government deregulation have facilitated such development (Knox and Taylor, 1995:5–6). The number of Japanese manufacturing TNCs increased from thirty-five in 1975 to ninety in 1987. The Tokyo Stock Exchange is the second largest in the world, after New York, in terms of market capitalization. As the number of Japanese TNCs increased, a globalization of regional banks followed. In providing better services to their clients, thirty-four of Japan's regional banks had seventy-seven overseas bases, mostly in New York, London, and Hong Kong. At the same time, the globalization of the Japanese economy has been paralleled by an influx of foreign companies in Tokyo. In 1989, of the 1,251 foreign companies, 84.6 percent had headquarters in Tokyo, especially in manufacturing, service, and finance (Fujita, 1991).

What is most notable during the past two decades is that countries in Pacific Asia have displayed greater structural interdependency from the standpoint of production and marketing. By the mid-1980s, Japan had already outstripped the United States in interindustrial relations with the Asian NIEs and Association of Southeast Asian Nations (ASEAN) countries in terms of finished goods and raw materials. A nontreaty trading bloc is fast becoming a reality along the western Pacific rim, and in this process the world cities in the region have been playing pivotal roles in advancing and restructuring their economies (Lo and Yeung, 1996).

For example, Hong Kong and Singapore have witnessed rapid growth as financial centers, transport nodes in air and container traffic, and providers of advanced services in the global and regional economies. The rise of Hong Kong as a financial center can be perceived in the transformation of its banking system during the period 1969–1990. For example, the balance-sheet size of the banking sector increased 263 times to HK$5,234 billion (U.S.$671 billion) while customers' deposits soared 100 times to HK$1,231 billion (U.S.$158 billion). At the same time, the amount due to banks abroad increased by 1,695 times, and loans and advances abroad increased 4,000 times. Of the largest 500 commercial banks in the world, 220 are present in Hong Kong in one form or another (Jao, 1993:51). Indeed, nineteen of the twenty largest banks in the world maintained a fully fledged licensed bank in Hong Kong in 1989. Apart from Hong Kong and Singapore, Taipei and Bangkok also have aspirations to be financial centers in the region.

As the Asian NIEs continue to accumulate wealth and technological know-how, they have become exporters of capital in their own right. Their global cities have become control and management centers in manufacturing and service provision in the region and beyond. Hyundai, Goldstar (now LP Group), and Samsung (South Korea), Singapore Airlines, and Hongkong Bank are eminent examples of TNCs from these countries. Thus, while Hong Kong is a major focus of foreign direct investment (FDI) from Japan, China, and the United States, it is an important exporter of capital to many parts of the world, most notably to China and ASEAN countries, with Indonesia and Thailand being the favored destinations. Between 1984 and 1988, the average outflows of Hong Kong FDI reached U.S.$2,536.5 million (H. Yeung, 1994).

The Changing Socioeconomic Milieu

As world cities have evolved and changed to enable them to discharge functions that are largely externally driven, they experience urban restructuring spatially, economically, and socially.

In terms of spatial outcome, an increase in control and management functions in a world city means that urban functions and land-use patterns have been transformed. In Tokyo, the main trends of spatial restructuring entailed, among others, the formation of space for global control functions, the expansion of space for domestic control functions in central area districts, the relocation of regional control functions from the central area to subcenters, and the location of an R&D division of high-tech industries in suburban areas. In essence, the urban functions that are worth locating in central districts are selected, old and unnecessary functions are removed, and new space for new functions is created. As a result, many districts within Tokyo have been forced to change their economic functions and spatial forms (Machimura, 1992:122–123). In general, there is a differentiation of urban land use and thus location for the functions of the global and domestic markets. A huge demand exists for land use for the global market, resulting in the rapid escalation of rent. The extraordinary increase in the rental of office space in the central areas of Hong Kong, Tokyo, and other cities in the region is a manifestation of this phenomenon. In 1994, Hong Kong had the dubious distinction of having the most expensive office rental space in the world, but the situation has since eased, as sales values reportedly have decreased by 32 percent from their peak to HK$10,500 per square foot in April 1995. Since late 1997, real estate values have continued to plunge in Hong Kong, which has also suffered from the ill effects of Asia's financial crisis. In addition, it has been observed that in Jakarta, Bangkok, and other world cities in Asia, periurban areas have witnessed more rapid growth than the city proper in a process that has been described as extended metropolitanization (Ginsburg et al., 1991).

The NIDL has redefined the employment structure of world cities. Whereas control, management, and service functions have increased, manufacturing has declined in relative importance. For Tokyo, Rimmer (1986:144) has shown, in contrast to industrial activities, wholesaling, and retailing, that finance, insurance, real estate, and a multifarious range of services continued to grow between 1960 and 1980; only the government sector has shown little or no growth. More than 200 foreign financial institutions, including eighty-two banks, have set up in

Tokyo, and the number of people involved in the market-oriented financial community was expected to grow from 25,000 in 1987 to 75,000 by 1997 (Fujita, 1991:280). Similarly, as they restructured their economy, both Hong Kong and Singapore have experienced a sharp decline in the manufacturing sector in employment and contribution to GDP. Only 288,887 people were employed in manufacturing jobs in 1997 in Hong Kong, compared with 907,463 in 1980.

Equally pronounced as an outcome of their global orientations has been the changing population composition of Pacific Asia's world cities. The presence of the Filipino population, working primarily as domestic maids, in the world cities of the Asian NIEs is widely accepted. They represent the largest concentration of foreign population in Hong Kong, totaling 90,700 in 1992. Filipinos, Thais, and Canadians have increased their populations, ranging from four to thirteen times in Hong Kong between 1980 and 1995 (Yeung, 1996). In Japan as well, international migration appeared for the first time in the mid-1980s. Illegal workers from Pakistan, Bangladesh, and the Philippines have grown rapidly in recent years. Many converge in Tokyo and other large cities, contributing to the phenomenon observed in New York and Los Angeles called the informalization of the core (Sassen-Koob, 1989). Excluding Koreans and Chinese, the legal foreign population in greater Tokyo has been estimated to be around 300,000, representing only 1 percent of its population (Masai, 1989:158). Since the mid-1980s, the Tokyo government has formulated a policy of "internationalization" that attempts to provide the physical and cultural conditions for accommodating foreign capital and foreign residents (Machimura, 1992:125).

Daily Life

The internationalization of Asian life that inevitably follows the development of world cities has its costs as well as its benefits. What are some of the negative dimensions?

One obvious consequence of the increased demand for space is the rapid appreciation of housing costs. This has been acutely felt by residents in Tokyo for the past three decades. They have been pushed further from Tokyo to the surrounding prefectures, as far away as 100 kilometers. Long commuting time and the distance to work and services have been increasingly painful, so much so that the Tokyo government has passed an ordinance that new office buildings must also have residential accommodation (Fujita, 1991:282). The cost of residential property has also risen dramatically in most world cities in Asia over the past two decades and has, as a result, sharpened social inequalities and tensions.

Although world cities in Pacific Asia have invested massively in infrastructure, growing affluence and the attendant widespread ownership of automobiles have led to horrendous traffic problems in Jakarta, Bangkok, Hong Kong, and other cities. Since 1975, Singapore has had in place a highly successful policy of limiting vehicular access to the central city area during the morning rush hour, and in 1997 the scheme was extended to a much wider area through electronic road pricing. When fully implemented, electronic road pricing will become an automated version of the area licensing scheme with the flexibility to vary charges at different times and places, depending on traffic conditions (Lim and Yuen, 1998). Nevertheless, most other world cities in the region prefer other, more palatable options supplemented with mass transit systems. Theoretically, advanced communication and telecommunications systems should reduce the need for face-to-face contact, but they have not lessened the demands for intraurban transport to date.

Subject to further research and verification, the globalization process has apparently led to growing polarization along class, gender, and ethnic lines. Where sizable foreign immigration has occurred, legal or illegal laborers earning less than normal wages and living in dilapidated and congested neighborhoods are bound to suffer. This has surfaced as a social problem in Tokyo, where ethnic segregation engenders social tensions (Machimura, 1992:125). On the other hand, despite the economic imbalance between rich and poor, most Tokyoites are more or less content with their present situation (Masai, 1989:157). The juxtaposition of wealth and poverty has never been a stranger to Asian cities, but the recent development in Hong Kong, Bangkok, and Jakarta has heightened social problems.

Another type of social tension has been reported in Tokyo. With the expansion of business space into traditional urban neighborhoods, a direct conflict arose between the central districts and the inner areas. Enormous land purchases by private developers have adversely affected living conditions and destroyed stable community relations nurtured over a long time (Machimura, 1992:126). Similar neighborhood disruptions have also been experienced in Singapore, Hong Kong, and Taipei, where urban redevelopment has proceeded. In the final analysis, one must question the meaning of development and for whom that development is intended.

On a daily basis, living in Pacific Asia's world cities means being part of global development, constantly exposed to global chains of mass consumerism, finding easy access to technological gadgets, being fully informed of political and economic events around the world, earning a comfortable salary, and living in decent quarters. These conditions apply especially to active participants of the global economy. As for other residents, they can still partake of some of them. For a minority, life is the same as before, mired in poverty (see Yeung, 1998c). However, as Prud'homme (1989:54–56) has observed for selected cities of the world, the quality of life has tended to improve over time, in the air we breathe, at home, and at the workplace. At the risk of simplification, the generalization is probably applicable to world cities in Pacific Asia.

A PROFILE OF ASIA-PACIFIC GROWTH

Globalization has affected individual cities as well as national urban systems. The relationships between, on the one hand, the economic structural adjustments experienced in individual countries and, on the other, globalization forces and urban transformation can be seen in a number of cases, as detailed in the following.

The clearest expression of the changing roles of a city in the region can be seen in Tokyo. Three stages of development can be distinguished. In the 1960s, Tokyo clearly emerged as a national magnet in the Japanese economy to which population and development were drawn. Then, in the 1970s, Tokyo developed and strengthened with greater contributions to the national economy by developing itself as a financial, telecommunications, and transnational corporation center. At the same time, decentralization of its manufacturing capacity, while keeping central managerial functions, became evident within Japan. However, its full integration as a world city emerged only in the 1980s, when Tokyo developed a new division of labor and industrial restructuring by relocating manufacturing production to cities abroad, especially in the Asia-Pacific region, again retaining key central managerial functions and R&D within Japan. The comparative advantage of Tokyo and cities within the Asia-Pacific region was being capitalized in the process. Japan emerged as one of the leading economies in the world. Tokyo's status as a world city grew as a consequence, for it had become increasingly integrated with the global and regional economies. Its importance within the Japanese urban system has also increased, as it has become a giant urban agglomeration of more than 27 million inhabitants within its daily commuting distance.

The recent development of Seoul and Taipei further epitomizes the regional response to economic globalization and the seizing of new economic opportunities as the Asian NIEs are in a position to seek development beyond their shores. In both cases, labor-intensive manufacturing has been decentralized to offshore locations, such as ASEAN countries, coastal China, and recently Vietnam, where labor and other costs of production are lower, leaving capital-intensive types of production within their countries. However, the urban pattern within South Korea and Taiwan has shown some interesting contrasts. Within South Korea, Seoul has emerged as the overarching urban agglomeration, and the problem has been to halt Seoul's unwanted growth since the 1980s. In Taiwan, on the other hand, Taipei has grown at a more subdued pace, with the southern port city of Kaohsiung exerting a countervailing effect to give rise to an urban corridor across the island from north to south. The kind of urban concentration exhibited in Seoul is absent in Taiwan.

Looking in a regional context and over time, Japanese offshore industrial relocation to the Asian NIEs in the 1960s and 1970s might be viewed as the first wave of regional economic development. Similar developments in the ASEAN countries in the 1970s and 1980s constituted the second wave. In the 1960s and 1970s, ASEAN countries had limited manufacturing development in import-substitution industries.

Rapid economic development actually began in 1985 with the Plaza Accord and the remarkable appreciation of the Japanese yen. Japan was anxious to relocate its manufacturing production abroad within the region to maintain its competitive edge. This was followed by a similar appreciation of the currencies of South Korea and Taiwan in 1986 and 1987. These countries were also keen to maintain their export manufacturing competitiveness and needed cheaper locations from which to do so. ASEAN countries presented just the right mix of conditions for this offshore manufacturing to take place. As a result, FDI in ASEAN countries increased sharply, facilitating a major economic restructuring of these countries from being commodity exporters to manufacturing exporters in the 1980s. Structural reorientation also occurred in the early 1980s, when commodity prices collapsed, providing the ASEAN countries with timely and critical relief from their previous overdependence on primary commodity exports for their national income. This new infusion of growth impulses has given renewed strength to their large cities. Thus, Bangkok, Kuala Lumpur, and Jabotabek have grown rapidly and in new functions. By virtue of their traditional and newfound importance, they have become well articulated with the new global economy. However, within these urban agglomerations, it is their fringe areas that have experienced the fastest rates of growth and the most rapid physical transformation. These areas have relatively more land and somewhat less stringent regulatory controls on manufacturing-related growth and investment by TNCs. The rapid growth and transformation of these urban fringe areas are components of physical and social change that have not been adequately dealt with by the governments concerned.

In contrast to the other ASEAN countries, the Philippines has been experiencing slow rates of growth for decades. Political instability and other problems have not made the island nation attractive to foreign investment compared with its neighbors, which experienced massive foreign investment, especially in the second half of the 1980s. In fact, because of economic stagnation, sustained emigration and labor migration to the countries of the Middle East have been occurring for two decades. Consequently, Manila has been bypassed by some of the positive effects of globalization, and until recently persistent neglect of social and economic infrastructure has resulted in the deterioration of the quality of life, especially for the urban poor.

The third wave of regional economic development refers to foreign investment and development in the coastal regions of China since the mid-1980s. The opening of China to the world for a new style of development began in 1978, with the adoption of an open policy and economic reforms, initially with the establishment of four special economic zones in Guangdong and Fujian. This was accelerated in the late 1980s, with the end of the Cold War, as similar development was pursued in other coastal areas of China, such as Dalian, Qingdao, Shanghai (Pudong), and other port cities in northern China. However, the focused and accelerated development along the coastal region has led to heightened economic and social disparity between the coastal and interior parts of China, with grave implications for policy formulation and the future. The coastal region's visible success and attraction have generated massive rural-to-urban and urban-to-urban migrations that have led to waves of floating population, variously estimated at 80 to 100 million, from less developed inland provinces and the rural areas within the coastal provinces. These population surges have created new opportunities as well as challenges for the coastal cities. China's coastal cities are being integrated with the economies within the Asia-Pacific region and increasingly with the world, but no world city in a functional sense has yet emerged.

2 Cooperative Regional Development

3 The Emergence of Growth Triangles

INTRODUCTION

The global restructuring that was triggered by the oil crises in the 1970s gathered momentum in the following decade as a consequence of several megatrends that affected many parts of the world. First, agricultural commodity and oil prices plunged, with deleterious consequences in many developing countries that depended heavily on their sales to realize national incomes. Especially hard hit were countries in sub-Saharan Africa and Latin America, where primary commodities accounted, respectively, for 98 and 83 percent of their exports in the 1980s. Second, concomitant with the decline in the role of material resources in production has been the rise of capital, in particular the internationalization of capital, as a major driving force in the global economy. In the Asia-Pacific region, transnational capital became a powerful force in spearheading development in the wake of the Plaza Accord in 1985 and the resultant realignment of the yen against the U.S. dollar and selected Asian currencies. Foreign direct investment (FDI) has been a key factor in influencing patterns of economic development. Countries and cities in the region have found themselves in a situation of changing comparative advantage whereby some are bound to benefit more than others. Third, a determinant of structural change has been technological change, which has been breathtaking in its speed and scope, especially in the late 1980s. The cluster of new innovations in computers, electronics and telecommunications, new materials, biotechnology, and robotics has been facilitating production processes, speeding up and revolutionizing business transactions, and permitting creativity (see chapter 2). The investment climate has been changing rapidly in regional and global terms. A global shift of manufacturing production and investment has fundamentally altered the economic relation of nations and has led to the rapid growth of some economies (Dicken, 1998).

Standing to gain the most from the global restructuring that has been briefly sketched here have been countries and cities in the Asia-Pacific region or Pacific Asia. Collectively, they project a robust future with the dawning of the twenty-first century. Although sustained and rapid economic development has taken many forms, the focus of this chapter centers on the growth of subregional/transnational economic regions that have been variously called natural economic zones and growth triangles. It reviews the global and regional context under which these regional cooperative modes have emerged. Existing and potential growth triangles are described and compared, and then implications for the future are drawn.

To date, growth triangles represent a uniquely Asian phenomenon that has apparently grown with a mix of spontaneity and government intervention, depending on situations. Some scholars (e.g., Parsonage, 1992) have viewed it as a subregional response to global transformation. Indeed, the push to this subregional response has taken into account the tendency toward regional trading blocs and protectionism that were strongly emerging in Europe and North America in the late 1980s. The collapse of communism in Eastern Europe in 1989, followed by the sudden demise of the Soviet Union in 1991, signaled the end of the Cold War and the triumph of geoeconomics over geopolitics. In this climate of détente and political liberalization, several subregions in Pacific Asia have evolved creative transnational economic zones that are designed to maximize their varied factor endowments and accentuate their comparative advantage. Often taking the form of contiguous geographic areas under different sovereignties, growth triangles are stronger in sum than in individual parts of countries. By design, growth triangles seek closer forms of economic cooperation among the geographic areas concerned and, by capitalizing on their different economic strengths, are in a better position to play a greater role in the increasingly interdependent global economy.

In a review of growth triangles in the Asia-Pacific region, Min Tang and Myo Thant (1998) identified four conditions that this form of regional economic cooperation has that may be considered superior to trading blocs. First, the growth triangle approach usually involves only contiguous parts of countries, thus reducing the economic and political risks and being expandable to other parts of the country. Second, in encompassing only some parts of a region, a growth triangle can be established at a relatively lower cost and in a shorter period of time. Third, growth triangles are export oriented and do not discriminate between internal and external markets. Fourth, growth triangles have the advantage of conferring economic benefits even on those countries that are not part of the triangle not only because of their nonexclusionary characteristics in terms of market access but also because of their policy to attract foreign investment.

What are the main factors that make a growth triangle successful? Again, Tang and Thant (1998) have outlined five features on the basis of existing triangles. (1) To be successful, economic complementarity must exist among the countries and areas concerned by being at different stages of economic development or with different factor endowments. Edward Chen and Joseph Lee (1998) have distinguished the former as complementarity in development versus the latter as complementarity in production premised on a division of labor. Both, however, are viewed as variants of vertical complementarity. (2) Geographic proximity is one of the key factors to minimize transport and communication costs. The additional affinity in the form of similar cultural and linguistic backgrounds would facilitate mutual understanding and business transactions. (3) Political commitment of the governments in question and policy coordination among governments are prerequisites for the success of regional cooperation. (4) Infrastructure development, especially in developing new areas for attracting foreign investment, is crucial in creating a propitious investment climate. Such development is expensive, but many models of infrastructure development exist, as experience so far suggests. (5) The importance and value of a growth triangle should be measured not only by its trade and investment linkages but also by its capacity to expand to other parts of a country. The successful example of the Southern China Triangle is derived, to a large extent, from the expansion of its initial focus of the four special economic zones (SEZs) to the whole of the provinces of Guangdong and Fujian when economic logic and geography pointed the way.

EXISTING GROWTH TRIANGLES

As a new form of regional economic cooperation, growth triangles emerged only in the 1980s. Strictly speaking, at present only two operating triangles exist—Southern China and Johor-Singapore-Riau (JSR)—but the third is close to becoming a reality in the Tumen River delta. Figure 3.1 shows the distribution of growth triangles in Pacific Asia at different stages of development. Whereas Table 3.1 provides a comparative profile of the three existing triangles, Table 3.2 summarizes the main reasons that the relevant countries or parts of countries want to pursue cooperative development through joint efforts. For the purposes of this chapter, it is instructive to highlight the salient characteristics of each of the existing triangles.

Southern China Growth Triangle

Southern China, here defined as inclusive of Guangdong and Fujian provinces, Hong Kong, and Taiwan, is the oldest and most successful growth triangle. It emerged at a favorable conjunction of political and economic circumstances prevailing in the three territories as well as in the world. It began in 1978, when China adopted an open policy and experimented with a market economy, initially in the four SEZs in the two provinces. Gradually, cooperative development spilled over to the entire area of the two provinces, leading to the formation of a sizable subregional cooperative entity from which all participating countries derived substantial benefit. It has now become a powerful economic unit to be reckoned with.

The teaming up of Hong Kong and Taiwan on the one hand and of Guangdong and Fujian on the other for economic development make eminent economic sense. The former are strong economies, having an

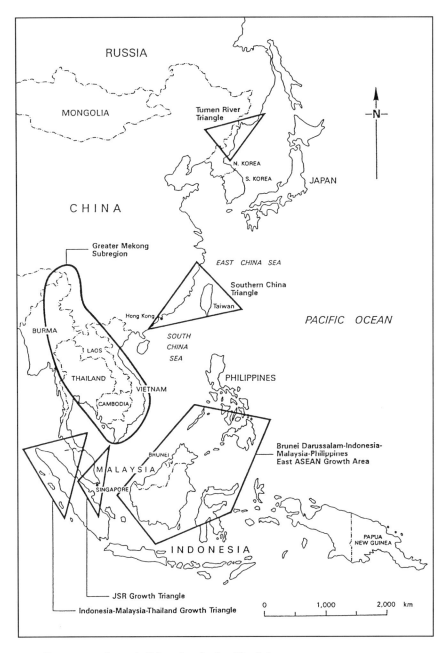

RUSSIA

MONGOLIA

Tumen River
Triangle

N. KOREA

S. KOREA

JAPAN

CHINA

Greater Mekong
Subregion

EAST CHINA SEA

Southern China
Triangle

Hong Kong

Taiwan

PACIFIC OCEAN

BURMA

SOUTH
CHINA
SEA

LAOS

THAILAND

VIETNAM

PHILIPPINES

CAMBODIA

BRUNEI

MALAYSIA

Brunei Darussalam-Indonesia-
Malaysia-Philippines
East ASEAN Growth Area

SINGAPORE

PAPUA
NEW GUINEA

INDONESIA

JSR Growth Triangle

Indonesia-Malaysia-Thailand Growth Triangle

0   1,000   2,000   km

■ Figure 3.1 Growth Triangles in Pacific Asia

■ Table 3.1 Growth Triangles in Pacific Asia: A Comparative Profile

	Attributes	JSR	SOUTHERN CHINA	TUMEN	
				River region	Delta region
Physical	Participating countries	Johor (Malaysia) Riau Islands (Indonesia) Singapore	Guangdong, Fujian (China) Hong Kong Taiwan	North Korea Northeast China Russia Far East	North Korea Northeast China Russia Far East South Korea Mongolia Japan
	Area	22,853 sq km	334,971 sq km	7,127,000 sq km	169,000 sq km
	Population	5.1 million (1991)	126.9 million (1995)	129.6 million (1990)	298 million (1990)
Economic	Strategic approach	Government led	Private sector led	UNDP led	
	Investment levels (U.S.$)	Singapore in Batam (1980–1990): 347M Singapore in Johor (1993–1990): 778.3M	Taiwan in China (1987–1992): 6.8B HK in S. China (up to 1991): 9.16M China in HK (up to 1992): 20B	Korean ODA Japanese ODA (in 1991): 10B	
	Land cost differential (U.S.$/m², 1989)	Johor: 4.08 Singapore: 4.25 Batam: 2.3	Factory rental per month HK: 24.7 Shenzhen: 2.8 Guangzhou: 3.45		—

	Imports/ exports (% of total)	Malaysia-Singapore trade: 40% through Johor	China to HK (1989): 48% HK to China (1989): 25.7% China to Taiwan (1991): 1.57% Taiwan to China (1991) 6.13%	Japan to the region: 9.2% South Korea to the region: 21.9% North Korea to the region: 83.7% China to the region: 23.0% Russia to the region: 6.6% (1990)
	Per capita GNP (U.S.$, 1995)	Malaysia: 3,890 Singapore: 26,730 Indonesia: 980	Guangdong: 965 Fujian: 788 HK: 22,990 Taiwan: 12,780	North Korea: 987 Norhteast China: 499 South Korea: 9,700 Mongolia: 310 Japan: 39,640
Social	Ethnic affinity	Chinese-Malay tension	Cantonese (HK-Guangdong) Fujianese (Fujian-Taiwan)	2 million Koreans in China and Russia
	Wage differential (U.S.$/month, 1989)	Unskilled worker Johor: 150 Singapore: 350 Batam: 90	Manufacturing worker Hong Kong: 700 Shenzhen: 100 Guangzhou: 140	—

Source: Adapted from Kakazu (1998); Asian development Bank (1997); Fujian Statistical Bureau (1997); Guangdong Statistical Bureau (1997).

■ Table 3.2 Motivations for Forming Growth Triangles in Pacific Asia

Growth triangle	Population (million, 1995)	Per capita GDP (U.S.$, 1995)	Motivations
SOUTHERN CHINA			
Fujian, China	31.6	788	Taiwan has heavily invested in the province, taking advantage of its proximity and common cultural background
Guangdong, China	67.9	965	The province initiated China's open policy. Hong Kong dollars have been circulating in the open economic zones.
Hong Kong	6.2	22,990	Hong Kong intends to maintain its economic status by promoting a market-driven economic integration with Guangdong before its return to China in 1997.
Taiwan	21.2	12,780	Taiwan wants to revitalize its economy through relocation of its labor-intensive industries to the mainland.
JSR			
Indonesia	195.3	980	Development of the Riau region has been an important agenda for many years. Looking for capital and technology from Singapore and others.
Malaysia	20.7	3,890	To aim at further development through strengthening economic ties with Singapore and Indonesia.
Singapore	3.0	26,730	To ease its development bottlenecks, such as labor, land, and water, and to relocate its less competitive industries to the region.
TUMEN RIVER			
North Korea	22.19	987*	With abundance of natural resources and labor, the ailing economy has begun to adopt market-opening measures, including the establishment of special economic zones.

Northeast China	99.30*	499*	With abundance of land and labor, a good basis exists for regional cooperation, many Koreans live in its northern provinces. People are now looking for open policies to catch up with advanced southern coastal zones.
Russia Siberia	6.90	5,810*	Although abundant in natural resources, the region lacks labor, capital, and technology. After the collapse of communism, the region, the least developed in Russia, is ready to accept market-oriented development.
South Korea	44.90	9,700	To secure natural resources as well as to diversify its markets through the regional division of labor. The zone will accelerate the development of its western coastal area.
Japan	125.00	39,640	Japan Sea littoral prefectures, notably Niigata, have positively supported the idea as part of regional development.
Mongolia	2.30	310	After the collapse of the Soviet economy, on which Mongolia heavily depended, it is now looking for new economic ties with its southeastern partners, especially China.

Note: Asterisks (*) denote 1989 figures.

Source: Adapted from Kakazu (1998); Asian development Bank (1997); Fujian Statistical Bureau (1997); Guangdong Statistical Bureau (1997).

enviable record of economic growth in the postwar period and considerable experience in export-oriented manufacturing, capital accumulation, entrepreneurship, and technology development. Hong Kong and Taiwan have been such fast-growing economies that they have earned the sobriquet "Asian dragons." However, they have been confronted with escalating land and labor costs, and having reached a certain stage of development, their economies were in need of basic restructuring. During the 1980s, Taiwan saw stock and property booms and the accumulation of a sizable trade surplus. The ratio of trade surplus to gross domestic product (GDP) reached nearly 20 percent in 1986. Consequently, the NT dollar went through rapid appreciation between 1985 and 1989, resulting in Taiwan's loss of some of its competitiveness. In addition, a growing concern about environmental pollution resulted in growing pressure on certain polluting industries to seek alternative locations outside the island. The need to seek economic opportunities offshore was paramount. Similarly, Hong Kong went through economic restructuring in the 1980s. The share of the service sector in GDP increased from 55.7 percent in 1980 to 66.1 percent in 1990, whereas that of the manufacturing sector declined from 23.8 percent in 1980 to 16.7 percent in 1990 (Chen and Lee, 1998).

In contrast, Guangdong and Fujian, as part of China's command economy for decades, have cheap land and labor that await development. Guangdong and Hong Kong share a common border and cultural and linguistic affinity; indeed, many Hong Kong residents have ancestral roots in that province. Fujian and Taiwan are separated by a strait that can be crossed in one hour in some parts, and people in these areas also speak the same Minnan language. Under China's open policy and a more flexible position allowed for the two southern provinces, the complementarity between them and Hong Kong and Taiwan appeared perfect for rapid economic growth to take place.

Rapid economic growth was precisely what followed after the three territories explored ways by which to cooperate. Hong Kong entrepreneurs began tentatively investing in the Pearl River delta in the early 1980s, but the move blossomed in the mid-1980s, as reflected in soaring two-way trade figures between China and Hong Kong after 1985. Hong Kong's exports to and imports from China have since increased astronomically. Hong Kong has remained the largest investor in Guangdong, and its companies were responsible for employing an estimated three million workers in the province, primarily in assembly types of manufacturing processes. This has led to a major restructuring of Hong Kong's economy that, with its large-scale relocation of labor-intensive industries to the Pearl River delta, has been increasingly oriented toward a service-dominated one.

In the same way, Taiwanese investors were quick to seize the opportunity to relocate their industrial plants to China. They tended to concentrate in Guangdong and Fujian, especially in Shenzhen, Xiamen, Guangzhou, Dongguan, and Fuzhou. The major industrial investment has been in footwear, electrical engineering, vehicles, plastics, and apparel. A distinctive feature of the Southern China Growth Triangle is that its emergence was driven largely by private-sector initiatives that explored factor price differentials. The driving force lay in the complementary nature of their comparative advantage. Especially in the period prior to 1985, the middleman role played by Hong Kong was critical in facilitating Taiwanese investment in China. Hong Kong's role has been described as a "nucleus," combining the role as a trading partner, a middleman, a facilitator, and a financier.

Although Hong Kong and Taiwan have derived substantial gains in the subregional cooperation, the most profound impact has been the physical and economic transformation experienced in Guangdong and Fujian. Both provinces have grown at rates and within such a short period of time that their miracle growth has surpassed the experience of the Asian dragons in a certain sense. Had it not been for the bottlenecks encountered in infrastructure development in these two provinces, especially in rail transport and energy supply, their growth rates could have been even more rapid. Although infrastructure development in southern China has lagged markedly behind demand, different levels of government have been allowed ample initiatives to meet their own requirements (see chapter 4).

Recent developments within the Southern China Growth Triangle point to the greater integration of the three economies. The resumption of sovereignty by China over Hong Kong in 1997 enhanced cooperation between Hong Kong and Guangdong that has been manifested in a variety of economic and cultural domains. Rapid increases in two-way trade and flow of people and goods have been matched by those in investment. The need for closer cooperation has been no more obvious than in infrastructural projects. Thus, the Infrastructure Coordinating Committee between Hong Kong and Guangdong was set up in December 1994 to facilitate such projects straddling the border. In fact, urbanologists have been predicting the emergence of a fast-growing urban agglomeration of 35 to 40 million inhabitants involving Hong Kong and Guangzhou and many smaller cities in between (see chapter 9). With the signals of direct trade and communication between Taiwan and Fujian already expressed by the people in early 1997, Taiwan will also be drawn closer to the growth triangle.

JSR Growth Triangle

Johor (Malaysia), Singapore, and the Riau Islands (Indonesia) (JSR) began their process of trilateral cooperation only in 1989, when the deputy prime minister of Singapore, Mr. Goh Chok Tong, stated that the three territories would form a "triangle of growth." This has provided an emerging form of subregional cooperation with a new term, and "growth triangle" has since gained currency in development circles, more readily capturing the imagination of policymakers and planners. In December 1994, the three governments formally signed agreements, and the name Indonesia-Malaysia-Singapore Growth Triangle (IMS-GT) was adopted.

   With Singapore as another Asian dragon taking a leading role in subnational regional cooperation, this triangle exhibits much the same kind of complementarity that the Southern China Growth Triangle does. Singapore as a well-developed city-state has the capital, technology, communication, marketing networks, and entrepreneurship that would complement the expansive land and cheaper labor that are available in the southernmost peninsular Malaysian state and the Indonesian archipelago. Nevertheless, the disparity in land and labor costs in these three territories is not as sharp as it is in the Southern China Growth Triangle. For example, skilled labor costs U.S.$200 per month in Batam compared with U.S.$400 in Johor and U.S.$600 in Singapore; land costs U.S.$2.3 per square meter in Batam versus U.S.$4.08 in Johor and U.S.$4.25 in Singapore (Lee, 1991:9; see also Table 3.1). These represent a smaller range of factor price differentials but are still large enough to attract investors.

In fact, the twinning of Singapore and Johor dated back to 1979, when Malaysia welcomed the relocation of labor-intensive operations envisaged by Singapore's second industrial revolution. This subregional division of labor was given a further boost when, in 1984, political endorsement of economic links resulted in cooperation between the Malaysian Industrial Development Authority and Singapore's Economic Development Board in facilitating industrial relocation and tourism linkages. In the wake of the recession in Singapore in 1985, the need to restructure its economy by moving up (upgrading production) or moving out (relocating) manufacturing production was keenly felt. Following Malaysian economic deregulation, the Johor state government announced a policy of "twinning" with Singapore in 1988. A clear testimony to the political endorsements of the governments concerned was that in 1988 the flow of investment from Singapore to Johor increased dramatically by 200 percent. Economic relations between Singapore and Johor grew closer, as 40 percent of Singaporean trade with Malaysia passed through Johor and 70 percent of Malaysia's tourist arrivals entered from Singapore by way of Johor (Perry, 1991; Parsonage, 1992).

Despite Johor's success in attracting capital to escape Singapore's land and labor constraints, its declining investment attractiveness was beginning to show in a number of ways. Singapore depends on Johor for the supply of water, which can be ensured only on the basis of amicable regional cooperation. Other strains in the bilateral relations were revealed in rising living costs in Johor, an increase in foreign ownership, and a widely held perception that the economic gains were captured by Malaysian Chinese. In its long-term interests, Singapore decided to pursue "regional reconfiguration" and looked for new directions. In particular, greater emphasis was to be given to local firms and services to seek a regional management role beyond production, an orientation that has been dubbed the third industrial revolution in Singapore. It was to look south toward the Riau Islands (Perry, 1991; Perry et al., 1997).

Indonesia has been promoting the economic development of the

Riau Islands since the 1970s, but the results have been only modest. After almost 20 years of promotional efforts, Batam, the main island in the archipelago about the size of Singapore, was little changed. Singapore and Indonesia shared the mutual goal of seeking more rapid development in the island group.

The success of Johor's twinning policy was used by Prime Minister Lee Kwan Yew in 1989 to persuade Indonesian President Suharto to agree to liberalize investment regulations in Batam. These changes allowed foreign investors, especially those based in Singapore, to retain 100 percent equity in Batam for five years, after which only 5 percent was to be transferred to Indonesian investors. This compared with the need to divest 51 percent of ownership after 15 years elsewhere in Indonesia. Indonesian deregulation included permission for private investors to develop industrial estates, previously the exclusive purview of the Trade Ministry. Batam was designated a free-trade zone, the only one of its kind in Indonesia. A Board of Investment Office was opened in Batam with decision-making autonomy from the head office in Jakarta. Singapore fell short of securing pioneer status for Batam, but the measures taken were sufficient to make Batam a privileged investment location in Indonesia (Perry, 1991; Parsonage, 1992). On June 29, 1991, Singapore and Indonesia signed a 50-year water agreement under which water resources in Riau will be developed to supply both Singapore and Riau (Lee, 1991:80). In so doing, Singapore has diversified its sources of water supply beyond that of Johor.

In a short span of a few years, Batam has witnessed rapid development. Approved foreign investment in Batam soared from U.S.$65 million in 1988 to almost U.S.$300 million in 1990, more than a fourfold increase in three years. Singapore accounted for about 45 percent of the cumulative foreign investment in Batam committed up to 1990, totaling U.S.$299.164 million, followed by the United States and the United Kingdom. During the period 1988–1990, the official workforce increased from 9,600 to 16,300, the value of exports from U.S.$44 million to U.S.$150 million, and the population from 80,000 to 107,000. Visits from Singaporean tourists increased from around 5,000 per month in the mid-1980s to over 30,000 in 1990. The most tangible proof of bilateral cooperation between Singapore and Indonesia was the U.S.$400 million joint venture, Batam Industrial Park, established in January 1990. It combined Singaporean state capital and leading Indonesian political and economic elites. Batam's economy is to be built on three main sectors: tourism, agrobusiness, and manufacturing industry. The physical and economic landscape of Batam has been transformed (Perry, 1991).

The formation of the JSR Growth Triangle represents a blend of private-sector initiatives and government intervention. Like any fledgling cooperative entity, it has its share of problems and challenges. First, as many observers would perceive, the economic logic for a growth triangle here is compelling, but the politics are complex. The Singapore-Johor nexus is especially sensitive in a political sense, as Johor operates as a state under a federal Malaysian government. Malaysia is concerned about a "dependent" relationship between Johor and Singapore, akin to a core-periphery setup. It is also concerned that the concentration of foreign investment in Johor will affect equitable regional development and even contradict its national development policy. Johor itself would like the state economy to leap forward into high-tech manufacturing, heavy industries, high-volume tourism, and services, which will pose direct competition with Singapore (Lee, 1991:70). Second, the triangular relationship is anchored in Singapore as two bilateral cooperative links. To date, little has brought the economies of Johor and Batam together, as they have very similar factor endowments. Planned and actual development flows between them are minimal (Thant et al., 1998:9). Third, the visible Singaporean influence in Johor and Batam is feared and to a degree resented. An ethnic dimension exists here, as much of the foreign investment from Singapore is derived from ethnic Chinese Singaporeans in territories where the population is mainly Malaysian. In Johor, everything from vice to the high cost of land is blamed on Singaporeans. In Batam, allegations exist of "dormitory capitalism." The Jakarta government has been reported to chafe at the influence that Singapore now wields on Indonesian territory (Vatikiotis, 1993a; Burton, 1994). The dilemmas facing the concerned territories perhaps can be summed up in this quotation on what they have to do to resolve their differences in the interest of their shared goals:

The present situation is a throwback to the historical period when the three areas were part of the same empire. The question now is whether, with such a historical heritage, the ASEAN [Association of Southeast Asian Nations] partners can overcome national political and economic interests and co-operate to enhance overall economic growth. The Growth Triangle offers an opportunity for three partners to test their political and economic commitment to a greater economic zone. (Lee, 1991:24)

The success of the JSR Growth Triangle is attested to by its recent expansion. In March 1996, it was expanded to include three additional states in Malaysia (Melaka, Negri Sembilan, and Penang) and one province in Indonesia (West Sumatra). In mid-1997, Indonesia proposed five more provinces to be included, namely, Bengkulu, Jambi, Lampung, South Sumatra, and West Kalimantan (Thant et al., 1998:9–10).

Tumen River Growth Triangle

The delta area focused on the Tumen River involving China, North Korea, and Russia has lately attracted considerable attention because of their common interest in seeking closer economic cooperation to develop it into a massive free-trade zone. Apart from the three riparian countries, Mongolia, South Korea, and Japan have shared their interest in cooperative development. They have been meeting since 1991 under the aegis of the United Nations Development Program (UNDP), which funded an 18-month feasibility study beginning in 1992. The central proposition of the U.S.$30 billion project is to transform the Tumen delta into an international free-trade area, ambitiously envisaged as the "future Rotterdam of the Far East" (Court, 1993).

China is strongly motivated in the project because at the mouth of the Tumen River its northeast provinces are denied direct access to the Pacific Ocean by a narrow 15-kilometer corridor. China was a Japan Sea littoral state until the Treaty of Aihun of 1858, by which China was forced to cede to Russia the entire Siberian coast, including the mouth of the Tumen River. North Korea and Russia share a border with China and see this as an opportunity to speed up development. North Korea is perhaps the most enthusiastic about the project, as it perceives an opportunity to attract investment. Landlocked Mongolia is keenly interested in the project as a prospect of having the shortest access to the Pacific Ocean. Japan and South Korea, for their own economic and strategic reasons, are keen on stability and economic cooperation in the area.

At the moment, conceptual designs for the project are still in flux. Three levels of development can be distinguished. At the first level is the Tumen River Economic Zone (TREZ), a roughly 1,000-square-kilometer free district, including China's Hunchun, North Korea's Najin, and Russia's Posyet. These are the sites for the free-trade zones of the three riparian countries, but whether they should be separate, contiguous, or merged under some sort of supranational administrative authority is yet to be decided (Clifford and Kaye, 1992). This zone is located at the mouth of the river and constitutes the core of the project (Kakazu, 1998:275–277). At the second level, farther away from the ocean, is the Tumen River Economic Development Area (TREDA), with about 10,000 square kilometers. Consisting of a hoof-shaped plain, it is bounded approximately by China's Yanji, Russia's Vladivostok, and North Korea's Chongjin. TREDA is subsumed under the Tumen River Area Development Program (TRADP), signed by the concerned countries under UNDP auspices in July 1991 (Kim and Wu, 1998). The third level of cooperation refers to an expanded region called the Northeast Asia Regional Development Area, occupying 370,000 square kilometers of the river valley and beyond, binding the border provinces of the three countries together (Li, 1992).

The geography of the Tumen delta is of strategic interest to Japan from the standpoint of transport. Niigata is only 850 kilometers from the Tumen River, and as a result this is viewed positively by many Japanese as an ideal transfer point toward the European market. A land bridge, if eventually constructed linking Hunchun to Europe, will save the existing Eurasia land bridge by way of the trans-Siberian railway at least 1,000 kilometers. Active development in the Tumen area will likely bring prosperity to western coastal areas in Japan.

The Tumen project is a concrete example of subregional economic cooperation that has emerged in Northeast Asia. At present, the concept and focus of cooperation are being defined and sharpened, but what distinguishes this project from other subregional cooperative ventures is the assistance provided by an outside body (the UNDP) and the possible funding by international development banks for some of its development projects. However, many obstacles need to be overcome before the project can move forward, including institutional and legal arrangements for cooperative development and a clearer expression of official commitment by the governments concerned. The Chinese government has agreed with Russia to invest more than U.S.$100 million and to construct a short rail link into Russia (Martinez, 1993). By early 1998, the UNDP-aided Sino-Russian border railway connecting Hunchun in Jilin province and Russia's Makhalino was nearing completion. Both sides agreed to start joint international transportation on July 1, 1998 (Clear Thinking, 1998a). In addition, North Korea designated the Najin-Sonbong port area a free-trade zone in 1992. China set up its latest SEZ in Hunchun in 1993, and Russian plans for Vladisvostok are already in place (Court, 1993). All signs appear to be pointing to a fair likelihood that something positive will emerge from the collaborative efforts.

Indeed, the first phase of the TRADP from 1991 to 1994 involved the UNDP spending about $4.5 million for general studies and the establishment of an institutional framework for cooperation. The second phase began in May 1995, when emphasis was placed on harmonizing existing projects, progress of which had been erratic (Thant et al., 1998:12).

In short, the development projects of the Tumen River basin for East Asian economies have been described as economically very attractive and yet politically complicated. The viability of any practicable strategy depends critically on a balance of opposing forces, as conceptualized by Kim (1992). Despite the Program Management Committee (PMC) countries having met twice in 1995 to establish two bodies and facilitate actual implementation of the TRADP, obstacles still impede the full implementation of subregional cooperation. Tumen delta development still remains a potential "growth pole" of converting formerly centralized economies into more dynamic market economies (Kakazu, 1998:291–293; see also Shiode, 1998).

NEWLY EMERGING GROWTH TRIANGLES

Against the background of rapid economic growth in the Asia-Pacific region and the strengthening processes of globalization, planners in many parts of the region have been encouraged by the positive demonstrative effects of the existing growth triangles. Under the aegis of the Asian Development Bank (ADB), three subregional groupings have been formed within the ASEAN region to further closer subnational economic cooperation. A short review of these new groupings follows.

IMT-GT: This growth triangle networks two Indonesian provinces of North Sumatra and Daerah Istimewa (DI) Aceh; the four northern Malaysian states of Kedah, Penang, Perak, and Perlis; and five provinces in southern Thailand: Narathiwat, Pattani, Satun, Songkhla, and Yala. Overall, the Indonesia-Malaysia-Thailand Growth Triangle (IMT-GT) covers almost 200,000 square kilometers, 70 percent of which is in Indonesia, and a population of over 20 million. The IMT-GT strategy followed an eight-month study supported by the ADB to explore subregional economic cooperation that began in late 1993.

These territories have several facets in common: a long and common history, a Muslim and ethnically related population, and a location on the fringe of their country considered relatively backward and remote. The synergies among the three subregions are generated in part by northern peninsular Malaysia, which has experienced rapid industrialization in Pulau Pinang, Perak, and Kedah, with the contribution by the manufacturing sector above the national average. In 1995, the per capita income levels of Indonesia, Malaysia, and Thailand were $980, $3,890, and $2,740, respectively. Thus, there is a difference in the level of development, and complementarity exists. Northern Malaysia experiences a labor shortage in contrast to surplus labor in the other two territories in southern Thailand and northern Sumatra.

The initial investigative study of the idea of subregional economic cooperation was undertaken by a joint Malaysian and Thai government effort. Some of the potential fields of collaboration include trade, human resources development, joint tourism promotion, natural resources development, energy development cooperation, infrastructure networks, transport and shipping services, and environmental protec-

tion and management (Economic Planning Unit Malaysia and National Economic and Social Development Board Thailand, 1993). The
ADB study went beyond this. A comprehensive set of policy, program,
project, and institutional actions, consisting of ninety-seven initiatives,
was recommended to facilitate the achievement of the main IMT-GT
goals and various sector objectives. Financing of the strategy was examined, with direct and indirect support required from government
and development agencies. It was concluded that IMT-GT had met a
number of key conditions for successful subregional cooperation. By
the end of 1996, sectoral working groups had met to discuss investment
proposals. By 1997, forty-seven memoranda of understanding worth
about $6 billion had been signed. From all indications, the IMT-GT
has taken off to a favorable start (Thant, 1998).

EAGA: Another part of Southeast Asia comprising the Brunei
Darussalam-Indonesia-Malaysia-Philippines East ASEAN Growth
Area (BIMP-EAGA, or simply EAGA) was identified by the four governments in March 1994 as an area of regional cooperation. Again, the
ADB funded a technical assistance study of EAGA for the purpose
of formulating a strategy of regional development to facilitate economic cooperation. This sprawling part of ASEAN is plentiful in natural and human resources, with the population in 1995 estimated to be
at 30 million. The population in these territories shares the Islamic
faith and is ethnically and linguistically related.

At first sight, complementarities do not appear to be strong among
the four territories, but labor export and tourism development are
viewed as two potential fields for cooperation. The EAGA strategy calls
for closer cooperation among the participating countries through productive and supportive activities. Productive activities directly create
wealth, such as agriculture, fisheries and forestry, industrial development, and tourism, whereas supportive activities facilitate the creation
of wealth, such as trade, investment and trade in financial services, human resource development, transport and communications, and energy. To implement the development strategy, 151 policy, program, and
project initiatives have been identified. A $300 million EAGA growth
fund is also being planned to finance various development projects.
Evidence of early success is that in 1996 EAGA already expanded its

geographic coverage by including seven more provinces in Indonesia at its government's request (Pernia, 1998).

GMS: Although the Mekong Committee was established in 1957 as a UN initiative, the concept of involving the six countries—Cambodia, the Lao People's Democratic Republic, Myanmar, Thailand, Vietnam, and Yunnan province of the People's Republic of China—in regional cooperation surfaced only very recently. On the basis of existing bilateral and multicountry initiatives and with technical assistance from the ADB, the six economies of the Greater Mekong Subregion (GMS) entered into a comprehensive program of subregional economic cooperation in 1992.

The GMS covers a land area of about 2.3 million square kilometers, with a total population of about 237 million in 1996. The region is rich in natural resources, with a fertile agricultural base, extensive timber and fisheries resources, considerable mineral deposits, and vast energy reserves in the form of hydropower, coal, petroleum, and gas. The ADB-assisted program is focused on project identification and preparation for financing. Some 100 priority subregional projects in seven sectors have been agreed to by the GMS countries and are currently at various stages of preparation and implementation. Since 1992, the ADB assistance process has been divided into three phases, with the third phase, on implementation, beginning in 1997.

As many areas are poorly developed, the GMS has emphasized its cooperative efforts on infrastructure and energy development. In this respect, public sector leadership and implementation are crucial, being financed from the international donor community and external private financiers, in view of the high capital costs of these projects and the very limited local financing from the private sector. The basic objective of GMS cooperation is to directly change the economic structure of the subregion through cooperative development in specific projects. Ultimately, subregional cooperation is aimed at reducing economic distance and enlarging economic space.

For many of the cooperative goals to be realized, resources must be mobilized successfully, especially financing. As financial requirements far exceed the capacity of governments and official sources of financing, the private sector and the GMS governments are presented with the challenge of seeking innovative and feasible forms of public-private partnerships and collaboration. Multilateral institutions such as the ABD can also play an effective role in resource mobilization (Abonyi and Pante, 1998).

Beyond these relatively new growth triangles, other less definite designs have been proposed as well. The region centered around Timor, Irian Jaya in Indonesia, Darwin in Australia, and Papua New Guinea has been suggested as a suitable candidate. Even the newly established states in central Asia, Pakistan, and Iran have been mentioned as a likely subregion for promoting transnational economic cooperation.

Related to growth triangles but conceptually covering a wider region have been territorial designs to enhance economic cooperation and regional integration for the benefit of all concerned. These groupings would mainly involve more countries encompassing a wider territory. One example is the GMS, which has involved six countries. Other propositions include the Northeast Asia Economic Zone, the Yellow Sea Economic Zone, the Japan Sea Rim Economic Zone, and the Greater ASEAN Economic Zone (see Figure 2.1). By and large, these are focused on a geographic region or a prominent physical feature, but the underlying spirit of regional cooperation parallels the one that has powered the growth triangles. Their proliferation has been viewed as evidence of the much vaunted peace dividend in the wake of the end of the Cold War (Thant et al., 1998:19).

DISCUSSION

Having reviewed the conceptual and operational milieu of growth triangles in the Asia-Pacific region, it is appropriate at this point to address some key issues. How could they be developed and planned or market led? What has been the role of national policies for regional cooperation? Does any conspicuous division of labor exist among participating countries? What is the legal and institutional basis of international cooperation for the successful development of a growth triangle? These issues can be tackled with reference to the empirical evidence that has been presented in this chapter.

Whether a growth triangle can be planned or market led should not be posed as a dichotomous question. It is often a question of degree rather than one of either-or. In the southern China experience, the initial spark came from China's adoption of an open policy and its willingness to embark on economic reforms that made things possible. However, the initial decision to move industrial plants to southern China by businessmen from Hong Kong and Taiwan was predicated on the proverbial entrepreneurial risk-taking and cultural affinity. Subsequent policy liberalizations by the governments merely took cognizance of an unstoppable tide of economic and cultural interactions. In the JSR Growth Triangle, it was largely a government initiative taken by Singapore that found favorable receptions in Malaysia and Indonesia in the spirit of ASEAN cooperation. The economic logic for Singapore, not unlike that for Hong Kong and Taiwan, was to relocate manufacturing industries to neighboring territories to remain competitive in the global market. In so doing, they were able to restructure their economies more toward services and high-tech. Finally, in the Tumen River delta, had it not been for the leadership provided by the UNDP, the scheme of transnational cooperation would move sluggishly in view of the historical animosity among the participating countries. The trilateral cooperation plan has not yet taken shape, but something positive is likely to emerge from the goodwill and efforts that have been invested to date.

The role of national policies in regional cooperation is important but can lead to frictions at the operational level if a flexible approach is not taken. In a small country such as Singapore, the need for national policies to project visions of the future is vital for its survival and sustainability. In this respect, the Singaporean government has done admirably well in being able to anticipate problems and to position itself in terms of changing global and regional economies. In countries such as China and Malaysia, with the provincial and state governments in charge primarily of implementing subnational economic cooperation, a measure of policy flexibility must be allowed if actual cooperation is to run smoothly. In the case of China, Guangdong and Fujian have been granted more autonomy than other provinces to pursue their target of accelerating development within prescribed policies (see Yeung and Chu, 1998), but the difference in federal and state government views on Singapore's investment in Johor occasionally tested the will of co-operative development.

The conceptual underpinning of a growth triangle is varied factor endowments, with the obvious corollary that a division of labor exists. The natural complementarities as witnessed in the Southern China and JSR Growth Triangles are the main reasons for their success. In essence, if growth triangles are viewed as a subset of the spatial manifestations of the global division of labor, such internal division is an expected and necessary characteristic of the subregional entity. In the current phase of globalization, the borderless economy has come to the fore, with transnational capital seeking locations globally for production and services that will produce the highest yields. The division of labor within growth triangles can be readily understood in this global context.

A legal system and the institutions to guide international cooperation in a growth triangle can protect investors and remove elements of uncertainty. In general, investors and entrepreneurs have been protected by the laws and institutions in the countries forming the growth triangle. For example, different perceptions of one's gain from regional cooperation may lead to parties being loath to institutionalize economic ties. Not surprisingly, Kuala Lumpur and Jakarta have been reported to stall on a trilateral government agreement on the JSR Growth Triangle (Vatikiotis, 1993b). In any event, it has been the Asian tradition of doing business through personal contact rather than bureaucratic rules and of relying on memoranda of understanding between participating governments rather than treaties (Burton, 1994). Essentially, minimal intervention, but within certain prescribed rules, would enable economic cooperation to proceed at an uninterrupted pace.

To conclude this chapter, the question of replicability and the future of growth triangles inevitably comes to mind. The existing triangles surely confirm the fact that in the continuing evolution of the global economy they have found a successful niche to harness new economic opportunities by increasing their competitiveness through subregional cooperation. They represent perhaps one mode of cooperation oriented toward export manufacturing. Their strong natural complementarities have enabled them to seek this pattern of development. However, this does not preclude other forms of economic cooperation, such as joint exploitation of natural and energy resources and infrastructure development, as some of the newly emerging growth triangles strongly suggest. At least within the context of ASEAN, it has been submitted that because growth triangles are not trade led but investment led, their multiplication and overlapping will eventually assist the goals of regional cooperation, as targeted in the ASEAN Free Trade Area (AFTA), to be in place in 15 years from 1993 (Naidu, 1998). From the trends and patterns of global and regional development, the Asia-Pacific region will most likely remain a strong growth center within which growth triangles will be important contributors to this growth. Asia's financial crisis since 1997 would inevitably have set back the pace of development in some of the growth triangles in the region. However, in the long run, their inherent bases of economic cooperation will carry them well into the twenty-first century to contribute to the economic growth and modernization of the region.

4 Infrastructure Development in the Southern China Growth Triangle

INTRODUCTION

Much of the rapid economic development in the Asia-Pacific region in recent years has taken place across national boundaries as economic agents have attempted to capitalize on differing endowments of land, capital, and labor. Economic hubs, or growth triangles, have been established to enable countries to maximize the advantages to be derived from the possession of these factors of production and to produce synergistic conditions conducive to economic growth. The objective of this chapter is to examine how economic growth in the Southern China Growth Triangle (consisting of Guangdong and Fujian provinces, Taiwan, and Hong Kong) has been facilitated by infrastructure development and how development planning has taken account of the political integration between the People's Republic of China (PRC) and Hong Kong in 1997.

The chapter is divided into five sections. The first section briefly traces the development of infrastructure in the Southern China Growth Triangle. Only cursory attention is devoted to Taiwan and Hong Kong, as information about these economies is readily available, and much has been written about their economic and infrastructure development. The emphasis on Guangdong and Fujian provinces is deliberate, with the four special economic zones (SEZs) within them being given special attention where appropriate. In this section and throughout the chapter, infrastructure is broadly defined to include facilities such as roads, railways, ports, airports, water, electricity, and housing. The second section examines the sequencing of infrastructure developments in the Pearl River delta area and looks at the prospects for future development. The costs of infrastructure development and financing arrangements are analyzed in the third section. The fourth section evaluates public policies relating to pricing, crowding out of investment, and environmental concerns. The fifth section spells out the lessons to be learned from past experiences and the prospects for future infrastructure development in the region. This section also discusses the role that bilateral and multilateral institutions can play.

For the purposes of this chapter, "South China" will refer to Guangdong and Fujian provinces of the PRC.

SURVEY OF INFRASTRUCTURE DEVELOPMENT

Rapid economic development in Hong Kong and Taiwan over the past decades has been based to a large measure on heavy but judicious investment in infrastructure. This has enabled these economies to reach their present preeminent positions, with their export-oriented manufacturing and service industries accounting for much of their growth.

Hong Kong

In Hong Kong, investments in infrastructure were gradual but consistent during the years after World War II, with the greatest burst of activity occurring in the 1980s after the adoption of an open policy by the PRC in 1978. In 1963, the PRC was approached about the possibility of supplying water to Hong Kong from the East River (Dong Jiang). This became the first in a series of agreements governing sales of water by Guangdong to help Hong Kong ease its water supply problem. The supply of water from the PRC will increase to 840 million cubic meters in the year 2000 (Yeung, 1992).

Other milestones in Hong Kong's infrastructure development were the construction of the container terminal at Kwai Chung port in 1970, the completion of the first cross-harbor tunnel in 1973, the opening of the mass transit railway in 1979, and the electrification and double-tracking of the Kowloon-Canton railway in 1983. However, the first systematic attempt to establish a coherent framework for the development of roads, railways, and ports came with the formulation of the Territorial Development Strategy (TDS) in 1984. The TDS partly addressed the lack of coordination between urban development and transport provision, notably in the towns that developed rapidly in the New Territories in the 1970s. This was followed in 1988 by the Port and Airport Development Strategy (PADS), which was designed to help the territory meet the projected growth in port and air traffic to the year 2001. Also in 1988, discussions on a "Metroplan" were initiated. The primary objective of the Metroplan was to enhance Hong Kong's role as an international port and airport. Thus, the White Paper on Transport Policy in Hong Kong in 1990 called for (1) the replacement of Kai Tak Airport with a new airport at Chek Lap Kok on Lantau Island and (2) the expansion of port facilities in Tsing Yi, Stonecutters Island, Tuen Mun, and North Lantau (Yeh, 1993; see Figure 4.1).

Although a memorandum of understanding between the Chinese and British governments was signed in 1991 on PADS, the ten core projects surrounding the new airport were dogged by controversy, with disputes stemming initially from the rapid escalation of the total cost estimates from HK$98.6 billion in March 1991 to HK$112.2 billion in April 1992 at March 1991 prices. Differences over political reforms called into question the validity of the contract award for Container Terminal 9, which was to have been commissioned in 1993. Protracted delay in reaching an agreement came to an end only in September 1996, when the concerned parties struck a deal to break the deadlock. Construction of the terminal began in the first half of 1998, and the first berths will be open for operation at the end of 2001. Meanwhile, traffic between Hong Kong and South China has been on the rise, with the average daily traffic through the three border crossing points with Shenzhen increasing from 13,450 vehicles in 1990 to 23,280 in 1995.

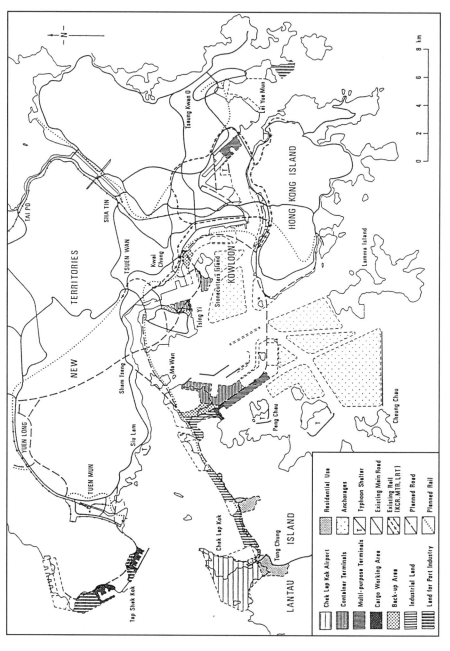

■ Figure 4.1 The Port and Airport Development Strategy (PADS), Hong Kong

Vehicles carrying goods accounted for 95 percent of the traffic, reflecting the massive relocation of manufacturing enterprises from Hong Kong (D. Chu, 1992).

Taiwan

Not unlike Hong Kong, Taiwan has been investing heavily in infrastructure development to bolster its economic growth. The most important breakthrough in this respect was the launching of the Ten Major Construction Projects in 1973 at a cost of NT$200 billion. Among the projects were six that focused on infrastructure development: the North-South freeway, Suao harbor, Taichung harbor, the railways electrification project, the Taoyuan International Airport, and the North-Link railway (see Figure 4.2). These projects contributed greatly to Taiwan's economic takeoff in a number of ways. For example, the North-South freeway and the railway electrification projects linked the major cities along the west coast of the island, shortened the travel time between the north and the south, and accelerated economic and social development in general. The North-Link railway provided the eastern part of the island with improved access to the Taipei metropolitan area, allowing greater population mobility. Taichung harbor facilitated the import and export of materials and products for Taichung's industrial development (Tsai, 1996). At the peak of Taiwan's economic growth in 1977 and 1978, investment in the Ten Major Construction Projects accounted for 13 and 8 percent, respectively, of total fixed asset investment (Executive Yuan, 1979). According to some estimates, the annual government expenditure on infrastructure may have been as high as 25 to 30 percent of total fixed asset investment during the past 30 years (Kao and Lee, 1991). Whatever the actual figure, the Ten Major Construction Projects involved massive government outlays and were a critical factor in bringing Taiwan out of an international recession and accelerating its economic and social development. This program was followed by the Twelve Major Construction Projects and the Fourteen Major Construction Projects, both of which emphasized infrastructure development.

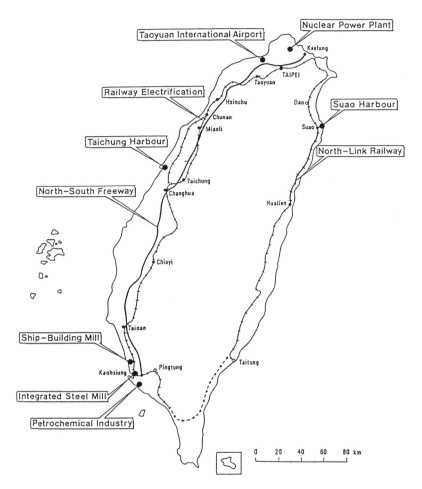

Nuclear Power Plant

Taoyuan International Airport

Kaelung

TAIPEI

Taoyuan

Railway Electrification

Hsinchu

Ilan

Suao Harbour

Chunan

Miaoli

Suao

Taichung Harbour

North-Link Railway

Taichung

North-South Freeway

Changhua

Hualien

Chiayi

Tainan

Ship-Building Mill

Taitung

Kaohsiung

Pingtung

Integrated Steel Mill

Petrochemical Industry

0   20   40   60   80 km

■ Figure 4.2 Location of the Ten Major Construction Projects
          in Taiwan

More ambitious than any of the earlier infrastructure development
schemes is Taiwan's Six-Year National Development Plan (1991–1996),
which involved a total expenditure of $303 billion. It was a compre-
hensive strategy that sought simultaneously "to rebuild economic and
social order and to promote all-round balanced development." It included 775 development projects that touched practically all aspects of
economic and social life. For the transport sector, the plan provided for

the construction of the Taipei Rapid Transit System, a second north-south highway, a high-speed railway along the island's western coast, and additional mass transit systems for the major cities of Kaohsiung, Taichung, Tainan, and others. Plans were made to build two additional nuclear plants, telecommunications facilities, and environmental protection projects (*Far Eastern Economic Review*, 1992a). Despite some of the construction plans being downscaled by decreased government spending between 1995 and 1997, the need for expanding and improving the island's transport infrastructure became more critical with the official approval of the Asia-Pacific Regional Operations Center's plan in early 1995 (Wu, 1997). Consequently, the largest-ever infrastructure project was launched in July 1998 to build a 340-kilometer rail link between Taipei and Kaohsiung, and another high priority, a NT$50 billion rail link between Taipei city and Chiang Kai-shek International Airport, was contracted out in the same year (*Far Eastern Economic Review,* 1998a:205).

South China

Since 1978, Guangdong and Fujian provinces have been attempting to develop their infrastructure after many years of neglect. Development across sectors has been uneven, but the past few years have seen feverish activities as the government has sought to keep pace with rapid economic growth.

Land Transport

In land transport, one of the most pressing needs is the extension of the railway network to unserved areas (see Figure 4.3). For decades, the eastern and western parts of Guangdong have been inaccessible by rail. In recent times, the national and provincial governments have tried to rectify this situation. Access to western Guangdong was improved in 1991 with the completion of the San-Mao (Sanshui and Maoming) railway. Double-tracking of the Hengyang-Guangzhou and Guangzhou-Shenzhen railways was also recently completed. The second Beijing-Kowloon railway, a 2,538-kilometer line that runs parallel to the

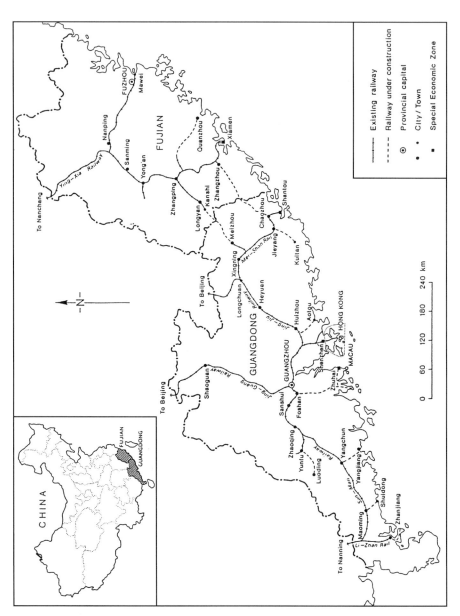

■ Figure 4.3 Rail Network of Guangdong and Fujian, c. 1997

existing line to the east through nine provinces by way of Tianjin and Jiaojing, was opened on September 1, 1996. However, the network in eastern Guangdong is still fragmented and awaiting the completion of lines to Meizhou and Shantou. At present, the two provinces are not linked by rail, but plans exist to make them accessible to each other. Guangdong has agreed to finance the 80.3-kilometer section from Meizhou to the border, whereas Fujian will construct the 44.2-kilometer section from Longyan to the border as a joint venture between its government and Hong Kong investors at a cost of $55 million (*Ta Kung Pao*, July 3, 1992). The most impressive project is the proposed 280-kilometer-per-hour bullet train, the first in the PRC, between Fuzhou and Xiamen, with the Itogawa Group from Japan jointly investing $2 billion with the Fujian government. The project, which is targeted for completion by 1998, will shorten the journey between Fuzhou and Xiamen from the current six to seven hours by car to slightly over an hour (Chor, 1992). However, it was ascertained during field reconnaissance in Fuzhou in July 1996 that the project had been abandoned. Instead, highway construction has proceeded apace.

In 1997, Guangdong had a total highway length of 91,862 kilometers. Even in 1995, almost all towns and 93.4 percent of the villages were linked by roads (*Guangdong Yearbook 1998*) (see Table 4.1). The road network in the two provinces is shown in Figure 4.4. The coverage by road is superior to that by rail, and highway construction has continued at a brisk pace. In Fujian, efforts have been made to accelerate the highway network centered around Fuzhou, with eight highways either being planned or now under construction. These are Fuzhou-Fuding, Quanzhou-Xiamen, Fuzhou-Quanzhou, Fuzhou-Minqing-Jianyang, Jianyang-Sanming, Putian-Meizhou Dao, Zhangzhou-Longyan, and Changting-Longyan (*Wah Kiu Yat Po*, September 20, 1992).

Water Transport

The long coastline in both Guangdong and Fujian makes marine transport viable. The presence of many rivers in both provinces also

■ Table 4.1 Main Indicators of Transportation, Postal, and Telecommunication Services in Guangdong Province, 1988–1997

Item	Unit	1988	1990	1995	1997
Operating railways	Kilometers	1,128	1,287	1,861	2,051
Highways	Kilometers	53,820	54,671	84,563	91,862
Navigable inland waterways	Kilometers	10,792	10,857	10,808	10,808
Civil aviation routes	Kilometers	81,706	107,979	296,226	463,953
Ship berths	Number	1,167	1,938	2,285	2,368
10,000-ton berths	Number	38	61	93	106
Berth length	Meters	42,930	81,605	111,262	128,668
Permanent highway bridges	Number	10,709	10,996	15,806	17,319
Civil motor vehicles	Number	324,195	402,086	1,147,348	1,234,317
Motor vessels	Number	37,775	40,473	33,117	29,250
	Net tons	4,944,417	7,611,980	7,888,261	6,567,844
Civil aviation aircraft	Number	68	73	97	94
Post and telecommunication office	Number	2,541	2,573	3,580	3,978

Direct-dial long-distance telephone lines	Number	16,042	38,030	449,548	530,068
Telephone exchange	10,000 lines	92.7	180.7	1,007.1	1,405.3
Urban telephone exchange	10,000 lines	58.1	108.9	569.8	881.0
Telephone sets	10,000 units	87.12	155.43	729.93	1,005.43
Per 100 persons	Number	1.47	2.45	10.63	17.75
Long-distance telephone lines	Number	10,211	20,845	159,162	205,748
Road passenger traffic	10,000 units	37,476	34,152	49,220	55,050
Per 100 million passengers	Kilometers	298.79	301.08	556.17	601.97
Road freight traffic	10,000 tons	19,173	18,792	24,636	24,664
Per 100 million tons	Kilometers	1,953.57	2,214.38	3,363.32	3,204.70
Seaport cargo	10,000 tons	11,582	11,904	18.933	20,358
Seaport passengers	10,000 units	3,166	2,686	2,795	2,144
Airport passengers	10,000 units	638	687	1,963	1,981
Operating volume of post and telecommunications (at 1990 prices)	RMB 100 million	13.46	26.30	204.93	330.38

Source: Guangdong Statistical Bureau (1991, 1998, table 14.1).

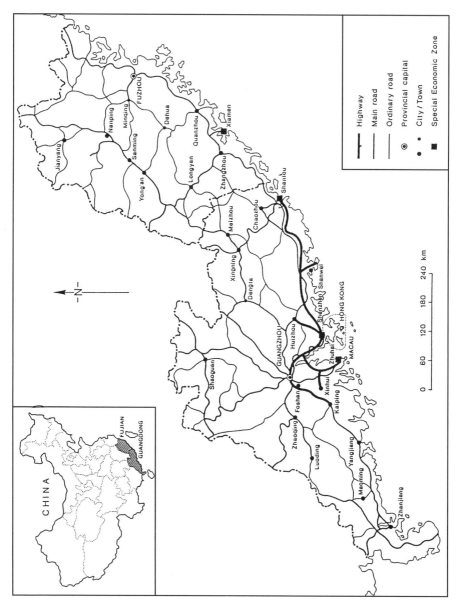

■ Figure 4.4 Road Network of Guangdong and Fujian, c. 1997

encourages the development of inland water transport (see Figure 4.5). Since 1978, Guangdong has built 2,368 berths along its coastal areas, 106 of which can accommodate ships of up to 10,000 deadweight tons. Its port-handling capacity had expanded annually from 44 million in 1978 to 204 million metric tons in 1997 (Table 4.1). As Figure 4.5 indicates, more ports exist along the coast of Guangdong than in Fujian, and three ports—Yantian in Shenzhen, Daya Bay's Oatou port, and Gaolan port in Zhuhai—have been approved by the central authorities for development into large, deepwater container ports (Liu et al., 1992). In contrast, Fuzhou, Xiamen, and other ports in Fujian lack modern handling facilities and do not have regular shipping schedules, so that many shippers prefer the more expensive three-day journey from Hong Kong's Kwai Chung port.

Air Transport

Figure 4.5 also shows the location of major airports in Guangdong and Fujian. Guangzhou's Beiyun Airport is the PRC's second-largest based on passenger traffic and the largest based on air cargo handling. With only one runway, it might reach the saturation point before 2000. Shenzhen's large Huangtian Airport, which began operations in 1991, will not need expansion in the foreseeable future, as capacity in the Pearl River delta is already high. Nevertheless, to cope with the rapid increase in air travel, existing airports are being expanded and modernized, and new ones are being planned or constructed. In 1995, new airports were opened in Zhuhai and Macau, which are neighboring cities sharing a common boundary. Most noteworthy for Guangdong is the explosion of air passenger traffic and civil aviation routes between 1988 and 1997 (see Table 4.1). In 1997 alone, Guangdong inaugurated 273 domestic routes and 34 international routes in addition to 21 scheduled chartered routes (*Guangdong Yearbook*, 1998:296).

Water Supply

As South China is situated in a subtropical climatic belt, it normally gets plenty of water from rainfall and rivers. However, periodic water

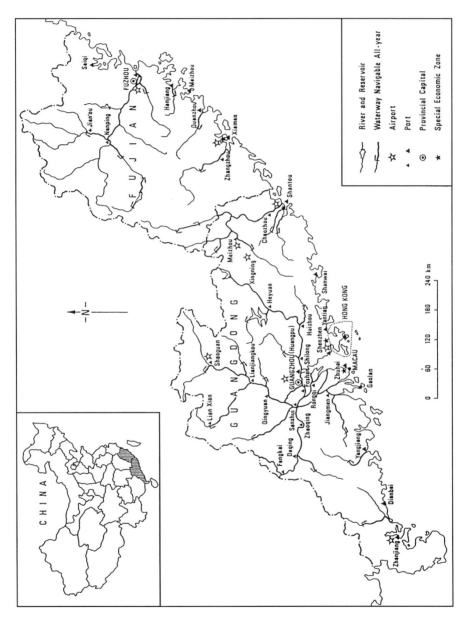

■ Figure 4.5 Water and Air Transport in Guangdong and Fujian

supply shortages occur in the burgeoning large cities on the eastern side of the Pearl River delta. Guangzhou, Shenzhen, Huiyang, and other cities must plan for the long term to ensure a steady supply of water. It has been suggested that it might be possible to divert water from the West River, which has an annual channel flow of 2,300 billion cubic meters, to the eastern parts of the delta (Cai, 1992). Over the past few years, significant progress has been reported in Guangdong in irrigation and channel improvement engineering works; however, because of silting and other problems, and despite seemingly incessant maintenance and improvements, the total length of navigable inland waterways in 1997 was below that of 1990 level (see Table 4.1).

Electricity

Hydroelectric power still constitutes a major source of power for the two provinces. In 1992, of the total power generation capacity in Guangdong of 8,070 megawatts (MW), some 3,330 MW was accounted for by hydroelectricity from the existing grid. The major power stations were Shajiao A (1,200 MW), Shajiao B (700 MW), Whampoa Addition (300 MW), Shaoguan Addition (200 MW), Conghua Pumped Storage (300 MW), Zhanjiang (600 MW), and Panyu (1,200 MW). Most of these are coal-fired or thermal power stations built with substantial investments from Hong Kong (To, 1992). In December 1992, Hopewell Holdings and other Hong Kong companies concluded a joint venture with a subsidiary of the Guangdoug General Power Company to develop three coal-fired generating units of 668 MW each at Shajiao C. The first generating unit began operation in December 1994 and would boost Guangdong's electricity supply by 13 percent (Manuel, 1992). Meanwhile, the first nuclear plant at Daya Bay, with a capacity of 1,800 MW, began operation in 1994. In September 1994, a committee was set up to deliberate on the construction of the second nuclear plant in Guangdong.

Even with these major projects, power shortages are likely to remain a problem in the Pearl River delta because of the increasing power requirements of the large number of manufacturing plants that have re-located there during the past decade. It is estimated that demand will soon outstrip supply by at least 40 percent (To, 1992). By 1997, Guang-dong's electricity-generating capacity reached 23,222 MW (Guang-dong Statistical Bureau, 1998 : 196). In 1998, Guangdong pressed ahead with its plans to invest another RMB60 billion[1] in new power projects on top of the budgeted RMB10.9 billion for that year. Thus, Guang-dong, along with Sichuan, reported power surpluses (Clear Thinking, 1998b). In Fujian, the authorities have realized the importance of tap-ping hydro and thermal sources, and preparations are being made for the building of nuclear plants. In the more remote areas, and especially in places not covered by the provincial power grid, attempts are being made to generate electricity from nonconventional sources, such as wind and tides (J. Chen, 1991).

Housing

A policy ensuring low-rent worker housing has been in existence in the PRC for decades. Since 1949, the government has viewed housing as a component of state welfare to be provided to all at nominal cost. In general, rents are the equivalent of only slightly more than 1 percent of the average household income, but prolonged subsidization has led to huge problems of poor maintenance, overconsumption, and limited in-centives for home ownership (Chiu, 1992).

More recently, the government has been encouraging home owner-ship, especially because savings realized from the rapid post-1978 eco-nomic growth in Guangdong and Fujian can be harnessed for housing development. At the same time, housing projects aimed at Hong Kong and overseas Chinese buyers have mushroomed in the Pearl River delta. In the first six months of 1992, as many as 12,956 housing units in the

[1] RMB stands for renminbi or yuan, the Chinese currency. In 1998 the U.S.$1 was converted to RMB8.2.

delta cities were offered for sale in Hong Kong. The majority of these were in Huiyang, Guangzhou, and Shenzhen (Ka, 1992).

Special Economic Zones

A survey of infrastructure development in South China would be incomplete without noting the status of the SEZs in Zhuhai, Shenzhen, Shantou, and Xiamen. The four SEZs were designed to spearhead national modernization efforts, and their success was predicated on providing adequate infrastructure to attract foreign investment. When the SEZs were established in 1980, the infrastructure was rudimentary; since then, many projects have been completed (see Table 4.2).

DEVELOPMENT OF THE PEARL RIVER DELTA

The Pearl River delta, which has been a critical part of the rapid economic development in Guangdong, could further boost its rate of growth if its infrastructure were better developed. A total of $1.5 billion was invested there in 1991 by Taiwanese businessmen (Goldstein, 1992a). Hong Kong investors have more than 10,000 joint ventures and full subsidiaries in Guangdong. Nearly 60 percent of Hong Kong's reexports in 1990 consisted of raw materials or semimanufactures destined for factories in South China, whereas 61 percent of Hong Kong's imports from the PRC came from these factories (Cheng and Taylor, 1991).

Electricity

Because the Pearl River delta still has a critical shortage of electricity, the establishment of many large-scale power stations has attracted Hong Kong investors. Many small-scale generation stations are being developed as well, such as in Shenzhen, Dongguan, Humen, Foshan, Shunde, Huizhou, and Nanhai. These will ease the power supply shortage, although they will be more costly to operate because of their reliance on oil and their small size (Liu et al., 1992).

■ Table 4.2 Infrastructure in Special Economic Zones (SEZs) in South China

	Zhuhai	Shenzhen	Shantou	Xiamen
Seaports	Jinzhou deepwater port opened in 1987 Xiangzhou port with 11 berths for fishery and trading	Total 78 berths in 4 ports: Yantian, Chiwan, Shekou, and Mawan Two 350-TEU container terminals completed in Shekou	7 berths as of 1988	4 deepwater berths, 1 designed for container traffic
Airports	Zhuhai heliport completed in 1983 New airport being planned in Sanzao Island in western Zhuhai	Huangtian Airport opened in 1991 Heliport at Nantou providing air service for oil exploration in South China Sea	Shantou Airport expanded at RMB60 million; 8 routes, including 1 international, by 1988	Xiamen International Airport opened in October 1983
Railways		Train service scheduled between Shenzhen and Zhaoqing in 1990 Second Beijing-Kowloon railroad being constructed Shenzhen West Branch railway linking Shekou container terminal to Guangzhou-Kowloon Railway; construction began in 1991 Guangzhou-Shenzhen railway. Construction began in 1991	Guangzhou-Meizhou-Shantou railway to be completed in Eighth Five-Year Plan period	Electrification of Ying-Xia (Yingtan-Xiamen) opened in December 1993

Roads	373.5 km of roads and 105 bridges constructed by 1988.	302 km Zhuhai-Guangzhou-Shenzhen superhighway completed in mid-1990s at a total cost of RMB3,500 million.	50 km of roads built by 1988. Highway linking Shenzhen and Shantou being constructed.	A new causeway to link Xiamen Island to mainland planned.
Communications	151 telephone lines linking Hong Kong and Macau established by 1988; linked to 150 countries by IDD	17,654 long-distance telephone lines by 1994	251,909 telephones in urban area in 1994	Digitalized telephone exchange introduced and microwave telecommunications system installed
Electricity	Nanping supply station with 35 KW began operation in 1988		10-KW power line linking urban district with SEZs built in 1991; 110-KW power station completed in Lunghu in 1985; thermal power plant approved for construction in 1988	Thermal power plant approved for construction in 1990
Water supply	7 reservoirs with holding capacity of over one million cubic meters in city; new reservoir completed in Kuichong with holding capacity of 952,000 cubic meters	2-km pipeline linking urban districts with SEZs constructed in 1982; 25.8 km of water pipelines available by 1988.		

Source: Various publications.

Land Transport

To alleviate bottlenecks in land transport, many highway and railway projects have been proposed or are now being implemented (see Figure 4.6). With the completion in September 1996 of the new Beijing-Kowloon railway, north-south rail services have improved, and traffic has increased. A second new line, the Guang-Zhu railway, will connect Guangzhou with Zhuhai through seven counties and bring a large part of the western area of the delta within reach of rail service. The direct rail service between Foshan and Hong Kong, inaugurated in January 1993, reflects the growing demand in many cities of the delta for more frequent and direct contacts with Hong Kong.

Ongoing highway construction plans can reshape the nature of land transport in the delta. The most important of these is the Guangzhou-Shenzhen-Zhuhai superhighway, whose six lanes will link Guangzhou with the two SEZs of Shenzhen and Zhuhai. The first phase, covering 123 kilometers between Guangzhou and Huanggang (in Shenzhen), was completed and opened on July 18, 1994 at a cost of $1.2 billion. Dubbed the "spine of the province," the road has reduced travel time between Guangzhou and Shenzhen from the previous four hours to only 90 minutes. The contract for the construction of the second phase (146 kilometers linking Guangzhou with Zhuhai) was signed in October 1992, with Hopewell Holdings as one of the seven contracting parties (*Economic Journal,* October 26, 1992; Goldstein, 1992b). The contract also provided for the construction of the 33-kilometer Boca Tigris Bridge, opened in 1997, which spans the Pearl River and connects Nansha in Punyu with Humen in Dongguan (see Figure 4.6). The bridge, which is on one of two routes being envisaged, should also facilitate the delivery of water from the West River to the eastern flank of the delta (Cai, 1992). Along with the superhighways on either flank of the delta, the bridge dramatically reduces the travel time between the two sides of the estuary. The second phase will be implemented at a cost of $1.4 billion.

A car-ferry service was launched in 1991 linking Nansha and Humen. Jointly financed by Henry Fok, Lee Shau-kee of Henderson Land in Hong Kong, and Guangdong Enterprises, it halved the travel time

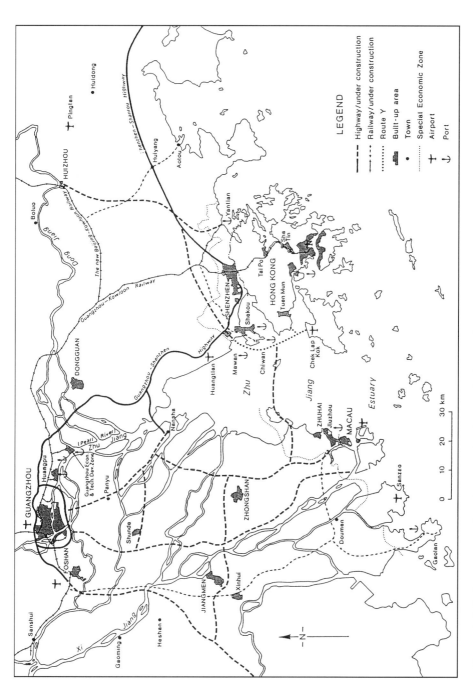

■ Figure 4.6 Infrastructure Development in the Pearl River Delta, 1997. Source: Variously derived information, 1997.

■ Table 4.3 Planned Highway Construction Projects
           in Guangdong, 1992–1998

	Length (km)	Total cost (million RMB)	Completion year
1. Yantian to Huizhou	64 (4 lanes)	600	1992
2. Foshan to Sanshui	32 (4 lanes)	4,200	1993
3. Guangzhou to Zhuhai (eastern lane)	76 (6 lanes)	3,400	1996
4. Foshan to Kai Ping	80 (4 lanes)	1,000	1996
5. Huizhou to Heyuan	67 (2 lanes)	800	1996
6. Guangzhou to Shaoguan	360 (4 lanes)	5,000	1997
7. Shenzhen to Shantou	286 (4 lanes)	3,200	1998

Source: K. Chu (1992).

across the delta by bypassing Guangzhou (Taylor and Cheng, 1991). An ambitious project to further improve the link between the two flanks of the estuary has been proposed by Hopewell, which plans to build a bridge-tunnel, one of the longest in the world, to link Zhuhai with Shekou, with a possible extension to the western New Territories in Hong Kong. The travel time between Hong Kong and Macau would be less than an hour along this bridge-tunnel link (Marriage and Chu, 1992). Other than the previously mentioned circular highway around Guangzhou, at least seven more major highway construction projects are under way, with two involving links to cities outside the delta in Guangdong (see Tables 4.3 and 4.4).

Ports and Airports

Port facilities in the Pearl River delta are relatively well developed and include fifteen deepwater ports (including both Guangdong and Hong Kong), with another three being planned (Nansha in Punyu, Shatin in Dongguan, and Gaolan in Zhuhai). Nevertheless, every city or county along the coast of the delta still aspires to have at least one port, even

■ Table 4.4 Types of Highways in Guangdong, by Length (km)

	1990	1994	2000 (projected)
Superhighways (3 lanes)	23	273	1,300
Class I highways (2 lanes)	106	1,575	2,500
Class II highways (1 lane)	1,900	4,656	7,000
Roads	52,571	69,212	65,200
Total	54,600	75,716	76,000

Source: K. Chu (1992).

though the density of container ports in the delta is already the highest in the PRC. Apart from Huangpu port in Guangzhou, ports in Shekou, Chiwan, Zhuhai, and others contribute to the container traffic. Their main function is to feed containers to Hong Kong's Kwai Chung port. In 1990, 281,000 20-foot equivalent units (TEUs) were ferried to Hong Kong by riverine vessels and lighters from different ports of the delta, compared with 805,000 TEUs through Shenzhen border checkpoints to Hong Kong in the same year (Chu, 1991). In 1997, Hong Kong handled 14.54 million TEUs, with about one-third handled in midstream compared with one-fourth in 1991 (D. Chu, 1992; Yuan, 1992).

As with port facilities, there is a high density of airports in the delta area. Within a 200-square-kilometer area, there are ten airports, including the international airports of Hong Kong, Macau, Guangzhou, and Shenzhen, as well as regional airports at Zhuhai, Huizhou, Foshan, and Jiangmen. These airports are relatively close to one another, thus raising questions about duplication and efficiency (Liu et al., 1992).

PRC–Hong Kong Integration

For much of the ongoing and planned infrastructure development in the delta area, the return of Hong Kong to the PRC in 1997 has helped. Hong Kong is already being integrated with the delta area and beyond, both economically and in terms of infrastructure. Every day, an estimated 75,000 (1997) Hong Kong residents cross the border to manage factories in South China. The number of Chinese officials and other visitors who travel to Hong Kong for business is increasing rapidly (Cheng and Taylor, 1991). In 1979, 5.65 million passengers crossed the Hong Kong–Shenzhen border, but the number soared to 64.17 million in 1997. The authorities are still struggling to cope with the rapidly growing traffic between the two territories, including extending border control hours from 6:30 A.M. to 11:30 P.M. from October 15, 1998. The increasing importance of Hong Kong in the delta and in the Asia-Pacific region is reflected in the fact that in 1990 alone, sixty-two multinational corporations opened new offices in Hong Kong to penetrate the Chinese and Asian markets (Szeto, 1992).

FINANCING INFRASTRUCTURE DEVELOPMENT
Hong Kong and Taiwan

One of the key requirements for the success of infrastructure development is access to adequate capital to finance projects. Both Hong Kong and Taiwan have generously funded their infrastructure development programs over the years, and their present systems of infrastructure provision are very sound. Looking toward the future, Hong Kong has the ambitious PADS that will make it ready for the twenty-first century. Financing of the far-reaching PADS (and especially the new airport at Chek Lap Kok) from local and international capital markets was not a problem, even though the British and Chinese governments had been mired in diplomatic problems stemming from the political reform proposals of Governor Patten in October 1992. Even before the political impasse, the Hong Kong government had made a commitment to spend HK$78 billion on capital projects over the 1992–1997 period, exclusive of the airport core projects. This represents a 42 percent increase (HK$23 billion) over the expenditure for the previous five-year period (Wong, 1992).

In Taiwan, attention has focused on the huge sums programmed for the Six-Year National Development Plan (1991–1996). The exact scope and justification for parts of the plan are still being debated, but with foreign exchange reserves of $90 billion, the country definitely has the means to raise funds through loans, bonds, and other channels (*Far Eastern Economic Review,* October 15, 1992). However, problems of allocating inefficiency and cost overruns have been identified by Jiayuan Cai (1991), who pointed out that even in the Ten Major Construction Projects of the 1970s, cost overruns had been a major problem. Of the six projects on transport infrastructure, four incurred costs of more than twice the original budgeted figures, and the North-South freeway cost 51 percent more. Only the expenditure for Taichung harbor was close to the original cost estimate.

South China

Infrastructure development needs in South China are enormous, and dependence on foreign capital to finance these plans will be great. To put the problem in perspective, Guangdong spent one and a half times more on fixed asset investments in the Seventh Five-Year Plan (1986–1990) than it did in the Sixth Five-Year Plan (1981–1985) (*Guangdong Yearbook,* 1991). In the Eighth Five-Year Plan (1991–1996), an estimated RMB20 to 30 billion was required for transport, raw materials, and technical upgrading (Taylor and Cheng, 1991). For the next 20 years, Guangdong will need $190 billion in foreign investment for its infrastructure projects and high-technology industries (Zheng, 1992). Thus, the capital requirements for infrastructure development in South China are escalating, and as the PRC moves more toward a market economy, it should diversify its sources of finance.

At the beginning of the open policy period, Guangdong and Fujian were equally dependent on government funds for infrastructure development. During the next 10 years, as economic growth in the two provinces accelerated, other sources of funding became relatively much more important. Since 1985, self-financing in infrastructure has been the most important financing modality. Nevertheless, the amount of foreign capital for infrastructure development has continuously increased (see Table 4.5).

■ Table 4.5 Financing Modalities for Infrastructure Development
          in Guangdong and Fujian (percent)

	1980		1985		1990		1995	
	Guang-dong	Fujian	Guang-dong	Fujian	Guang-dong	Fujian	Guang-dong	Fujian
Government funds	48.6	52.2	13.6	29.3	6.4	18.9	2.2	3.7
Domestic loans	10.9	11.5	22.2	31.7	16.7	19.0	14.1	21.6
Self-financing	34.3	35.7	38.6	33.1	33.9	41.8	49.6	42.7
Foreign capital	6.2	0.6	15.7	1.5	21.4	10.7	24.0	15.4
Other sources	0.0	0.0	9.9	4.4	21.6	9.6	10.1	16.5

Source: Guangdong Statistical Bureau (1992, 1996); Fujian Statistical Bureau (1992, 1996).

Local Investment

Government funding for large-scale infrastructure projects has tradi-tionally been determined at the central and provincial levels, where competing demands are weighed against one another and decisions are not always made strictly on the basis of a project's own merits. Conse-quently, an attitudinal change has come about at the local level. Local governments have adopted a strategy of self-reliance, following the dic-tum "using road to sustain road, using port to sustain port, and using bridge to sustain bridge." Under this strategy, funds are raised locally, and user charges are utilized to recoup initial investments. Many of the roads and bridges in the Pearl River delta were constructed and paid for in this way.

In the mid-1980s, local governments showed creativity in meet-ing their transport, energy, and telecommunications needs. However, this would not have been possible without the devolution of decision making to their level. For example, since 1980, Shunde has invested RMB1.35 billion in transport, telecommunications, and other infrastructure development, so that it now has its own electricity generation station of 130 MW, a container port at Rongqi, and many bridges and roads (Guo and Chen, 1992). Another good example of local initiative is provided by Dongguan, which made significant infrastructure improvements on large tracts of land in this manner. Similar local initiatives have been encouraged in Fujian, as substantial Hong Kong interests have invested in Meizhou Bay and Fuzhou. In Fuzhou, the Lippo Group has set up a HK$1 billion joint investment company with the city government to work on infrastructure development. As far as cooperative ventures are concerned, two modalities are usually considered: build-operate-transfer (BOT) and build-operate-own (BOO) (Tyson, 1992).

Foreign Investment

For large-scale projects, more conventional sources of funding from overseas are needed. Thus, multilateral agencies, such as the World Bank and the Asian Development Bank (ADB), have been approached for various projects. For example, the World Bank funded several projects in Guangdong and Fujian, including the Foshan-Kaiping and Shenzhen-Shantou highways for $200 million (*Wah Kiu Yat Po,* September 17, 1992) and the Xiamen-Quanzhou highway for RMB100 million (*Wen Wei Po,* May 30, 1992). The ADB has lent $200 million for the construction of the Changping-Shantou single-track railroad (*Wen Wei Po,* June 26, 1992). Likewise, the ADB has financed the second phase of the Conghua Pumped Storage Power Station (*Wen Wei Po,* February 27, 1992). Soft loans, which are preferred by the Chinese government and by end users, and other foreign investments are estimated to meet up to one-third of the financial needs of infrastructure development in Guangdong in the Eighth Five-Year Plan period. Noteworthy as well is the fact that almost half of the $12 billion that the World Bank has lent to the PRC has been spent on roads, highways, and power plants (*Far Eastern Economic Review,* 1992b).

Bonds constitute another vehicle for raising funds. This can be done through the local banking system, as has been reported by Taylor and Cheng (1991). Money can also be raised through overseas bonds. For example, Guangdong International Trust and Investment Corporation (GITIC) was reported to have floated 15 billion yen worth of bonds in Japan (Zheng, 1992).[2] Since 1986, Guangzhou has issued $343 million in infrastructure-related bonds in the financial markets of Hong Kong, Tokyo, and London.

Another more direct way of raising funds overseas is simply by setting up new banks or by purchasing existing ones. Guangdong Development Bank, a local provincial bank, negotiated with several nongovernmental financial institutions in Taiwan for the purchase of a bank in Hong Kong (Zheng, 1992). Many Chinese banks are already operating successfully in Hong Kong, and local provincial banks could also gain access to the thriving Hong Kong financial market.

Yet another source of foreign funding is bilateral aid from countries such as Japan, France, and Germany. The Conghua Pumped Storage Power Station, the first of its kind in the country, is now being built at a cost of $470 million, of which $250 million has been lent by the ADB. Electricite de France is the principal contractor to provide all the power station equipment. French firms are also involved in the construction of the Daya Bay nuclear plant.

On the other hand, Western commercial banks are reported to have avoided lending for infrastructure development because of the PRC's poor legal structure and the perceived long-term risk of investing in large-scale projects. For example, Hopewell Holdings faced considerable difficulty in raising $800 million for the first phase of the Guangdong-Shenzhen-Zhuhai superhighway, ultimately tapping the resources of twenty-nine international banks. Viewed from the perspective of the overall development of Guangdong, foreign investment has thus far been inadequate. In the period 1979–1990, Guangdong had 501 infrastructure projects involving foreign investment, with infrastructure

---

[2] On October 6, 1998, the Beijing authorities, reacting to GITIC's staggering foreign debts (RMB36.175 billion, or U.S.$4.4 billion) and reckless management, shut the firm down. As a consequence of this, it has become increasingly difficult for Chinese strategic projects to raise foreign funds.

ranking fifth in attracting such investment, after industry, agriculture, real estate, and commerce (Zheng and Ni, 1992).

Resources of overseas Chinese have also emerged as an important source of capital, especially in Guangdong, where Hong Kong investors, such as Gordon Wu of Hopewell Holdings, Cheng Yu-tung, Lee Shau-kee, Li Ka-shing, Henry Fok, the Y. K. Pao family, and others, have invested heavily in infrastructure and related projects.

Outstanding Needs

More highways are needed, as by one estimate more than 1,600 towns in Guangdong are still not accessible to motor vehicles. Highway construction projects invariably need intricate financing packages. Construction of the seven highway projects emanating from Guangzhou requires an estimated RMB19 billion (K. Chu, 1992; see Table 4.3). In addition, six other high-speed highways—Shanwei-Shantou, Shantou-Raoping (Huanggong), Guangzhou-Hai'an, Qingyuan-Shaoguan, Guangzhou-Huizhou, and Guangzhou-Huaxian-Qingyuan, totaling 1,104 kilometers—are to be built mainly with foreign capital. The foreign investors will be given favorable terms, including the right to operate a highway for 30 years, with the profits in the first 10 years accruing to the investor. The profit in the following 10 years would go to the investor and the local government at a 60-to-40 ratio; for the last 10 years, the ratio would be 30 to 70 (*Wah Kiu Yat Po*, September 17, 1992).

The four SEZs in South China were able to greatly improve their infrastructure within a relatively short period through self-financing and the use of foreign capital. When the SEZs were just starting up, the government allocated only limited funds for infrastructure development; this appropriation has shrunk progressively over the years. The pattern of financing for infrastructure development in the SEZs differed from that of the larger administrative areas where they are located (see Table 4.6). However, sustained infrastructure development over the past 14 years in these relatively small areas has yielded impressive results.

■ Table 4.6 Financing Modalities for Infrastructure Development
in Special Economic Zones (SEZs) (percent)

	1985				1995			
	Zhuhai	Shenzhen	Shantou	Xiamen	Zhuhai	Shenzhen[a]	Shantou	Xiamen
Government funds	1.6	1.6	0.0	6.3	0.7	—	2.4	4.3
Domestic funds	27.6	20.4	—	—	4.2	16.6	5.6	20.2
Self-financing	41.9	45.8	30.2	20.5	63.2	50.6	57.2	41.6
Foreign capital	26.2	13.1	11.7	—	17.2	19.7	30.4	10.8
Other sources	2.7	18.1	58.1[b]	73.2	14.7	13.1	4.4	23.1

Note: Data for Zhuhai (1985, 1988) and Shantou (1995) refer to the entire city, whereas those for the other SEZs pertain to the special territorial units.

[a] Data for Shenzhen in 1995 included both infrastructural and real estate development.

[b] Bank loans.

Source: Statistical yearbooks for the SEZs (various years).

POLICY CONCERNS

Since 1978, and especially after 1990, significant progress has been made in infrastructure development in South China. However, the demand for infrastructure far outstrips supply, raising numerous questions about the formulation of policy.

Planning Coordination

Although local governments have been lauded for taking the initiative for infrastructure improvement, a serious problem exists regarding the duplication of work resulting from a lack of coordination. Every local government essentially plans for itself, yet provincial governments lack the mechanisms to coordinate local efforts. This problem manifests itself in duplications such as the simultaneous construction of deep-water container ports in Shenzhen (two ports), Zhuhai, and Daya Bay. It would be more efficient to have one large container port to complement Hong Kong's Kwai Chung port rather than four facilities within a relatively small area. Not surprisingly, the port projects have attracted less foreign investment than have power plants, highways, railways, and telecommunications. This also highlights the sensitivity of foreign interests to the long-term economic prospects of different infrastructure subsectors (Liu et al., 1992).

Another problem is a glut of airports, with new airports in Hong Kong, Shenzhen, Zhuhai, and Macau all completed and operational. The recently released Twenty-Year Socioeconomic Development Profile of Guangdong indicates that the largest international airport in South China will be situated in Guangzhou, with airports in Zhuhai, Shenzhen, and other areas taking secondary roles (*Wah Kiu Yat Po*, February 2, 1993).

Environmental Impact

As noted in the previous section, two of the present bottlenecks in South China's infrastructure development—land transport and power supply—have attracted considerable foreign interest and investment. However, it is doubtful whether due consideration has been given to environmental concerns. In Guangdong, congestion on the railroads is very serious, as loaded railway cars line up for hundreds of miles to enter Guangzhou from as far away as Hunan province (*Wen Wei Po*, June 8, 1992). Such congestion leads to higher production costs and forces shippers to use other means of transport. Increased land transport also causes environmental degradation and puts pressure on limited energy reserves.

Similarly, Renqun Cai (1992) emphasizes that the Pearl River delta now has an unusually large concentration of electric power–generating stations because of the rush to meet power demands. On two sides of Humen in Dongguan, there are five large-scale, coal-fired stations and one oil-fired station with total capacity of 6,000 MW. The Daya Bay nuclear plant, which began operation in 1993, will bolster this capacity. Hong Kong's power stations, with a capacity of 5,000 MW, are also located on the eastern flank of the delta, giving a combined power generation capacity of 13,000 MW. The large number of power stations and their geographic concentration has raised concerns about air pollution, acid rain, and the risk of environmental disasters in densely populated areas.

Competition for Resources

Infrastructure development has to compete for funding with other key economic sectors, such as agriculture, industry, and state enterprises in need of restructuring. However, the crowding out of investment does not seem to pose a serious problem, as Guangdong and Fujian have been reducing their dependence on government funds for infrastructure development, as previously noted (see Table 4.5). Nor are other sectors within the two provinces adversely affected by infrastructure projects. At the national level, South China with its SEZs has traditionally not received heavy investments from the central government. Thus, the question of other provinces being adversely affected by infrastructure development in South China does not arise.

Other Concerns

The general policy concerns that pertain to infrastructure development in the delta area and that are also applicable to South China as a whole have been summarized well by E. G. Pryor (1991):

> Development within the Special Economic Zones has generally been well planned but elsewhere in the Delta much new development has been opportunistic and, at best, loosely coordinated. This has led to difficulties in upgrading transport networks, in the control of pollution and in the provision of utility services, especially power supplies. . . . Within the Delta area itself it would seem that the principal needs in the medium term will be the expansion of power supplies, the extension and upgrading of road networks and cross border links, the expansion of feeder port and domestic air service facilities, the rationalization of urban development patterns and the wider implementation of environmental protection measures. (4)

Pricing and subsidizing infrastructure projects must be viewed within the context of broader economic reforms and policies related to those reforms. By and large, it is observed that with price liberalization and the gradual development of free markets, explicit subsidization of infrastructure services has been declining. This is especially true of many of the local initiatives in which repayment is contingent on the principle of user charges, and it is true of projects that depend on foreign investment. Pricing questions are more complicated because, on the one hand, the costs of raw materials and other inputs are rising faster than returns on infrastructure projects and, on the other, prices cannot be raised drastically without general and fundamental price reforms in the Chinese economy.

CONCLUSIONS

The experience in infrastructure development in the Southern China Growth Triangle can yield important lessons not only for the economies concerned but also for other nations wishing to engage in cross-border collaborative productive enterprises. Hong Kong and Taiwan have shown wisdom and foresight in their massive investment in infrastructure development, which in turn has enabled their economies to take advantage of new opportunities as the world economy has moved toward greater integration. Infrastructure development enabled both places to attain their preeminent status as transport, communication, manufacturing, and service centers in the region. Their experiences also provide a good example of effective partnership between the government and the private sector.

In South China, infrastructure investments were neglected until recently. For example, in 1982 in Guangdong, modern highways were only a very minor part of the total road network. Only recently were plans drawn up for road development to 2010, when it is projected that 90,000 kilometers of highways will exist, of which 2,800 kilometers will be superhighways, 5,000 kilometers class 1 and class 2 highways, and 83,000 kilometers roads (*China Cityscape*, June 21, 1992).

Annually, the Chinese government provides only RMB6 million to Guangdong for transport infrastructure development. This is a pittance, considering that it costs RMB2,000 to build a one-meter portion of a bridge and RMB200,000 to build one kilometer of roadway. Thus, it is impressive that in the period 1981–1990, Guangdong built more than 1,200 bridges, a rate of construction that was unimaginable during the earlier command economy period. This can be attributed partly to the efficacy of devolving decision making to the local level and partly to savings from the agriculture sector, both of which have proved to be an important source of funds for investment not only for infrastructure but also for schools, hospitals, and housing (Cheng and Taylor, 1991).

Another important lesson from Guangdong relates to the potential for infrastructure development to help reduce sectoral or geographic income imbalances. As the province's coastal areas attained a measure of success in economic development, efforts were directed toward helping poorer mountainous areas, effecting, in essence, a redistribution of wealth. The forty-nine mountain counties, which account for 65 percent of Guangdong's land area and 40 percent of its population, saw an increase in agricultural output from RMB8.9 billion in 1980 to RMB44.9 billion in 1990. In 1991, coastal cities and counties assisted the mountainous areas in 318 projects, with capital investment of almost RMB200 million. This was accompanied by a transfer of technology.

The foregoing analysis of infrastructure development in the Pearl River delta and beyond has highlighted the problem of a lack of coordination in certain key sectors. Although this problem always existed among cities and counties within the delta area, the need for coordinated infrastructure development has lately assumed greater importance because of the return of Hong Kong and Macau to China in 1997 and 1999, respectively. Various proposals have been made on how to better coordinate infrastructure development across the territories by forming expert groups, joint management structures, and joint investment companies (*Wen Wei Po*, March 16, 1990). To complement one another's strengths and weaknesses, a wide scope exists for cooperation not only among the governments but also among private enterprises and nongovernmental organizations (Lei and Chen, 1990). Cooperation is complicated, especially given the different political systems and administrative cultures that prevail in the territories. The challenge of collaboration is further compounded by recent political controversies. In the final period of Hong Kong's transition to Chinese rule, there appeared to be a more immediate concern in taking into account infrastructure plans in the region beyond Hong Kong's immediate territory. This was a basic premise of the 1996 TDS review to the early twenty-first century.

On the whole, infrastructure development in South China still lags behind overall economic development. Infrastructure standards are uneven but are constantly being improved. Infrastructure development presents opportunities for foreign investors as well as local entrepreneurs. The main goal in the 1990s and beyond will be the systematic development of large-scale projects to take infrastructure development to a higher level, with wider networks, more modern facilities, and increased scope for international trade and cooperation.

One conclusion that can be drawn from the foregoing analysis is that bilateral and multilateral foreign assistance and investment is obviously necessary in Guangdong and Fujian provinces. Development at the national and provincial levels has many competing demands, and infrastructure development using government funds in the two provinces must necessarily be accorded a low priority. Thus, local initiatives are important, but there is a limit to what local resources can finance and build.

International assistance is needed for a wide range of highway, railway, port, airport, and telecommunications projects in Guangdong and Fujian. Already, the World Bank and the ADB are providing loans for a number of projects, but more needs to be done. Foreign assistance is especially critical for projects such as power stations and nuclear plants, which must take account of the environmental concerns of neighboring territories and the Asia-Pacific region at large. Because environmental concerns are not yet high on the agenda of planners in the PRC, bilateral and multilateral donors might include environmental conditions with the assistance that they render.

Priorities also need to be assigned within the PRC regarding the development needs of South China in relation to those of other provinces; further, infrastructure projects must be weighed against projects in other sectors. Even within South China, and especially in the Pearl River delta, external assistance might prompt the local authorities to evaluate their infrastructure needs in a more rational, holistic manner.

Individual cities and local authorities should be dissuaded from their present practice of planning within narrow territorial perspectives, with decisions driven by concerns about prestige rather than the economic viability of projects. External assistance can provide the impetus for large projects to be better coordinated and harmonized.

Finally, China has been actively seeking membership of the World Trade Organization (WTO). Should its efforts prove successful, it will surely lead to further integration of the members of the Southern China Growth Triangle. Hong Kong's pivotal role as the efficient middleman between South China and Taiwan will be enhanced. Expansion in trade and economic relations can be anticipated from China's admission to WTO, and inevitably this will spill over to infrastructure investment, which underpins any accelerated cooperative development (Sung, 1995).

3 China and Hong Kong

5 Metropolitan Planning and Management in China

INTRODUCTION

China is not only the most populous country in the world but also the one with the largest urban population. The 1990 Census of Population recorded a total urban population of 301.91 million, or 26.4 percent of the total population. Since the People's Republic of China came into existence in 1949, four censuses of population have been undertaken. Between the first census in 1953 and the latest one in 1990, the number of urban places almost doubled from 7,068 to 12,391, of which the number of cities almost tripled from 166 to 456, and the number of towns more than doubled from 5,402 to 11,935. The increase in the number of both cities and towns since 1978, when China embarked on a bold program of economic reforms and adopted an open policy, has been rapid and significant. In particular, the number of newly designated towns rose sharply from 2,781 in 1983 to 6,211 in 1984 and continued to rise to about 9,000 in 1987. It stabilized for a few years before rising again to 11,935 in 1990 (Chan, 1994a).

China's urban population is huge as well as inordinately difficult to count. It has continued to baffle Chinese and foreign scholars. The size of China's urban population is affected by three factors, namely, the urban designation criteria, the urban boundary, and the household registration classification. These factors have changed many times over the years, and despite the assiduous efforts of scholars (Chan and Xu, 1985; Ma and Cui, 1987; Chan, 1994a), the size of urban population in China remains an enigma. For example, China's urban population in 1990 has been shown, by various definitions, to range from 202.53 to 604.47 million, accounting for 18.5 to 52.9 percent of the total population (Chan, 1994a:247). To underscore the confusion in calculating China's urban population, another scholar working on a similar series of data came up with slightly different figures (Kirkby, 1994:133).

This chapter does not attempt to unravel the statistical mystique surrounding China's urban population. Instead, it focuses on the challenges and opportunities inherent in planning and managing China's large cities, which have always played key roles in that country's administration and development. In the current stage of openness and transition from a socialist to a market economy in China, the importance of its large cities cannot be overemphasized. Certainly in the context of globalization and world cities, China's large cities must be kept in focus.

From a historical perspective, it has been the policy of Chinese decision makers to keep their large cities in check for much of the period since 1949. In the 1950s, the National Construction Committee advised, "Don't develop large cities. The small cities and industrial towns should be the focus. The large city development will not receive support without particular reasons" (Cui, 1995:2). There was a "small-towns" consensus in the early 1980s. Indeed, the often quoted slogan for the urban distribution policy was to control strictly the growth of large cities (over 0.5 million in population), rationally develop medium-size cities (0.2–0.5 million), and actively promote small cities (under 0.2 million). This was the guiding policy, notwithstanding severe criticisms from academics. More or less the same "control large cities" goal was embodied in a modified policy objective that was written into the Urban Planning Ordinance in 1990. However, scholars, mindful of the vast regional disparities and the inappropriateness of a city size guideline for the whole country, have been advocating the notion of comprehensive efficiency rather than size for its own sake. In the future, large-city development will depend on policy reform and economic liberalization if it is to thrive (Ye et al., 1988).

This chapter consists of four sections. The first section discusses the character of large cities in China. The second section systematically examines the salient problems in managing these large cities. The third section deals with the planning and management framework for China's large cities, with particular reference to the challenges being faced by the ongoing economic reforms and the systemic changes that are required in the cities. The fourth section highlights the two case studies on Shanghai and Guangzhou to show what recent changes they have undergone in planning and management terms so that they can move ahead.

GROWTH AND PRODUCTIVITY OF LARGE CITIES

City size is an important variable in urban development in China. The designation of "city" and "town" carries with it certain administrative and fiscal power and responsibilities. The pursuit of a planned distribution of urban population has been predicated on the managed growth of cities by size, at least by administrative guidelines.[1] At the apex of the urban hierarchy are four megacities—Shanghai, Beijing, Tianjin, and Chongqing—which are special municipalities equivalent to the status of a province. Large cities are of special importance in China because of the heavy concentration of industrial, financial, commercial, administrative, and intellectual power in them. To a large degree, they dictate the pace, direction, and character of national development and economic growth. In addition, they are largely China's windows to the world and vice versa.

Prior to the introduction of economic reforms, much of the period 1964–1980 was characterized by large and extralarge cities growing at below national urban rates. However, in the period 1980–1989, these

---

[1] Customarily, Chinese cities are classified into large cities (populations more than 0.5 million), medium-size cities (0.2 to 0.5 million), and small cities (less than 0.2 million). The huge- or superlarge-city grade was added by the State Statistical Bureau in the compilation of *China's Urban Statistics 1985* (London: Longman).

■ Table 5.1 Population Growth Rates by City Size, 1964–1980
and 1980–1989

City size	No. of cities in 1964	Annual growth rate 1964–1980 (1)	No. of cities in 1980	Annual growth rate 1980–1989 (2)	Index of growth rate (2)/(1)
Above 2.0 million	5	0.36	7	2.42	6.73
1–2 million	8	1.09	8	2.54	2.32
0.5–1 million	18	1.49	30	2.85	1.91
0.2–0.5 million	43	2.36	70	3.42	1.45
0.1–0.2 million	51	2.68	62	4.49	1.68
Below 0.1 million	42	3.81	46	7.04	1.85
Average/total	167	1.59	223	3.16	1.99

Source: Zhou (1993:108).

cities witnessed much faster growth rates of population despite the smaller cities growing at even higher rates. Consequently, the index of population growth when the two periods are compared has revealed the relationship that the larger the city size, the greater the growth propensity (Table 5.1). This clearly shows that China's large cities have grown more rapidly than smaller cities in the reform period compared with the past decades. However, when viewed in another way, cities with population of more than 0.5 million have declined in relative terms in both number and population nationally. More specifically, these cities accounted for 20.2 percent of the total number of cities in 1980 versus 12.6 percent in 1990; they also accounted for 63.3 percent of China's urban population in 1980 versus 54.2 percent in 1990 (Cui, 1995). This highlights the fact that despite their recent rapid growth in population, large cities in China have decreased in relative weight against the background of a rapidly growing urban population and the multiplication of cities.

To expand the theme of the growth of cities by various size categories under China's open policy, Table 5.2 shows that the growth of small cities of 0.2 million or fewer inhabitants has been exceptionally

■ Table 5.2 Growth of China's Cities, 1980–1996

		1980	1985	1990	1996
Extralarge cities (above 1 million)	Number	15	22	31	34
	Population (millions)	35.09	47.47	62.60	95.11
Large cities (0.5–1 million)	Number	28	30	28	44
	Population (millions)	22.20	21.92	19.00	42.99
Medium cities (0.2–0.5 million)	Number	70	94	119	195
	Population (millions)	21.12	28.99	37.03	155.53
Small cities (below 0.2 million)	Number	108	178	289	393
	Population (millions)	11.94	19.88	31.66	221.48
Total	Number	221	324	467	666
	Population (millions)	90.35	118.26	150.28	515.11

Source: State Statistical Bureau (various years).

rapid; they more than tripled from 108 in 1980 to 393 in 1996.[2] The total number of cities increased by more than 200 percent in the same period.

Table 5.3 places the largest cities in China in 1996 into three categories. Whereas China had only nine cities with a population of more than a million in 1953, these "million" cities grew to fifteen in 1980 and thirty-four in 1996. The ten largest cities in China are shown in Tables 5.3 and 5.4, in which Harbin, Nanjing, and Xian can be seen to have experienced rapid growth in population in the 1980s, enabling them to become superlarge cities with more than two million inhabitants by 1996.

The distribution of "million" cities in China is shown in Figure 5.1, where such cities are positioned relative to the three main regional divisions in the country as well as the time at which they attained "million" city status. Despite its relatively small area, by 1994 the coastal

---

[2] By a broader definition of urban population, China had ninety-five cities with population greater than one million in 1991 (Pannell, 1995).

■ Table 5.3 Large Cities in China, 1996

Rank	2 million or above	Population (millions)	1–2 million	Population (millions)	0.8– 1 million	Population (millions)
	Extralarge cities				Potential extralarge cities	
1	Shanghai	8.42	Changchun	1.99	Handan	0.96
2	Beijing	6.27	Dalian	1.91	Luoyang	0.95
3	Tianjin	4.75	Taiyuan	1.72	Hefei	0.93
4	Shenyang	3.84	Qingdao	1.70	Wuxi	0.91
5	Wuhan	3.82	Jinan	1.68	Nanning	0.89
6	Guangzhou	3.22	Zibo	1.42	Datong	0.88
7	Chongqing	2.81	Zhengzhou	1.39	Yantai	0.82
8	Harbin	2.55	Lanzhou	1.37	Benxi	0.81
9	Nanjing	2.30	Changsha	1.30	Yichun	0.80
10	Xian	2.21	Hangzhou	1.29	Suzhou	0.80
11	Chengdu	2.05	Kunming	1.28		
12			Anshan	1.28		
13			Shijiazhuang	1.27		
14			Fushun	1.26		
15			Nanchang	1.22		
16			Urumqi	1.19		
17			Guiyan	1.19		
18			Tangshan	1.16		
19			Jilin	1.15		
20			Qiqihar	1.11		
21			Baotou	1.06		
22			Fuzhou	1.01		
23			Xuzhou	1.00		
Total		42.24		30.95		8.75

Note: Data on population refer to the urban population and not to the total population of the urban agglomeration.
Source: State Statistical Bureau (1997:31).

region had sixteen of the thirty-four "million" cities in China, a reflection of the enhanced importance of the coastal region in national and economic development, where recognition was given to the comparative advantage of coastal cities in spearheading economic development. Indeed, China's coastal cities have been acting as effective agents for

■ Table 5.4 Urban Population (in millions) of China's Ten Largest
            Cities, 1951–1996

	1951	1981	1990	1996
Shanghai	5.90	6.09	7.50	8.42
Beijing	4.01	4.67	5.77	6.27
Tianjin	3.22	3.83	4.58	4.75
Shenyang	2.41	2.94	3.60	3.84
Wuhan	2.15	2.66	3.28	3.82
Guangzhou	1.84	2.34	2.91	3.22
Chongqing	2.12	1.90	3.27	2.81
Harbin	1.55	2.09	2.44	2.55
Nanjing	1.42	1.70	2.09	2.30
Xian	1.31	1.58	1.96	2.21

Source: State Statistical Bureau (various years).

modernization since 1978, and the spread effects are being radiated to
other interior provinces and regions (Yeung and Hu, 1992).

Regarding the impact of the open policy on the regional distribution
of urban population by large and extralarge city categories, Table 5.5
provides evidence that nothing of importance has occurred in the decade 1979–1996. About half the total urban population and nearly
half the population in large cities still resided within the eastern region.
However, the relative proportion of population living in large and extralarge cities has increased rapidly in the central region. Nationwide,
the northern and northwestern tiers of provinces have the highest levels of urbanization, whereas the southwest and south-central tiers have
the lowest (Pannell, 1986:302).

Although recent rapid growth of smaller and medium-size cities has
helped balance the urban hierarchy, the economic disparity between
the coastal and interior regions has widened as a result of the policy of
decentralization of power to the local level and economic liberalization
as part of the open policy (Yeung, 1993). Nevertheless, for a large
country such as China, the degree of metropolitan dominance is low.
Demographic primacy of the large cities is lower than most smaller
countries in Asia (Kim, 1991). Xiangming Chen (1991) in his regional

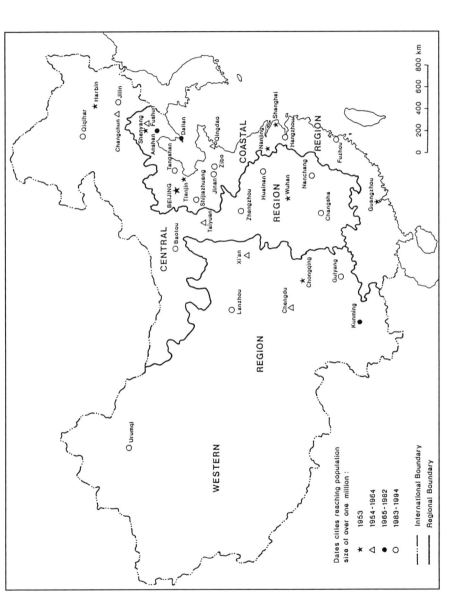

■ Figure 5.1 "Million" Cities in China, 1953–1994

■ Table 5.5 Urban Population by Regional Division, 1979, 1989,
             and 1996

Year	Regional division	National urban population (%)	Extralarge city population (cities of above 1 million) (%)	Large city population (cities of 0.5–1 million) (%)
1979	Eastern	50.1	64.3	50.4
	Central	34.0	19.9	36.1
	Western	15.9	15.8	13.5
1989	Eastern	49.4	61.5	51.7
	Central	35.3	23.2	40.3
	Western	15.3	15.2	8.0
1996	Eastern	51.4	50.0	47.7
	Central	33.8	29.4	50.0
	Western	14.7	20.6	2.3

Source: Zong (1993:169); *Yearbook of China's Cities* (1997:63).

analysis reveals that other than Shanghai, which has some demographic and industrial dominance over the cities in the eastern region,
China's urban system in the 1980s remained distinctly nonprimate and
relatively stable. Except for industrial output, the growth of cities in the
eastern region exceeded that of the inland cities. In addition, China's
new spatial development strategies have encouraged interregional interaction between coastal and inland cities, mainly through joint ventures,
for their mutual benefit.

For the most part, large cities in China are more efficient and better
provided for in basic services than smaller cities. The higher productivity of large cities is often seen as justification for their existence and
for government investment. The positive relationship between city size
and economic productivity is borne out by the selected indicators
shown in Table 5.6. The indicators appear to be consistent in pointing
to the large cities as being more productive, and their residents enjoy
higher quality of urban services. However, Won Bae Kim (1991:158)

■ Table 5.6 Economic Efficiency of Cities in China, 1996

City size	GDP per capita (RMB)	Agricultural output value per capita (RMB)	Industrial output per capita (RMB)	Pretax profits per capita (RMB)	Pretax profits per RMB100 assets (RMB)	Industrial output value per industrial worker (RMB)	Higher education-students per 10,000 persons	Doctors per 10,000 persons	Annual wage per worker (RMB)
Above 2 million	15,812	836.7	23,846.6	1,911.9	7.1	86,508.2	221	104	5,901.1
1–2 million	14,456	956.7	20,846.6	1,543.8	7.2	69,551.6	196	104	4,319.0
0.5–1 million	13,060	1,110.7	21,628.8	1,621.8	7.7	64,859.1	97	86	3,623.4
0.2–0.5 million	8,400	2,099.6	14,151.3	666.3	6.4	73,797.3	33	48	1,896.0
Below 0.2 million	6,281	2,569.5	10,108.1	419.9	9.1	74,179.9	7	31	935.4
Average of all cities	9,139	1,995.5	14,588.4	840.8	8.1	74,002.7	60	54	2,344.6

Source: State Statistical Bureau (1997:338–341).

has pointed out that higher productivity in large cities might not necessarily be attributable to size alone; other factors, such as a higher capital-to-labor ratio, the concentration of highly skilled manpower, and better industrial infrastructure, might have played their part.

In a more detailed and rigorous analysis, Z. H. Zhang (1991) has revealed the agglomeration economies characteristic of large cities in China. A positive correlation exists between city size and economic efficiency. By means of an efficiency index, the correlation shows that large cities, each with a population of two million or more inhabitants, are more than twice as efficient as the small ones. Large cities are capable of generating higher output with less cost, on average, than cities of lower order. Moreover, from the standpoint of occupancy of land, large cities are superior to small ones. The output per unit of land in large cities is about 100 times that in small ones. Priority should be given to large cities, it is argued, if efficient utilization of land resources is the main concern in formulating guidelines for urbanization in China. Given the high performance of large cities in China, a strong case has been built for the development of large rather than small cities.

Against the backdrop of their higher productivity, Table 5.7 attempts to portray the changing economic structure of the largest fifteen cities in China in the period 1991–1996. Nearly all the fifteen largest cities, except Beijing, Tianjin, Harbin, and Taiyuan, experienced a decline in the share of the secondary sector. By contrast, the tertiary sector increased at double digits in percentage terms in the same period, and the increase in trade employment was rapid, especially in Beijing, Dalian, and Wuhan.

The transformation of the urban economy is closely associated with economic reforms and structural adjustment, especially the role of state enterprises and that of collective and individual enterprises. In the period 1991–1997, growth in employment in state enterprises occurred in Chinese cities although the percentage share has declined (Table 5.8). Collective and jointly owned enterprises during the period decreased in employment both in number and in relative importance, especially with the former. On the other hand, urban employment in shareholding enterprises increased sharply during the period since 1993. Total urban employment in the span of six years increased by almost 20 percent.

Despite the declared policy of controlling large cities in China, few

■ Table 5.7 Employment by Sector of the Fifteen Largest Cities in China, 1991 and 1996

	Secondary				Tertiary				% change 1991–96	
	1991		1996		1991		1996			
	(1000s)	(%)	(1000s)	(%)	(1000s)	(%)	(1000s)	(%)	Secondary	Tertiary
Shanghai	2,285	54.5	2,835	51.0	499	11.9	2,534	45.6	−3.5	33.7
Beijing	1,487	33.3	1,845	40.3	509	11.4	2,687	58.7	7.0	47.3
Tianjin	1,440	51.2	1,925	54.6	271	9.6	1,424	40.4	3.4	30.8
Shenyang	1,250	55.3	1,537	49.2	282	12.5	1,315	42.1	−6.1	29.6
Wuhan	966	46.6	1,371	44.7	165	8.0	1,352	44.1	−1.9	36.1
Guangzhou	694	38.4	867	36.3	451	25.0	1,285	53.8	−2.1	28.8
Chongqing	770	54.8	1,212	37.2	129	9.2	944	29.0	−17.6	19.8
Harbin	783	46.8	1,010	49.2	330	19.7	889	43.3	2.4	23.6
Nanjing	668	50.4	803	50.3	254	19.2	700	43.9	−0.1	24.7
Xian	600	47.2	753	43.9	275	21.6	808	47.1	−3.3	25.5
Chengdu	539	43.6	753	42.4	262	21.2	659	37.1	−1.2	15.9
Changchun	518	47.0	648	40.3	141	12.8	692	43.0	−6.7	30.2
Dalian	537	49.3	546	41.7	143	13.1	672	51.3	−7.6	38.2
Taiyuan	522	49.4	815	53.0	100	9.5	658	42.8	3.6	33.3
Qingdao	64	48.1	613	46.1	40	30.1	576	43.3	−2.0	13.2
Total of 15 cities	—	—	17,533	45.6	—	—	17,195	44.8	—	—

Source: State Statistical Bureau (1992:82–91, 111–129); Yearbook of China's Cities (1997:131–149).

■ Table 5.8 Urban Employment by Ownership of Selected Regions in China, 1991–1997

Year/Region	Urban workers (1000s)	State owned (1000s)	(%)	Urban collective owned (1000s)	(%)	Joint owned (1000s)	(%)	Shareholding (1000s)	(%)
1991	169,770	106,640	62.81	36,280	21.37	490	0.29	—	—
1992	172,410	108,890	63.16	36,210	21.00	560	0.32	—	—
1993	175,890	109,200	62.08	33,930	19.29	660	0.38	1,640	0.93
1994	184,130	112,140	60.90	32,850	17.84	520	0.28	2,920	1.59
1995	190,930	112,610	58.98	31,470	16.48	530	0.28	3,170	1.66
1996	198,150	112,440	56.74	30,160	15.22	490	0.25	3,630	1.83
1997	202,070	110,440	54.65	28,830	14.27	440	0.22	4,680	2.32
Beijing	4,996	3,547	71.00	685	13.71	32	0.64	193	3.86
Tianjin	3,188	1,962	61.54	582	18.26	20	0.63	62	1.94
Shanghai	5,277	3,082	58.40	795	15.07	21	0.40	322	6.10
Jiangsu	9,951	5,845	58.74	2,424	24.36	88	0.88	216	2.17
Zhejiang	6,007	2,905	48.36	1,471	24.49	22	0.37	236	3.93
Fujian	4,321	2,217	51.31	556	12.87	28	0.65	89	2.06
Guangdong	11,565	5,566	48.13	1,814	15.69	58	0.50	287	2.48
Chongqing	3,690	2,153	58.35	622	16.86	4	0.11	118	3.20
Sichuan	7,940	5,182	65.26	1,325	16.69	6	0.08	361	4.55
Qinghai	740	565	76.35	76	10.27	3	0.41	2	0.27

Source: State Statistical Bureau (1998:130).

mechanisms have been implemented that can support this policy. On the contrary, Yuan Cheng (1990) has identified the following factors as favoring large-city growth:

- The living standard of urbanities, kept artificially higher than that of villages, creates centripetal forces.

- The larger the city, the stronger its position in the national economic system.

- Until a land market is in place, there is no price mechanism to reflect the efficiency of urban services and infrastructure servicing the land.

- Under the traditional system, enterprises are indifferent to cost because they are all public and often subsidized.

- City governments are generally ready to accept investment projects from outside and view this as a vehicle to grow. (74–75)

These push factors were at the base of the economic growth of large cities in China; large cities of coastal areas have been accorded a special role since 1978, in reversal of the earlier policy of favoring inland urban and regional development for strategic and ideological reasons. The pattern of growth of large cities in China to date and the way forward has been summed up well by Mike Douglass (1988):

Since large cities have demonstrably greater comparative efficiency vis-à-vis smaller towns, attempts to prevent the growth of large cities through mechanisms in the past would only result in a lower capacity of the urban system to provide new employment for a still rapidly growing labor force.

Taken to its extreme, and when combined with new efforts to open up China's coastal regions to foreign investment in export-oriented manufacturing, this view tends to suggest that the future direction of urbanization in China will be less differentiated from the general development path being pursued by other Asian countries. The large coastal cities would aggrandize their economic positions, and economic growth would be expected to start from these centres and diffuse inward from the coast in a "staircase" manner down the urban hierarchy to the periphery. (2)

PROBLEMS OF METROPOLITAN MANAGEMENT

Managing China's large cities has always been a challenging and critical dimension of governance, given the huge size of the country and immense regional differences. Yet for centuries, they have been the control and administrative centers for the main directions of economic development and social organization of the country. Since 1949, stringent control was effected on the growth of urban population and, in particular, on large cities, through the effective mechanisms of household registration and grain ration. The almost religious adherence to these mechanisms until the onset of economic reforms had allowed China to pursue relatively rapid industrialization alongside slow urbanization. In the early 1980s, the control mechanisms began to crumble, and, with the market economy and the attendant systemic changes yet to be put in place, the challenges being confronted by the large cities are especially poignant. At the same time, new opportunities exist for China's large cities to restructure, reorganize, and reposition themselves for a more effective and commanding role—culturally, economically, and technologically—in the country, the Asia-Pacific region, and indeed the world, at the dawn of the twenty-first century. The overriding issues of metropolitan management in China can be highlighted as follows.

Transition to a Market Economy

Under the traditional socialist system, China's large cities were held in check with controlled growth, and unfettered urbanization was avoided. The policy tended to increase urban-rural disparities and accentuate the attractions of urban living. In addition, the policy sought to suppress per capita urbanization cost, increase the industrial labor output ratio, and decrease the urban multiplier all at the same time (Chan, 1989). However, most serious in terms of its effect on later development is the notion of a socialist city that emphasizes its productive mode at the expense of its consumptive functions. As a consequence, the neglect of basic infrastructure investment in Chinese cities was a common problem to which large cities have found themselves to be most vulnerable and have found it difficult to deal with as the country adopted an open policy. Even now, after two decades of economic reforms, Chinese cities that are led by those in the vanguard of reforms are only at various stages of transition to a market economy in which markets in land, labor, and capital are evolving. Already, the pros and cons of urban market reform have become apparent. For example, urban resource allocation has become more efficient, and the urban-rural gap in income ratio was reduced to 1.5 by 1985 (Perkins, 1990). On the other hand, urbanization cannot be easily contained, and acute competition for resources and development opportunities between cities has surfaced (Chen, 1991:360–362). China's large cities are at the forefront of these changes, and they need skills and determination to be on top of the situation.

Rural-to-Urban and Temporary Migration

Migration has become a critical component in Chinese urbanization, owing to the fact that natural increase has become markedly moderated since the adoption of the one-child policy in the late 1970s. In the period 1978–1982, of the 9.0 million average annual growth in urban population, 6.96 million, or 78 percent, was attributable to net in-migration. In the subsequent period, 1983–1990, net in-migration again accounted for 74 percent of the average annual growth of urban population of 10.9 million (Chan, 1994b:36). Of course, the expansion of urbanized areas also contributed to the significant growth.

A prominent facet of urban growth in the postreform period has been in-migration in two ways. One is the traditional rural-to-urban migration, which, counted by the State Statistical Bureau, amounted to only 13 million in the period 1982–1987. This covered the critical year of 1984, when China officially relaxed its migration policy of allowing rural dwellers to change residence to towns as long as they were self-reliant in grain. However, Kam Wing Chan (1994a:264–264) challenged the official figure on migration and suggested a substantially higher figure of net rural-to-urban migration between 1983 and 1987 at 48.9 million. Even discounting the element of reclassification of rural settlements as urban, the net rural-to-urban migration for 1983–1987 would still total 29 million. This would be comparable to the 35 million in the preceding five years, which included the sudden surge of returned, rusticated urban youths of more than six million in 1978 and 1979. The year 1977 was important, as the nationwide examination for university entrance was reinstituted after being abandoned for years during the Cultural Revolution. It sparked a massive return of rusticated urban youth from the rural areas (Kojima, 1987:41).

Another component of the in-migration is what has been called a temporary, or floating, population that has been gaining in size and visibility in recent years. By their very nature, these migration streams are seasonal and converge on fast-growing and employment-generating cities, such as those in the coastal areas after the Chinese New Year. The most comprehensive nationwide study on the floating population sponsored by the Ministry of Construction covered eleven of the largest cities between 1988 and 1990. It reported a total floating population in these selected cities of eight million, ranging from 70,000 in Jilin to 2.09 million in Shanghai (Li and Hu, 1991). Extrapolated to the nation, the total floating population was estimated to be in the order of 70 million in 1989, comparable to similar estimations by other sources (Chan, 1994a:267). The study also reported that 60 percent of the floating population was from the countryside and the balance from other urban areas. In the selected cities under study, the floating population constituted 23.7 percent of the urban population (see Table 5.9). This compares well with the figures of an independent study of temporary migrants in fifteen extralarge cities by Lin Zichun in 1990, but the average was 14.22 percent of the population in the cities. However, the average of floating population in the fifteen cities studied in 1990 had increased from 5.02 percent in 1981 and from 11.02 percent in 1985, indicating an unmistakable trend of the increasing proportion of temporary migrants in urban population (Wang, 1992:21).

It is safe to conclude that the migrant population reached more than 10 percent of the population of many large cities in the early 1990s. It is at once a bane and a bonus to large cities. Although it is a source of almost inexhaustible cheap labor, it is also taxing the urban services to

■ Table 5.9 Floating Population in Selected Cities in China,
           1988–1994

City	Floating population (millions)	Growth rate (10,000 people/day)			
		1988	1989	1992	1994
Shanghai	2.09 (1988)	209	—	—	330
Beijing	1.31 (1988)	131	—	150	167
Tianjin	—	112	—	—	—
Wuhan	1.20 (1990)	—	75	120*	—
Guangzhou	1.30 (1989)	117	130	—	—
Chongqing	—	67	—	—	—
Chengdu	0.42 (1989)	—	53	—	—
Taiyuan	0.36 (1989)	29	36	—	—
Zhengzhou	0.37 (1989)	—	37	—	—
Hangzhou	0.50 (1989)	—	50	—	—

*This number refers to the floating population in Wuhan in 1990, not 1992.

Source: Li (1996, table 6); Li and Hu (1991), cited in Chan (1994a).

their limit. Increasingly, temporary migrants constitute an underclass of marginally and temporarily employed persons, reminiscent of similar phenomena in other developing countries (Pannell and Torguson, 1991). Other scholars have observed potential cultural conflicts between new migrants of farmer-workers and their host urban communities. The separate identity of the new cultural groups is underscored by their being described as "islands in cities." In a sense, this is an expression of the increasing integration of urban and rural areas, which is a characteristic of contemporary Chinese urbanization (X. Q. Zhang, 1991).

Shortage of Developable Urban Land

The average developable urban land in 1985 totaled 56 square meters per person in large cities of over 0.5 million inhabitants (and 52.2 square meters per person in extralarge cities of over one million inhabitants), which was only two-thirds of the average of all cities. Among the large cities, one-third was below the average, such as Shanghai (with only 26.2 square meters), Taiyuan (29.4 square meters), Chongqing (35.2 square meters), and Chengdu (41.0 square meters), a reflection of the gravity of the situation. The problem has arisen in part because of years of emphasizing production to the detriment of livability in Chinese cities. As a consequence, the average urban population density reached 16,800 persons per square kilometer and a peak of 43,100 persons per square kilometer. For three decades prior to 1978, despite the huge amount of land developed, only a relatively small proportion was used to enhance urban livability. The situation was aggravated by a rapid increase in population in some large cities (Zong, 1988:171).

Housing Shortage

In recent years, all cities have achieved considerable progress in improving housing provision, with the resultant average living space per person having increased from 4.1 square meters in 1981, to 5.2 square meters in 1985, and 9.0 square meters in 1997. Among cities, large differences exist in the standard-of-housing provision. Large cities are especially plagued by problems of housing shortage, residents living in congested conditions, and sizable parts of the housing stock considered unfit for living. The proportion of households with no accommodation in large cities exceeded the average for all cities by seven times. In extralarge cities, the proportion was ten times as large, underlining the acute shortage of housing. For example, more than 50,000 households did not have accommodation in each of the following cities: Beijing, Shanghai, Tianjin, Harbin, Changchun, and Chongqing. Households with special housing problems of having living space of less than two square meters per person totaled more than 10,000 in more than ten large cities (Zong, 1988).

The problem of housing hinged on insufficient funding for housing construction. New housing was continuously undersupplied before the 1970s. During this period, housing was supplied by the government or work units and was state owned, constituting part of the social welfare system. Rent was set at exceptionally low levels. Housing scarcity created allocation problems, especially in large cities, where people had flocked in search of economic and other opportunities. Since 1979, the traditional welfare system began to disintegrate. Suburban farmers began to rent their houses to urbanites or newcomers. Housing was gradually viewed as a commodity. Changes in the concepts of rent, home ownership, and housing finance spurred private investment in the emerging housing industry. However, massive funding will be needed for the projected 300 million square meters of urban housing required by the year 2000 (Kojima, 1987).

The paradox of planning a new housing system is that housing is taken to be a merit good and a wage good at the same time. People were dissatisfied with the supply and allocation of housing, whereas the government was concerned about the costs of housing investment. The World Bank is in favor of free-market reform whereby housing is treated as a commodity. It has recommended a comprehensive reform strategy in property rights, rent, housing production, and housing finance. Housing reform must fit into the wider economic reform of the cities and the nation (World Bank, 1992).

This line of thinking argues for privatization in housing as a means to achieving the broader goals of economic reform, including efficiency and equity. The central issue is how to privatize the housing stock in the work units and housing bureaus. Wages of workers must increase in step. Factors affecting tenure choice include rent levels, lending terms, property rights, and saving-portfolio decisions. Impediments to housing reform are manifold, including the remnants of a rationed rental market, inflationary credit arrangements, increased bureaucratization, and the lack of vision. The practicality of a drastic approach to housing reform—divorcing housing from work units—should not be ruled out (Tolley, 1991).

Poor Infrastructure

Decades of neglect and minimum investment have led most Chinese cities to suffer from inadequate infrastructure services, ranging from transport, water supply, gas supply, sewerage, and energy supply to communication. The inadequacies have led to bottlenecks and slowdowns in development, even in the rapidly developing areas of southern China (see chapter 4). A picture of catching up to the late 1980s has been painted by Deci Zou (1990) as follows:

> According to the statistics of 1988, the investment in urban infrastructure in China was about 13.6 times of that in 1978. The water, gas and central heating supplies agencies in urban areas had undertaken a series of large construction projects, including, to name a few, the diversion works of a trans-regional river course in Tianjin and Qingdao, the water supply and the under river tunnel project in Shanghai, and the high speed underground railways in Beijing and Tianjin, as well as the construction of flyovers. All these had become the foci of people's attention. The gas supply in urban areas had expanded very quickly. It was estimated that more than 5 million households, about 20 million persons, had access to the gas supply. Seventy-three cities were recorded to have central heating supply. . . . Coastal cities and special economic zones were able to plan and construct their infrastructures ahead of development, which proved desirable and effective. However, old cities were not so fortunate and they generally experienced serious infrastructure problems. For instance, cities in North China were largely suffering from the water supply problem, and some cities experienced drainage, traffic and energy problems. (5–6)

In addition, Reeitsu Kojima (1987) has reported China's urban transport as having grown from bad to worse in the 1980s. Large cities were beset by the problem of "bicycle pollution," which led to serious traffic congestion. Traffic in Chinese cities is generally characterized by having to accommodate vehicles of varying speeds, driven by mechanical power and human muscles. He attributed the urban transport problem to four factors: relative delay in investment, low revenue generated by public transport, low depreciation rates for fixed capital in public transport, and illegal road occupation.

The situation of infrastructure provision in the largest fifteen cities in China in the mid-1990s is depicted in Table 5.10. Paved road space per capita is still very much on the low side. By international comparison, paved road space per capita in China's largest cities is only a frac-

■ Table 5.10 Basic Public Services in the Fifteen Largest Cities in China, 1996

| | Per capita | | | Public buses per 10,000 persons |
	Paved road (sq m)	Electricity consumption (kWh)	Water consumption (tons)	Telephones per 100 persons	Public buses per 10,000 persons
Shanghai	5.4	365.0	104.6	41	11.8
Beijing	4.7	—	90.8	35	9.3
Tianjin	6.0	287.6	46.8	28	4.3
Shenyang	5.7	176.6	97.9	19	4.7
Wuhan	2.8	204.7	122.3	20	6.8
Guangzhou	5.2	545.1	223.3	41	9.6
Chongqing	2.2	192.5	64.2	10	4.1
Harbin	3.1	359.8	62.9	23	10.7
Nanjing	5.4	245.1	203.7	40	8.8
Xian	3.5	179.2	87.4	18	3.8
Chengdu	3.2	80.5	98.6	20	4.8
Changchun	3.4	259.2	85.1	19	7.0
Dalian	4.4	243.3	50.7	22	7.9
Taiyuan	5.0	163.5	57.7	14	5.5
Qingdao	6.0	331.7	52.3	21	9.0

Source: State Statistical Bureau (1997:331–349, 391–409).

tion of other large cities in the world. For example, Tokyo and Paris had 9.6 and 9.3 square meters per person, respectively, whereas the provisions for Seoul (65.0), London (26.3), and New York (28.0) were far more generous. Water consumption approximates the level of cities in developed countries. However, the situation in 1996 (Table 5.10) varied among cities. Large cities in northern and inland China, such as Tianjin, Dalian, Taiyuan, and Qingdao, have a relatively low level of residential water consumption, especially during the dry season, when water pressure runs low.

Electricity consumption is relatively low for China's cities, in which residential use accounted for only 13 percent of the total supply. The variability in electricity consumption among the largest cities in 1996 was large, with Shenyang, Chongqing, Xian, Chengdu, and Taiyuan especially poorly supplied in electricity. Electricity is in short supply, but it is one that foreign investors are more likely to be interested in funding (see chapter 4). In terms of communication and telecommunications, Chinese cities are only on the threshold of development. Most large cities are only beginning to develop their telephone systems. A common, street-corner facility for long-distance phone calls in many Chinese cities today is evidence enough, on the one hand, of the acceptance of and reliance on the telephone as a means of communication and, on the other, of the general shortage of the facility in many homes. For example, Shanghai, as the largest and earliest developed city in telecommunications, had only one-tenth the number of telephones that Hong Kong did (Zong, 1988:175–181).

Finally, inadequate provision of public buses is symptomatic of the urban transport malaise. Yet many large cities are sparing no costs in improving urban transport by investing heavily, with or without foreign investment, in intracity expressways, subways, bridges, airports, container ports, and other constructions. A classic example of foreign investment in infrastructure projects in large cities relates to Hong Kong's Wharf Holdings and New World Development in Wuhan, where its central location and potential for growth are being recognized. They plan to build a commuter-train line, an elevated railway, a shopping and office complex, Tianhe International Airport, a 17.8-kilometer airport expressway, and a massive toll bridge spanning the Yangzi River. Unfortunately, bureaucracy has stalled some of these projects (Huus, 1994:60).

Urban Environmental Degradation

Along with rapid economic growth, many of China's large cities have experienced environmental degradation. China's natural environment—rainfall and wind patterns and the topography of the coastline—and industrial sites in coastal and inland locations are vulnerable to industrial pollution. As economic development accelerates, industrial pollution increases rapidly. Other forms of pollution, such as wastewater, solid waste, chemical fertilizer, and coal fuel pollution, have grown in severity and scale. For example, Smil (1984:199) has called attention to China's staggering mistreatment of the environment and has viewed it as a major impediment to its efforts in sustainable development. Yeung (see chapter 8) has surveyed the situation for Chinese cities and pointed to institutional and attitudinal hindrances in overcoming problems.

The geography of China is such that some large cities are susceptible to water pollution along river courses. For example, along the Yangzi River, water bodies near large cities are prone to pollution. Chongqing, Wuhan, Nanjing, and Shanghai have polluted-water stretches of 70, 42, 70, and 50 kilometers, respectively. Pollution at Shanghai is especially serious, far exceeding that in the other cities. Similarly, Hun He flows through Shenyang and Fushun in Liaoning and has been a source of pollution for the two cities (Zong, 1988:174).

Degradation of the urban environment is serious, and the authorities are tackling the problem in many ways. Since 1979, China has implemented environmental protection legislatively and by improving management methods. It has been reported that the decision of introducing quantitative tests for a comprehensive urban environmental treatment by the State Environmental Commission and the endorsement of the Environmental Protection Act, formally published in 1989, have played an important part in improving the situation (Zou, 1990). Be that as it may, pollution in large cities in China is more serious than that in other urban places. Pollution levels in large cities are comparable to those in developed countries in the 1950s and 1960s. What is worse, the environmental quality in large cities has continued to decline, reaching levels below human tolerance and capable of creating social problems (Zong, 1993:164).

Other Issues

The problem of in-migration toward large cities has been mentioned earlier, with the floating population having become a growing phenomenon to be dealt with. This development should be seen in a broader context of limited arable land and a growing rural population in China. Rural surplus labor will become a growing national issue, and the pressure generated on large cities will loom large. Streaming this surplus rural labor is necessary, and large cities must be prevented from abrupt, massive inundations. The phased and managed in-migration is necessary, given that large cities are restructuring themselves, with the development of the tertiary sector destined to absorb their own surplus labor rendered redundant by modernization and technological upgrading of their productivity capacity. Finally, against the background of China's aging population, the large cities will be the first ones to confront the changing demographic structure.

PLANNING AND ADMINISTRATIVE FRAMEWORK

For much of the period since 1949, China followed two cardinal principles in the controlled growth of its cities: the household registration system and the criteria of city designation (Yeh and Xu, 1990:12–14). This has allowed China's large cities to avoid the worst pitfalls that have afflicted similar cities in the developing world. For China, the goal of its urban policy has been to create, for many decades, a more dispersed urbanization. However, this policy has been open recently to debate, and the emphasis on high efficiency has implied a policy that favors large cities. Thus, the Eastern Economic Region has grown more rapidly, bolstered by three rationales in a spatial development strategy in favor of the coastal cities: a stronger industrial base along with a more comprehensive infrastructure, a superior ability to attract foreign investment, and a disposition to explore the international market in view of the intensifying competition between coastal and inland areas (Chen, 1991:354). However, scholars have argued that apart from efficiency, other planning goals, such as securing distribution, maintaining social integrity, and protecting the environment, should not be given short shrift (Douglass, 1988).

In reviewing recent policies on urban growth, Sun Sheng Han and Shue Tuck Wong (1994) found that industrial growth and city planning were the most influential factors in providing impetus for Chinese urbanization in the 1980s. Indeed, urban planning as a tool to a structured space economy gained currency only after the onset of economic reforms. To the extent that it has helped evolve a more rational framework for the planning and management of Chinese cities, the following salient trends are worthy of elaboration.

The Notion of "Key Point City"

Richard Kirkby (1985:222–228) has noted that after a lapse of 20 years, the notion of the "key-point city" *(zhongdian chengshi)* system was resurrected in the late 1970s. The purpose of key-point status is to systemize preferential access to resources and to increase autonomy of key cities beyond what is usual for other cities. With the open policy gathering momentum, the translation of this concept into implementation came in quick succession. First, four special economic zones (SEZs) were established in 1980 at Shenzhen, Zhuhai, and Shantou in Guangdong and at Xiamen in Fujian. Then, as a new initiative in the new urban and regional policy, a move took place to establish macroregions whose boundaries are functionally rather than administratively defined. The Shanghai Economic Zone (74,000 square kilometers) and the Pearl River Delta Open District (42,600 square kilometers) are examples of this construct. A third strand of this policy tends to enlarge the spatial domain of the existing cities by the administrative rearrangement of transferring all *xian,* currently under the prefectures, to the cities. In effect, the prefectural *(diqu)* tier of the Chinese administrative field system is abolished. Consequently, all provincial-level cities and many prefectural cities, such as Guangzhou and Chongqing, also administer a number of counties called "suburban counties" *(jiaoxian* or *shixiaxian)* outside their urban areas. The number of counties under urban administration soared from 173 in 1981 to 689 in early 1988, accounting for one-third of all the counties (Chan, 1994a:249–250). This administrative reorganization is premised on the notion of enhancing "horizontal" integration and polar growth of the more developed cities and the surrounding rural areas.

Contradictory Policies?

At various times, the government has pursued urban policies that are contradictory. More specifically, some policies encouraged the growth of large cities under the policy involving economic reforms and under policies that restricted the growth of large cities such as those that prevailed as recently as the early 1980s. Other policies were intended to promote the growth of large cities and to encourage the growth of small cities. The coordination of reform with prereform policies and the balance of market-driven forces with government control form an indispensable element of current urban policy (Han and Wong, 1994). This transition of policies and their implementation from one period to another is not easy, as many obstacles must be surmounted, a fact that is well summed up by Yukun Wang (1993):

> China's economic activity has already begun to change from supply-driven to demand-driven. But in urban planning, "supply-driven" still has a strong influence. Planning continues to proceed from the total volume of state investment, and not much thought has been given to the preferences of consumers and to investors. Planning habits still lean towards unified state allocation for construction, and little attention is paid to the problems brought about by pluralization of investment sources. Not much importance has been attached either to the demands on housing and urban infrastructure by the floating population. Planning still proceeds from a static concept with little attention paid to basic economic concepts such as inflation, land rent prices, the supply and demand of land market, labour cost, land value increase and shortages. (70)

In fact, the transition is not limited to urban policy and urban planning in practice. A need exists as well for a basic reorientation of functions and a repositioning of China's large cities toward external demands from the region and beyond. Won Bae Kim (1991) has pertinently observed the following:

> Compared with other metropolises in Asia, China's large cities are not very specialised in their modern services and management functions. Given the important role of metropolises in the national economy of China, they should be encouraged to specialise in information-related industries, management functions, business services such as finance, banking, insurance, professional services, and research and development activities, rather than rudimentary

services and standardized production. . . . Restructuring of the urban economy and internationalisation of the Chinese economy, however, imply an increasing demand for office space, hotels, housing, and urban amenities in the metropolises. (174–175)

Urban Planning in China

Urban planning in China in the 1980s emphasized implementation, and the long-advocated ideology that planning was "an ideal blueprint of final state" was discarded. However, the most important achievement in urban planning was the introduction of the City Planning Act and its adoption by the Standing Commission of the central government in 1989. It was the first planning act for the country, meaning that urban planning had become statutory. Two principal features of the act should be noted.

First, the act defines the "city planning area" for the first time as "city districts, inner suburban districts, and areas needed for urban development within the city administrative region. The boundaries of the city planning are to be determined by the local government in the course of formulating a comprehensive plan for the city." The definition of the "city planning area" is crucial for the management of the city, especially in regulating land use.

Second, the act defines five powers of urban planning, namely, the powers of participation, ratification, approval, modification, and examination. These powers strengthen the concept of urban planning and the mechanisms of land management. Furthermore, in addition to the City Planning Act are the Act of Land Control and the Act of Environmental Protection, which are mutually reinforcing in the planning and management of Chinese cities (Zou, 1990).

Land-Use Management

One of the critical components of urban change in China focuses on land-use management. Since 1984, Chinese cities experimented with a series of land-use management policies. These tended to proceed faster in the southern and central coastal cities and the SEZs, well ahead of their counterparts in the north and the interior. By 1992, evidence was seen of an acceleration of urban reform, with land leasing being adopted at an unprecedented scale in selected cities. Other notable changes included the creation of profit-oriented real estate development companies, the promotion of economic development zones to attract foreign investors, the selective use of land-use lease mechanisms, the introduction of land-use development fees and taxes, the promotion of spot redevelopment of inner-city areas, and the reintroduction of land and building registration cadastres. These were the beginnings of a comprehensive urban land reform strategy. The objective of the reform is to create property markets in which land and structures are traded at competitive prices and explicit land price signals govern land-use behavior choices (World Bank, 1993).

Ultimately, these efforts are aimed at establishing in Chinese cities demand-driven urban planning, which is sensitive to changes of economic activities and the needs of consumers and investors. Wang (1993) has outlined the characteristics as follows:

> Demand-driven urban planning should attach importance to the changes in the market of key factors of labour, land and capital as well as changes in the commodity, cultural and service markets. Without understanding the trends in these markets, it would be difficult to let urban planning be the "locomotive" of urban construction. (71)

Recommendations

For urban planning with specific reference to large cities in China, a recent and important Chinese study has made a number of practical suggestions, as listed here (Ye et al., 1988):

- Through national land use planning, regional planning and urban development strategy, the nature of large cities can be determined. There should be individual plans for economic structure, spatial distribution and population size. There should not be one model of development.

- The urban economy needs restructuring. Through economic means, the development and control of large cities can be adjusted. Large cities are made attractive as well as repulsive, with land use and infrastructure facilities being used as the main tools, in such a manner that it would cost more in large cities than in smaller ones.

- In restructuring the urban economy, particular attention should be given to high-tech industry and the tertiary sector.

- Develop horizontal economic linkages, with large cities offering talents, technology and capital to embark on joint construction projects with other places to increase production and elevate the economy.

- Natural increase of population in large cities should be lower than the national urban average. However, the actual rate of growth should be determined by economic planning and by the carrying capacity of the cities.

- The present relationship of the larger the city, the smaller the average developable land should be changed. Flexibility should be adopted in large cities.

- The floating population has already become an inseparable part of large cities. Such population should be welcome but must be carefully monitored and managed.

- Strengthen the planning and management of large cities. In the central city area, no one must be allowed to establish heavy polluting, energy-consuming, water- and land-wasting, and transport-oriented industrial enterprises.

- In the vicinity of large cities establish a number of well-endowed medium-sized cities for the purpose of alleviating the pressure on large cities. (625–626)

CASE STUDIES OF URBAN MANAGEMENT: SHANGHAI AND GUANGZHOU
Urban Profile

Having reviewed China's large cities as a whole and the main factors that have shaped their past and recent growth, it is instructive to examine more closely two such cities to better understand the salient characteristics of metropolitan planning and management in China. The selected large cities are Shanghai and Guangzhou, located at the heart of the Yangzi River delta and the Pearl River delta, respectively, the foci of the two most rapidly developing regions since China adopted an open policy in 1978. Although both cities are special in their urban history and role in Chinese development, their recent experience in urban development and innovation will provide valuable lessons to other large and smaller cities in China in the years ahead.

Shanghai and Guangzhou present two especially fascinating case studies, with their linked and contrasting fortunes in China's experience of opening to the world for trade and development. Prior to the Opium War (1839–1842), Guangzhou was the second-largest city in China, with a population of 0.8 to 0.9 million, second only to Beijing. For almost a century since 1757, Guangzhou was the only Chinese city open for trade to the outside world. However, since Shanghai began its modern development as one of five ports open for trade as a provision of the Treaty of Nanking in 1842, its transformation in 150 years from a third-rank town to a leading megacity in Asia and the largest metropolis in China is phenomenal. The tale of two cities since 1843 is one of explosive and miraculous growth for Shanghai and of continuous relative decline for Guangzhou as foreign investment, domestic resources, and fortune seekers converged on the new city of opportunity at the mouth of the Yangzi River. Since 1949, Shanghai has lost its former vitality, and Guangzhou did not find dynamism for growth. However, since 1978, Guangzhou began to find fresh impetus and a new magic to surge ahead. With Pudong being declared an open development zone in 1990, Shanghai has forged ahead powerfully and is poised to recapture some of its former glory and status (Le, 1994).

Shanghai is the largest city in China, with a total population (urban agglomeration) of 13.05 million in 1997 and an area of 6,340.5 square kilometers. It is probably the best-known Chinese city to the Western world, as it likely was the leading financial, cultural, and commercial center in the Far East in the early part of the twentieth century. By the 1930s, it attained national prominence in manufacturing industries. However, Shanghai quickly lost its luster as an eminent urban center in the Asia-Pacific region after 1949, when national and urban strategies in China favored other locales. Shanghai lived on its past laurels, and even after China reopened again to the world in the late 1970s, it remained on the sidelines. It was only after Shanghai was made one of fourteen open coastal cities in 1984—but more important, after 1990 with the announcement of Pudong as an open zone—that the metropolis has quickened its pace of development and reform. To date, development has been so rapid that the anticipated rejuvenation of Shanghai and, with it, the Yangzi delta and its hinterland is seemingly on the way.

Guangzhou, as the "gateway to South China," had a total population (urban agglomeration) of 6.66 million in 1997 and an area of 7,434 square kilometers. It has traditionally played a crucial role in exposing China to Western influence in being the only port of external trade for 100 years prior to the Opium War. Thus, it has always been in the vanguard of introducing new ideas and technology to China from the outside world, and, consequently, its political and cultural leaders had been ahead of their times. For centuries, Guangzhou had been at the apex of an urban hierarchy, representing cities of diverse sizes and functions in the Pearl River delta. This dominant role remains, although many medium-size cities mushroomed and developed spectacularly during the 1990s and are capable of posing competition to Guangzhou in some economic functions (see chapter 10). Guangzhou is one of the fourteen open coastal cities announced in 1984, but its reform platform has been erected on a wider foundation.

Both Shanghai and Guangzhou experienced population growth resulting from national policies. For example, during the Cultural Revolution Shanghai was at the vortex of political change and was responsible for sending thousands of educated citizens, including youths, to the countryside rather than outside the city. When the one-child policy was adopted in the late 1970s, Shanghai was among the first to implement it. Thus, by the early 1980s, signs were being seen of an aging population in Shanghai. This also explains the subsequent rapid decline of the natural growth rate of the population, which has stabilized at around 10 per 1,000 in both cities. Natural increase is no longer a major factor of urban population growth, although migration is. The floating population has become a sizable yet officially unrecognized component of the population. This has given rise to a burgeoning informal economy that operates largely outside the ambit of official plans and statistics. Shanghai has attempted to grapple with the problem, at least in part, by introducing the "Blue Card" for managerial and scientific personnel and employment licenses for general purposes. The problem is likely to exacerbate as economic and urban reforms continue to unfold.

Urban Change in a Transitional Economy

Since the 1980s, both Shanghai and Guangzhou have witnessed momentous physical and economic changes that have touched almost every aspect of the daily lives of their citizens. In Shanghai, a gradual but basic restructuring of the economy has taken place, with the tertiary sector gaining in importance in its share of both employment and gross domestic product (GDP). Even with the rapid growth of village and township enterprises, unemployment has emerged as a social issue in Shanghai. However, female participation in the labor force has remained high, and the growth of nonagricultural employment in the rural areas has been notable. As a consequence, the income differential between the urban and rural areas has narrowed. The contribution of Shanghai to the national economy has been significant in its revenue generated for the central government and the production and distribution of a wide variety of goods and commodities for the country. Its national role in economic leadership has been rapidly growing. It possesses one of the two stock exchanges in China, and eight futures-market exchanges were established in 1992 and 1993.

Guangzhou has expanded and intensified its economic functions since the late 1970s. The economic restructuring entailed a declining relative importance of manufacturing industry in employment and GDP and a corresponding rise of the tertiary sector. However, C. P. Lo (1994) has found that despite a reorientation of Guangzhou's role as a trade center and port, employment is still found mainly in the secondary sector with a strong emphasis on heavy industry. Tertiary activities have only recently reached the level prevailing in the early 1950s and are still lagging far behind in advanced forms of services, such as finance, insurance, and professional services. It is a city in transition from a planned to a market economy and exhibits the political-ideological conflicts of urban development.

The planning and provision of basic services in both cities have been guided by master plans, a common tool adopted by socialist cities. The latest Master Plan of Shanghai, ratified by the State Council in 1986, included many objectives, including the renewal of the central city, the development of satellite towns, new expressways linking the central city to suburban counties, and others. It also included detailed zoning plans designating industrial districts and residential quarters and the establishment of three economic and technical development zones in Minhang, Hongqiao, and Caohejing. What it did not contain was a blueprint to develop Pudong, which was announced by the central government in 1990 as a new open area for investment and development, with indigenous as well as foreign participation. The Pudong development plan has spurred accelerated infrastructure investment in Shanghai, in particular linking Pudong and Puxi across the Huangpu River. The construction of two new bridges—Nanpu Bridge and Yangpu Bridge—in 1991 and 1993, respectively, testified to the speed and efficiency of construction. The first line of the Shanghai subway was opened in mid-1995. Other elements of urban infrastructure have also been the object of active improvement, although decades of neglect and extreme population concentration are important barriers.

Since 1949, urban development in Guangzhou had been prescribed by a sequence of master plans. Looking retrospectively, the first thirteen master plans up to 1978 can be criticized for their lack of long-term planning for urban development because they were restricted by five-year plans of the central government or yearly plans of municipal governments. The first systematic and complete master plan was the fourteenth one, ratified in 1984. It defined the role and nature of future Guangzhou to the year 2000. Future development of the city will be mainly in two directions: north and southeast. Guangzhou also actively seeks to improve its infrastructure provisions, often with foreign participation. For example, the Daya Bay nuclear plant is a joint venture with China Light and Power of Hong Kong, and the Guangzhou-Shenzhen superhighway is a joint venture with Hong Kong's Hopewell

Holdings. For the most part, both projects are not in the city, although Guangzhou directly benefits from them.

Urban Reforms

One of the often heard rationalizations of the slow pace of development in Shanghai in the prereform period was the excessive burden shouldered by the municipality in revenue contribution to the central government. In the spirit of reform and to allow the municipality a greater latitude to pursue its development programs, a breakthrough was achieved in 1988. In that year, the central government granted Shanghai "a contract system" in finance, using Shanghai's revenue of RMB16.5 billion in 1987 as the base. Shanghai needed to contribute only RMB10.5 billion to the central government, keeping the balance under the control of the municipality for capital and recurrent expenditure. Having achieved this financial breakthrough, the municipality similarly devolved financial authority to the district and county levels, allowing them an incentive for economic development and change. This cycle of change has apparently worked wonders, although its abuse has been reported, such as the construction of expensive and duplicative subcity centers and shopping centers.

In Guangzhou, financial autonomy has been achieved much earlier. In 1980, Guangdong province had already reached an agreement with the central government to pay RMB1 billion annually. Since 1985, the fixed-amount system has been replaced by one of "steadily increasing responsibility" (see chapter 6). In any event, this early devolution of financial autonomy in Guangdong has greatly helped Guangzhou pursue its more freewheeling style of development. For example, it has been able to impose user fees for sewage drainage and tolls for using bridges and superhighways. In other words, Guangzhou has already begun to change the mentality of its citizens to accept a market-oriented style of delivery of urban services over the former welfare system of service provision. The commodification of housing, with the encouragement of housing units sold to tenants at cost, is an example of the market economy achieving progress in this city.

To speed up urban reforms, Shanghai and Guangzhou have been

experimenting with a number of measures, with good effect. In Shanghai, in view of the sharp demand for additional urban infrastructure and services, a new form of urban construction financing came into being in the early 1980s. It can take one of three forms (World Bank, 1993:82). Wang (1993:65) has described one of these "land rent in kind" as the municipal government being the only collector of land rent. Through the deal, the government will obtain not only infrastructure such as roads, pipelines, and green areas but also public facilities such as primary and secondary schools, kindergartens, and police stations. This practice has been successfully utilized in Shanghai in three stages since 1982 and in Guangzhou since 1979 (Wang, 1992:254–258). Other sources of revenue are from land leasing and transfer of land-use rights. In Guangzhou, a fairly conservative policy has been followed in leasing land. Between 1988 and 1991, twenty sites covering 14 hectares, were leased, mainly to foreigners, in the Economic and Technological District in Huangpu. Land lease sales in the rest of the city began officially in 1990. In two years, 1990 to 1991, a total of seventy-one sites were leased, yielding a total revenue of RMB211 million (World Bank, 1993:54).

CONCLUSION

From the recent experience of Shanghai and Guangzhou, it appears that they have made quite remarkable progress in transforming their cities physically, economically, and socially since 1978. The transition to a market-oriented economy is well under way, but the institutional and psychological impediments to change still exist, and these must be overcome. As both cities are in the throes of rapid change, urban reform can be carried out only in a spirit of experimentation. The success or failure of these urban innovations will assist China in its search for a systemic framework to plan and manage its cities, especially its large cities. In the final analysis, whether the open policy can be sustained and how rapidly China can develop depend on the success of its urban reforms and the demonstrable role of its large cities. The next two chapters examine how China's openness and economic reforms have transformed two key economic centers along its coast and shed further light on urban-regional change in coastal China in the age of globalization.

6 Guangdong's Rapid Change as a Coastal Province

Twenty-one years after a historic decision attributable to Deng Xiaoping in 1978, China has made truly remarkable economic strides through its economic reforms and open policy. World attention is once again focused on China's economic upsurge, to such an extent that a "China craze" reminiscent of the early 1970s appeared to have resurfaced. Leading China's bold and ambitious drive toward modernization and development has been Guangdong province, which has applied, with ingenuity and dexterity, a range of reform policies that have yielded astonishing and positive results across a broad front of economic and social life. The scope, pace, and prospect of life in Guangdong have changed so much that the effects are being felt in many parts of the country.

Visitors and students of Guangdong cannot help but marvel at the breadth and depth of the change that has occurred in the province in recent years. Comparing the situation in 1978 with that in 1999, the transformation of Guangdong is almost complete; the physical landscape, economic structure, institutions, and mind-set of the people and, indeed, man and society have undergone almost a complete reversal. Guiding socialist philosophy notwithstanding, signs of the market economy are everywhere. The rapidity of change in Guangdong is worthy of study in its own right, but the importance goes further. Not only are other open areas of China looking toward Guangdong as a barometer of change, but overseas scholars and political leaders alike harbor no less interest in whether the largest remaining communist country has, in fact, succeeded in a smooth transition from a centrally planned to a market economy and whether the switch is durable.

The objective of this chapter is to address the myriad physical, economic, and social changes in as encompassing a manner as possible. The emphasis is emphatically placed on explicating and analyzing the evolving physical and human panorama in Guangdong over the past two decades, coinciding with the period of China's economic reforms. The first section provides a brief overview of Guangdong, drawing out some of its salient characteristics. The second section highlights the main elements of its economic transformation. The third section discusses how Guangdong is viewed in relation to a broader context in the neighboring territories in Asia and what the future has in store for it. The fourth section addresses Guangdong's specific roles in the twenty-first century.

OVERVIEW OF GUANGDONG

With the exception of Hainan Island, which was separated from Guangdong into a new province and a special economic zone (SEZ) in 1988, Guangdong is the most southerly of the twenty-two provinces and five autonomous regions in China. It has an area of 177,901 square kilometers, representing merely 1.85 percent of China's total area. However, its coastline is the longest of all provinces, amounting to 3,368 kilometers, or 10.52 percent of the country's total. This is important for coastal and riverine shipping as well as for providing fishing and other marine resources. Guangdong's population in 1997 reached 70.51 million, accounting for 5.70 percent of China's population. This gives a population density of 382 persons per square kilometer, which is the ninth-densest province in China.

The special character of Guangdong is manifested in many ways—in its physiography, climate, language, folklore, and products. Topographically, it is separated from the rest of China by the east-west Nan

Ling range. This factor, together with its long coastline, its contact with other countries through its overseas emigrants, and its being exposed early on to Western influence through the port of Guangzhou, has the province historically associated with a degree of self-sufficiency and a tendency for separatism. Indeed, for a long time throughout Chinese history, until the Song dynasty, Guangdong was viewed as nothing but a semicivilized frontier to which disgraced officials were exiled as a punishment.

The geomorphology of Guangdong is diverse, being made up mainly of rounded hills, cut by streams and rivers, and scattered and ribbon-like alluvial valleys. Much of northern Guangdong consists of dissected uplands, but of the greatest economic value are the alluvial and deltaic plains formed by the three major rivers of the Pearl River (Zhujiang) system—the West (Xi), the North (Bei), and the East (Dong) Rivers. The Pearl River delta, referring to the area of the West River beyond the confluence, has been one of the fastest-growing areas in China since 1978. Since 1984, the so-called small and large deltas have been differentiated, occupying 11.1 and 21.7 percent of the provincial area, respectively.[1] The Han River in eastern Guangdong is the most important river outside the Pearl River system.

Much of Guangdong lies south of the Tropic of Cancer and thus is the only province, along with Hainan, with tropical and subtropical climates. What distinguishes Guangdong from most parts of eastern China are not its summer temperatures, which range from 28 to 30 degrees Centigrade in July in the West River valley, but its much higher winter temperatures, which range from 13 to 16 degrees Centigrade. Rainfall displays a pronounced summer maximum, with the rainy season lasting from mid-April to mid-October. Typhoons coincide with this rainy period, during which their occurrence can cause widespread human and physical destruction. The mild winter means that

---

[1] The "large delta" refers to eight cities (Guangzhou, Foshan, Zhongshan, Jiangmen, Huizhou, Zhaoqing, Shenzhen, and Zhuhai) and twenty-four counties. The "small delta" includes only six cities (Guangzhou, Foshan, Jiangmen, Zhongshan, Shenzhen, and Zhuhai) and thirteen counties. See Yeh et al. (1989).

two crops of rice can be grown everywhere in the province, and monsoon rains weave a pattern of agricultural land use that has been perfected for untold generations. Rain-fed rivers are not only a major source of water for the burgeoning population but also a cheap and common means of transport.

The administrative system in Guangdong has undergone many changes since 1949. However, since 1978 a tendency has existed for many counties *(xian)* to upgrade themselves to cities. Many city-administered counties thus came into being. At present in Guangdong, seventy-six counties are administratively under twenty-one cities, forming what might be viewed as city regions. An idea of the administrative hierarchy around 1997 is given in Figure 6.1. At the apex of this hierarchy is Guangzhou, which is the provincial capital. Guangzhou once was the unrivaled metropolis in Guangdong, dominating its economic and cultural life to a very large extent. Since 1978, because of the rapid rise of secondary cities in the delta area through economic growth and population influx, Guangzhou's relative importance has declined. Major cities have followed divergent paths of transformation but have tended to converge in the diversified functions that they perform in trade and the tertiary sector. Urban regions in their inchoate forms are also being established.

Beginning in the seventeenth century, a deteriorating man-to-land ratio and a weakening Manchu rule gradually led Guangdong to become an area of emigration. Emigrants from the province went afar and settled in many parts of the world. Despite the long physical and temporal separation, these emigrants have never forgotten their roots and have actually forged enduring links with their places of origin. The importance of this linkage can be appreciated by the fact that returned overseas Chinese totaled about 10 million in the mid-1980s, or about 15 percent of the total population (Wu, 1986:81). The vital overseas links that Chinese provide in technology transfer, capital accumulation, and information access have been critical in Guangdong's recent transformation. In this way, Hong Kong Chinese have been playing, since 1978, the role of Guangdong's window to the world exceedingly well.

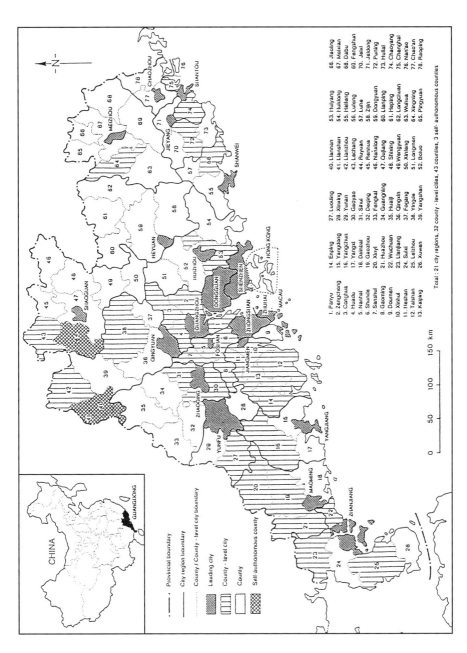

Total : 21 city regions, 32 County - level cities, 43 counties, 3 self - authonomous counties

1. Panyu
2. Zengcheng
3. Conghua
4. Huadu
5. Nanhai
6. Shunde
7. Sanshui
8. Gaoming
9. Doumen
10. Xinhui
11. Heshan
12. Taishan
13. Kaiping

14. Enping
15. Yangdong
16. Yangchun
17. Yangxi
18. Dianbai
19. Gaozhou
20. Xinyi
21. Huazhou
22. Wuchuan
23. Lianjiang
24. Suixi
25. Leizhou
26. Xuwen

27. Luoding
28. Xinxing
29. Yunan
30. Gaoyao
31. Sihui
32. Deqing
33. Fengkai
34. Guangning
35. Huaiji
36. Qingxin
37. Fogang
38. Yingde
39. Yangshan

40. Liannan
41. Lianshan
42. Lianzhou
43. Lechang
44. Ruyuan
45. Renhua
46. Nanxiong
47. Qujiang
48. Shixing
49. Wengyuan
50. Xinfeng
51. Longmen
52. Boluo

53. Huiyang
54. Huidong
55. Haifeng
56. Lufeng
57. Luhe
58. Zijin
59. Dongyuan
60. Lianping
61. Heping
62. Longchuan
63. Wuhua
64. Xingning
65. Pingyuan

66. Jiaoling
67. Meixian
68. Dabu
69. Fengshun
70. Jiexi
71. Jiedong
72. Puning
73. Huilai
74. Chaoyang
75. Chenghai
76. Nan'ao
77. Chao'an
78. Raoping

Figure 6.1 Administrative Divisions of Guangdong, c. 1997

The early exposure to Western influence with Guangzhou as the only port of external trade for 100 years prior to the Opium War (1839–1842), coupled with the overseas Chinese link, has traditionally facilitated Guangdong to nurture political and cultural leaders whose thinking was ahead of their times. Prominent leaders of political movements include Hong Xiuquan, Kang Youwei, Liang Qichao, and Sun Yat-sen. They have left indelible marks on the history of modern China. Of special interest is the historical development of Guangdong from an economic perspective. The rise of Guangzhou and Foshan was due largely to the flourishing commerce and trade that the province experienced as a result of the single-port policy and the use of the Meiguan Pass as the sole north-south conduit for the movement of goods between Guangdong and other parts of China.

A PROFILE OF SOCIETAL TRANSFORMATION

Over the past two decades since China adopted an open policy, Guangdong has become a transfigured land. Hardly any facet of society has been left untouched by the people's passion for change, so much so that a societal transformation has occurred in the province. From the abyss of stagnation in the late 1970s that was the bitter legacy of the Cultural Revolution, Guangdong has dramatically turned the corner and, by the late 1990s, could proudly show its face of modernity and breathtaking economic gains in its SEZs and in the bustling cities in the Pearl River delta and elsewhere. All this has been achieved amid such a climate of experimentation and hesitation, with the rules of the game hardly delineated, that China's economic boom has been likened to a "modern gold rush." Chinese businessmen's enthusiasm for change has been compared with the gold-rush fever that opened up the West Coast of North America in the 1800s (Dalgish, 1993).

The best way to bring home Guangdong's startling economic progress made in recent years is to cite some comparative statistics. Between 1991 and 1995, real economic growth in Guangdong averaged 19.1 percent per year, as opposed to 12 percent per year for China, or fully 7.1 percentage points above the national rate for five years. In the period 1985–1995, Guangdong's gross domestic product (GDP) multiplied 9.73 times. In 1980, Guangdong's gross national product (GNP) per capita was lower than the national average but by 1995 was 67.6 percent above it. Whereas Guangdong had ranked seventh in its contribution to China's GDP in 1978, it soared to the top rank by 1995 (beginning in 1989). Guangdong is now the foremost province in foreign capital utilizations, exports, investment in fixed social assets, and agricultural production. The share of Guangdong in China's production of consumer durable goods has similarly soared. Guangdong's share in the country's production of cameras has increased by many orders of magnitude, from 10 percent in 1978 to 82 percent in 1997. Likewise, Guangdong was responsible for producing a sizable proportion of China's hi-fi sets (84.9 percent), telephone sets (81.8 percent), and electric fans (81.8 percent) in 1997 (*Guangdong Yearbook,* 1998).

One primary factor that enabled Guangdong to grow as rapidly as it did was the decisive policy adopted at the Third Plenum of the Party's Eleventh Central Committee in December 1978 whereby economic reforms and an open policy would be pursued. Guangdong, through the three SEZs of Shenzhen, Zhuhai, and Shantou, was allowed to implement "special policies and flexible measures." The relationship between Guangdong and the central government has had its ups and downs, buffeted by the jostle for political power between the pro-reform and conservative groups in Beijing. Many dimensions exist to the fascinating tussle for political power and economic concessions. One breakthrough that permitted Guangdong to achieve a greater measure of fiscal autonomy was the agreement, in 1980, of a five-year fixed-amount quota system whereby Guangdong would pay the central government RMB1 billion annually. Since 1985, the fixed-amount system has been replaced by one of "steadily increasing responsibility." Many other facets of the central-provincial relations exist that touch on foreign trade, taxation power, and economic policymaking power.

In proceeding with its economic transformation, Guangdong initially focused its attention on the rural sector between 1979 and 1983. Agricultural production reached a record in the mid-1980s with diversification and specialization. Since then, production has remained stagnant. However, forestry productivity is relatively low by national and world standards, its development being hampered by backward technology. The rural landscape has witnessed drastic changes as a consequence of land disturbances and technological breakthroughs. Most disconcerting is the rapid loss of cultivated land, which amounted to 3.3 million *mu* in the period 1980–1990.[2] Guangdong had in the early 1990s only 0.61 *mu* of arable land per person, the second lowest of all provinces in China. In 1994, this decreased further to 0.51 *mu*.

In the period 1984–1988, after successful economic reforms in the rural sector with the adoption of a responsibility system, development was concentrated in the urban sector. This was the beginning of what can be described as an economic takeoff. From the mid-1980s, all economic indicators began to show a sharp upward swing. Advances in industry and trade can be ascribed to the stimulus that resulted from marketization and the emergence of a free-enterprise system. Collectively or privately owned enterprises grew phenomenally at the expense of state-owned enterprises (SOEs). In the period 1983–1988, the value of industrial product from SOEs consistently declined, losing 19 percentage points and thus falling to less than 50 percent of the total. The proportion of industrial SOEs decreased from 59.3 to 41.2 percent from 1983 to 1988 (Zhang, 1992). In the explosive growth of Guangdong's industrial capacity, the vital role played by township and rural enterprises is clearly shown in their staggering increase from 80,000 in 1978 to about 1.2 million in 1989, a 25.2 percent increase per year over 11 years (Wen and Zhang, 1992).

In fact, in the heart of the Pearl River delta, a new entrepreneurial spirit—a delta spirit—that has propelled the exceptionally fast growth in the area can be detected. In the "Four Small Tigers"—Shunde, Nanhai, Zhongshan, and Dongguan—the growth in GDP in the period since 1978 averaged over 20 percent per year, considerably above the provincial average. These provinces certainly are in the forefront of economic reforms. To make up for previous neglect and to keep in step

---

[2] One *mu* is equivalent to 0.06 hectares, or 0.165 acres. The other side of the coin in the loss of agricultural land is the rapid increase of built-up area in the Pearl River delta. The period 1978–1984 saw an increase of 40.3 percent in built-up area, but the explosive increase occurred later.

with the recent economic renewal, service industries have boomed in a variety of forms. A structural shift of the economy has taken place toward services, which at present account for one-third of the GDP of the province. The nascent consumer market in Guangdong is the envy of many transnational corporations that have diverse goods and service to sell. It has been suggested that domestic consumption will likely replace exports as the motor of China's development (Cheng and Taylor, 1991). Tourism has also become an important income producer. In the midst of economic prosperity, a real need exists for Guangdong to evolve new ways to manage banking and finance. Guangdong is "above average" in money and banking in China. For example, it is evolving new forms of financial intermediation by developing in Shenzhen one of China's two stock markets. In fact, both Shenzhen and Zhuhai are pioneers in financial reforms in China. The sustainability of economic reforms depends largely on financial reform.

As the delta region prospers economically, the wage differentials between that area and other counties in Guangdong and other provinces increase. Although the wage differentials between Guangdong and its neighboring provinces were only 10 percent in 1978, the gap was magnified to between 35 and 70 percent by 1990. This induced intra- and interprovincial labor migration into the delta region in search of work and economic opportunities. In fact, most of the farming in the prosperous delta region is undertaken by outside workers. The scale of migration has been massive and unprecedented. Understandably, most migrants move for economic reasons. In addition, a sizable mobile or temporary population exists in many of the cities in the delta region. In Guangzhou alone, the mobile population totaled 0.91 million in 1989, or about 25 percent of the city population. It has been estimated that Guangzhou's mobile population increased annually at 12.9 percent in the period 1979–1989 (Li and Hu, 1991:192).

To keep pace with the spurt of development, Guangdong has found it difficult to provide the necessary supporting infrastructure. Considerable progress has been made in improving all modes of transport and communication. Construction of highways, airports, and seaports has been ambitious, but coordination of such megaprojects at the provincial level or within the delta region itself is seriously lacking. Similarly, energy shortages prove to be a bottleneck that has the effect of restraining development. Demand for energy has been increasing rapidly and, despite foreign investment and participation, will remain insatiable for some time. Often viewed as a component of infrastructure, housing has been rapidly evolving from being a welfare provision to a tradable commodity in the market. Guangdong is still a long way from the full commodification of housing, but the beginning of housing reforms has been made, with the SEZs leading in such reforms and the development of housing markets. Fundamental problems have yet to be overcome.

Guangdong's headlong economic development has also spilled over into domains not directly related to income generation. It has been concluded that a rudimentary takeoff in education has occurred, with the early signs of market forces already at play. However, economic opportunities as a result of the open policy have lured many teachers from the schools, resulting in a crisis in the teaching profession. A related problem is the alarming wastage of some 1.12 million students to the job market in the period 1985–1989. The growing materialistic orientation in society has likewise caused a change in the content of education, with vocational education being given greater emphasis. Higher education as well is changing in fundamental ways, and even the meaning of education is a subject of debate. With respect to health, one negative side effect of rapid industrialization relates to occupational health problems associated with township and rural enterprises that are omnipresent while health services are poorly provided for or not provided for at all. Migrant workers, especially those engaged in "dirty jobs," are also prone to occupational health problems. The health system as a whole has undergone radical changes, and with the aging of Guangdong's population, the health of the elderly is a subject requiring special attention. Several important changes have occurred in social provisions incorporating social insurance, social relief, social welfare, and privilege security. A system of shared responsibility with the government has arisen as new enterprises are established. In addition, new social problems emerge as Guangdong moves toward a market economy, such as the reappearance of prostitution, another deleterious byproduct of opening the province for which no ready solution exists.

GUANGDONG IN A WIDER CONTEXT

The success of the Guangdong's economic reforms is probably beyond the expectations of the original proponents of the open policy. By the early 1990s, plenty of signs of prosperity were seen in the province, and the future path of development in Guangdong will be keenly watched in China as well as abroad. The meaning of Guangdong's economic leap can be grasped at three levels.

At the first level, within Guangdong itself the impulse of economic growth has been spatially differentiated, with the Pearl River delta viewed by some as a marvel of the open policy but many of the outlying mountainous counties scantily affected in material ways. The huge and widening personal income gap between the delta and the mountainous regions has been emphasized by Guangdong officials. However, the provincial government as well as the cities that have developed the fastest have faced up to the responsibility of helping the laggard counties catch up and narrow the difference.

Before the reforms will have a good likelihood of sustaining themselves, two sectors in particular require urgent attention. One is related to the legal system, which at present is chaotic and arbitrary, leaving little recourse to the wronged investor and trader. Progress is slow in legislative reforms, although Shenzhen has been allowed freedom in enacting local regulations. As economic development has accelerated, the Guangdong courts are saddled with a skyrocketing increase in the number and variety of commercial litigation cases. An interim solution is for many of the economic disputes to be settled in mediation centers that have been established. A disturbing concern appears to be that even the judiciary is not immune to corruption, a phenomenon that is widespread, undermining the administrative and social systems. Equally deserving of immediate remedial measures is environmental degradation in many forms. The pollution that comes especially with industrialization has become a serious problem. Despite the existence of environmental legislation and standards, their weak enforcement and the dispersed pattern of polluting industries have posed chronic difficulties. Environmental control is more relaxed outside the major cities of the delta, and the main threat has come from industrial development in small and medium-size cities and towns and rural areas. However, Guangdong plans to spend up to RMB14.4 billion during the Ninth Five-Year Plan (1996–2000) on environmental protection in the Pearl River delta, with fourteen large projects to be implemented (Kwan, 1996).

At the second level, Guangdong's experimentation with economic reforms is part of the national design to bring China out of its previous self-imposed isolation from the world community and economy. As Ezra Vogel (1989) has aptly put it, Guangdong's attempt at modernization and development is merely one step ahead in China. What is indisputable are the impressive gains that economic reforms and the open policy have brought to Guangdong, especially to the three SEZs, all of which started from very humble foundations. Shenzhen is the epitome of what the open policy has created. It grew at an average of 500 percent per year during the 1980s and is now the city with the highest standard of living and wages in China. In 1995, it had a population of 3.45 million, of which 2.46 million were temporary residents. Consequently, Guangdong, especially the SEZs, has been a major destination for the migration of skilled and unskilled labor from many parts of China. In fact, it has been observed that since 1978, a relative shift of China's center of gravity has occurred, involving the movement of capital, talent, technology, and labor to the south.

Indeed, the substantive and symbolic meaning of what happens in Guangdong is viewed seriously across China and other open areas in particular. Thus, the visits of top political leaders to the SEZs in Guangdong in 1984–1985, 1987–1988, 1990, and 1992 were planned to synchronize certain critical stages of the open policy and were widely publicized to the nation. These visits contributed in no small way to formulating the "socialist market economy" policy that culminated in Deng Xiaoping's visit to the south in January 1992.

With the passing of time and as other open areas succeeded in obtaining the special status that the SEZs and open cities in Guangdong had to pursue their economic development, the SEZs are no longer as special as they were. Although the development of other areas of China is needed and fully justified, a problem of duplication and redundancy has arisen among the coastal cities in the adoption of their development policy and direction. What had succeeded in Guangdong was, in some cases, blindly replicated without taking into account the local circumstances or comparative advantage.

Whatever the role of Guangdong as a pacesetter in China's transition to a market economy, the decision in 1990 to set up Pudong in Shanghai as a free-trade zone, with policies similar to the SEZs, was inspired by Guangdong's scintillating achievements in the 1980s. In part, the Pudong plan was conceived of as a countermagnet to the economic pull of Guangdong and as a "major economic base" from which to launch an economic rejuvenation of Shanghai and its surrounding region. From the signs that are emerging to date, Pudong will likely be another center of economic growth for China in the 1990s and beyond (Yeung and Sung, 1996).

At the third level, Guangdong's recent development must be viewed against the background of the neighboring territories, Asia, and the world. The original choice of Shenzhen and Zhuhai as SEZs was surely predicated on their advantage of geographic proximity to Hong Kong and Macau. At least for Hong Kong, its lucrative symbiosis with Guangdong that began hesitantly in 1978 has flowered into massive trade flows, two-way investments, and all-around explosive growth since 1984. Hong Kong has fully utilized the cheap land and labor costs in the delta region and relocated en masse the bulk of its industrial capacity north of the border. Guangdong has essentially become Hong Kong's workshop, employing around three million workers in factories owned by Hong Kong investors. Hong Kong capital accounts for Guangdong's overwhelming share of external economic activity, amounting to 80.9 percent in trade and 70.0 percent in investment. Hong Kong investors are involved in more than 10,000 joint ventures and derive their products from 20,000 processing factories in the province. Guangdong-processed goods offer a 70 percent profit margin against 20 percent in Hong Kong, providing a strong economic motivation to Hong Kong firms to effect their industrial relocation. In turn, Hong Kong's advanced transport, communication, financial, and service sectors serve Guangdong well to market its products overseas and to gain access to the latest market information. Hong Kong investors' willingness to take a chance in the face of uncertainty to provide capital for Guangdong's development in the 1980s provided the critical initial momentum that was later sustained as other investors also joined in.

The obvious and substantial mutual benefit that Guangdong and Hong Kong reaped from the open policy has given rise to other conceptual designs for "Greater Hong Kong," "Southern China," and other permutations. The southern China proposition involves the broader area of Guangdong, Fujian, Taiwan, and Hong Kong capitalizing on the Hong Kong–Guangdong link and the close Taiwan-Fujian linguistic and geographic relations (see chapters 3 and 4). In fact, it is one of several existing and potential growth triangles in the Asia-Pacific region, in which several contiguous countries are anxious for economic cooperation across national boundaries for the common object of accelerating development. A variant of the same theme is a newly industrializing Cantonese economy, involving Hong Kong, Macau, the neighboring SEZs, Guangzhou, and the inner delta, as Vogel has envisaged (Vogel, 1989).

Regardless of which extended territorial design is more appropriate, the development of Guangdong being linked to a wider region means that the fortune of the province is subject to the vicissitudes of the world economy. By leading China in the open policy, Guangdong has already been partially integrated with the world economy. China's openness has coincided with a period of globalization of production and more open economies since the 1980s. A recent Australian study has perceived propitious opportunities for economic change in Northeast Asia, including China, which has shown signs of greater openness and integration into the regional economy. China is anxious to rejoin the General Agreement on Tariffs and Trade (GATT), which has been replaced by the World Trade Organization (WTO), but it must further its economic reforms in trade, currency, and other spheres before it can succeed.

Looking toward the future, Deng Xiaoping, in his tour of Guangdong in January 1992, called on the province to become another "Little Dragon" of Asia in 20 years. At the Fourteenth National Party Congress held in October 1992, this statement spurred the creation of objectives for development that required Guangdong to realize modernization goals in two decades. Concrete development targets have been set in two stages, to 2000 and 2010. Guangdong has since adopted seventeen ways to open more areas to the outside, including declaring Meizhou, Shaoguan, and Heyuan as part of the coastal open areas. Guangdong's recent record of growth is any government's envy, as it has become one of the most rapidly developing regions of the world. It has already successfully translated, ahead of schedule, an early development goal set by central planners in China to quadruple GDP between 1980 and 2000. However, to be on par with the "Four Little Dragons" is a different proposition. A recent assessment is that Guangdong can realistically catch up with Taiwan and South Korea in 20 years, but to reach the level of Hong Kong and Singapore would be a different matter (Sung et al., 1995). In any event, it is an admirable development goal that, even if not entirely attained, will be an inspiring target toward which forces of energy and enterprise should be purposefully directed, as they have been in the recent past.

TOWARD THE TWENTY-FIRST CENTURY

During the period of the Eighth Five-Year Plan (1991–1995), Guangdong achieved tremendous growth, with annual growth of GDP averaging 19 percent, 6.5 percent higher than the previous plan period and 7.3 percent higher than the national average. It marked the period of the most rapid growth in Guangdong since 1949. The delta area grew even more phenomenally, averaging 26.2 percent during the period 1991–1994. However, beginning in late 1993, with the implementation of macroeconomic adjustment policies, growth began to moderate. The year 1995 marked the last year of rapid growth, with the annual growth of GDP at 15 percent (Chen et al., 1995).

However, for the period of the Ninth Five-Year Plan (1996–2000), Guangdong has set for itself more subdued rates of growth, with annual growth of GDP projected at 10 to 13 percent. Per capita GDP is projected to increase from RMB5,166 in 1995 to RMB8,610 in 2000. In addition, the plan has set specific goals for the province to achieve slightly faster growth in heavy industry versus light industry, to lean more toward export growth than economic growth, to emphasize the upgrading of technology, and to coordinate development among regions, specifically to minimize the disparity between development in the two flanks of the delta area and between the northern hilly region and the rest of the province.

Indeed, on the theme of technology upgrade, SOEs will form an obvious target. Guangdong's SOEs have the highest asset value among all provinces, estimated at RMB260 billion in 1997, with an indebted rate at 76.9 percent. Most of these SOEs are scattered and inefficient and have a high degree of duplication. Guangdong has been reported to have lagged behind Shanghai and Shandong in SOE reform during the past few years. Thus, this should be a major focus for the current plan period. A total of 250 SOEs have been identified for experimental reform, so that smaller enterprises will come first and all enterprises will eventually have to adjust to the demands of the market economy.

One of the key factors in furthering Guangdong's development in the years ahead is the return of Hong Kong to Chinese sovereignty in 1997. Closer integration across a broad front can be anticipated. In fact, the Guangdong authorities have plans to stitch Hong Kong and Macau into the infrastructure of southern China. By 2010, more than twenty-five expressways crisscrossing Guangdong are expected to be completed, providing better access not only to Hong Kong and Macau but to neighboring provinces as well. In the current plan period alone, some RMB90 billion is earmarked for the construction of sixteen expressways (Wallis, 1997). These include the Boca Tigris (Nansha-Humen) and Lingdingyang bridges. The latter bridge will connect Hong Kong and Macau over a distance of 37.9 kilometers at an estimated cost of HK$13 billion. A business consortium is reported to be actively pursuing the project with a completion date of 1999 (Batha, 1997), but nothing concrete has yet begun. Thus, it is certain that at the dawn of the twenty-first century, Guangdong will be much better provided for in terms of infrastructure and other facilities so that it can play a leading role in China's development and modernization.

A recent study comparing Guangdong to Shanghai reveals that, by 1994, Guangdong had increasingly outdistanced Shanghai when measured in terms of their share of national importance. For example, in the share of GDP, Shanghai accounted for China's 7.5 percent in 1978, but it decreased progressively to 4.4 percent in 1994. Conversely, Guangdong's share of the national GDP total increased progressively, from

5.1 percent in 1978 to 9.4 percent in 1994. Similar statistics have been assembled for exports, utilized foreign capital, and trade over time. Although details of their relative importance in the national picture might differ in the selected indicators, the trend is unmistakable that Guangdong has gradually garnered a greater national share in all the dimensions under review (Sung, 1996). Despite the special policy and resources allowed for Pudong, the recent rapid growth of Shanghai has, surprisingly, not changed the general tendency. Thus, it is clear that Guangdong is already in a commanding position to lead China to a period of sustained growth and development. A reflection of Guangdong's success in economic transformation is the fact that, in 1996, it provided a quarter of China's individual income tax revenue, at RMB1.53 billion (Economist Intelligence Unit, 1996).

The future outlook for Guangdong is distinctly robust, but its planners and policymakers must be fully aware of the possibility of its being a victim of its own success. As Guangdong will become more saturated with foreign and domestic investment, competition for land and labor will become more intense. Higher costs could price Guangdong out of the international market, much analogous to what Hong Kong and the other "Little Dragons" have experienced, triggering their economic restructuring. Already Hong Kong firms have been looking beyond Guangdong to Wuhan, Shanghai, and elsewhere for expansion and long-term investment (Goldstein, 1992c).

With the rise of Pudong, Sichuan, and other open areas in China, Guangdong has essentially lost its previous special advantages in terms of favorable policy. It must now create for itself new comparative advantages related to generative mechanisms and economic development to supplant its former privileged position bestowed on it by the central government. Deng Xiaoping's death in February 1997 has not had any negative impact on China's open policy. To be sure, this is reassuring to Guangdong and other open areas, as it has resulted from careful planning by top decision makers, including Deng himself. As the open policy further unfolds, China's development and modernization in the twenty-first century will be spatially more diffuse and substantively more broad based. Undoubtedly, Guangdong will continue to play a critical role in advancing China's development goals and modernization program.

THE NAME *summons up a world of compradors and foreign concessions, gunboat diplomacy and opium, afternoon tea at the Cathay Hotel and death by starvation in the streets outside Western cantonments. It recalls a landscape of gangsters, sweatshops, strikes and revolution, fierce intellectuals and vengeful Red Guards. (Walsh, 1992:19)*

7 Shanghai's Transformation and Modernization under China's Open Policy

Shanghai, literally meaning "on the sea," which is vividly described in the opening quotation, is China's largest city. It symbolizes the clash between Western and Chinese civilizations. After it was named one of five open cities by the Treaty of Nanking in 1842 following the Opium War (1839–1842), Shanghai was opened to Western trade and residence. It was a combination of unfettered Western capitalism, boundless Chinese entrepreneurial spirit, and an unrivaled geographic location that witnessed more than a century of unprecedented and dramatic growth at the mouth of the Yangzi River.

Yet Shanghai is a city of anomalies and paradoxes because, as a semicolonial city on Chinese soil, it marked the triumph of Western mercantilism and its most successful incursion in Asia in the nineteenth century. The result was truly startling and remarkable, as in less than a century Shanghai had transformed itself from a third-class, local town to a thriving and leading metropolis of the world. In 1936, Shanghai was the seventh-largest city in the world, with a population of 3.81 million. In addition, in its prime in the 1930s and 1940s, Shanghai was China's most urbane conurbation, a metropolis that exhibited all the hues of the human character. It was "as crowded as Calcutta, as decadent as Berlin, as snooty as Paris, as jazzy as New York"—in short, a giant among cities. No modern Asian city, not even Tokyo or Hong Kong, has been able to match Shanghai's cosmopolitan and sophisticated reputation from these vintage years (Editorial, 1995).

Development in Shanghai since 1949, after the People's Republic of China (PRC) was established, was radically different. The record of growth prior to the economic reforms and open policy initiated in 1978 is well summed up by Rhoads Murphey (1988):

> During the first three decades of Communist rule, Shanghai was periodically viewed officially as more problem than promise, an unwelcome leftover from a humiliating and resented semicolonial past. There was official talk in the early 1950s of dismantling Shanghai and distributing its factories and experts over the previously neglected rest of the country. Shanghai was never dismantled completely, but skilled workers, technicians, machine goods and tools, and some whole factories were reallocated from the city to aid in developing new inland industrial centres, and Shanghai's own growth was sharply restricted. (158)

Indeed, even after 1978, when certain parts of southern China (especially Guangdong and Fujian) surged ahead in economic transformation, Shanghai experienced rather modest growth. However, with the announcement in April 1990 of Pudong, the land to the east of the Huangpu River measuring some 350 square kilometers, as an open area for development, attention in China and, in fact, the world at large is focused again on Shanghai. In only several years, massive physical and economic transformation has occurred, propelled by the dynamism of Pudong. Officially, Shanghai has been designated as the "dragon head" to lead the Yangzi delta and basin and, more broadly, China into the twenty-first century through rapid economic growth and a new phase of openness, modernization, and development.

This chapter is divided into three sections. The first section provides a short overview of Shanghai, focusing on some of its key elements. The second section highlights Shanghai's ongoing reforms in the 1990s, which are traced back to the beginning of the open policy in 1978. The third section discusses the importance of the current reforms in Shanghai, focusing on whether they will rejuvenate the city to such an extent that it will recapture some of its former glory and on the relative roles of Hong Kong and Shanghai in the future.

OVERVIEW OF SHANGHAI

Located strategically at the mouth of the Yangzi River, Shanghai lies expansively, together with the island of Chongming, on a large deltaic plain formed by centuries of alluvial sedimentation. For the most part, the city constitutes the southeastern quadrant of the Yangzi River delta, fringed on the north by the Yangzi River and on the south by Hangzhou Bay. Bordered by Jiangsu province on the north and west and by Zhejiang province on the south, much of the boundless deltaic plain has an average elevation of three to four meters. The deltaic plain centered around Shanghai is crisscrossed by a dense network of canals and waterways, most of them man-made, that connect the city to Tai Lake (Tai Hu) to the west.

Shanghai enjoys a mild climate because of its subtropical latitude (30°23′ to 31°27′N) and its maritime location. The average January minimum temperature is 3 degrees Centigrade, and the average July maximum is 27 degrees Centigrade. Shanghai's winter temperatures are markedly higher than Nanjing's because of the moderating maritime influence on the former, notwithstanding their similar latitudes. Similarly, Shanghai is spared the extreme high summer temperatures in the Yangzi River basin for which Nanjing, Wuhan, and Chongqing are infamous. Shanghai has plentiful rainfall, amounting to 1,143 millimeters per year, with a good spread throughout the year and a maximum in June and a minimum in December. Over the years, farmers in the area have been more fearful of floods than of droughts for their harvests. Floods result from the heavy rains and sluggish drainage along the level and meandering waterways.

The importance of Shanghai is due largely to its location midway along the China coast. It serves as an effective link not only between port cities of North and South China but for cities in Japan and Korea and in the Asia-Pacific region as well. In air transport, Shanghai is about one hour's travel time to Tokyo, Seoul, Taipei, and Hong Kong. Although Shanghai's own market is already quite sizable, its hinterland is enormous and unequaled in China. It is estimated to reach 77.7 million inhabitants in the Yangzi River delta and 360 million inhabitants in the Yangzi River basin. Recent developments in infrastructure, such as the completion of the missing links in the rail link between Shanghai and Wuhan and the launching of the Three-Gorges Dam project, are positive factors that enhance the regional importance of Shanghai. Likewise, the recent easing of international relations would enable Shanghai to play a more active role in China's continuing open policy and to engage in economic interactions with countries in Northeast Asia and beyond.

Administratively, Shanghai, with a population of 13.05 million in 1997, is one of the three special municipalities in China with a status equivalent to a province. From an area of only 636.18 square kilometers in 1949, the city has successively expanded, most notably in 1958, to its present area of 6,340 square kilometers, of which 280 square kilometers are occupied by the central city and 6,060.5 square kilometers by suburban districts and counties. The city is made up of three parts: the central city with its ten urban districts, namely, Huangpu, Nanshi, Luwan, Jing'an, Xuhui, Changning, Putuo, Hongkou, Zhabei, and Yangpu; the four suburban districts of Baoshan, Minhang, Jiading, and Pudong New Area; and the six suburban counties of Songjiang, Qingpu, Jinshan, Fengxian, Nanhui, and Chongming (Figures 7.1 and 7.2).

As the cradle of the Chinese Communist Party in 1921, Shanghai is inextricably a part of China. For the past 150 years, the history of China has often been associated with Shanghai. Much has been written about the historical highlights of the development of Shanghai (see Murphey, 1953; Howe, 1981; Wei, 1987). In particular, the context of Shanghai's development as a special city, in comparison with some of the world's largest and most famous cities, has been traced from the nineteenth century to the reform period (MacPherson, 1996). The "Shanghai model" is unique in the history of China.

A major factor that sets Shanghai's development apart from that of other cities in modern China is its entrepreneurial spirit and its bold drive for innovation. Entrepreneurship, it has been maintained, is the driving force for economic dynamism, and Shanghai still lacks an external pattern of entrepreneurship as found in Hong Kong. Both Hong

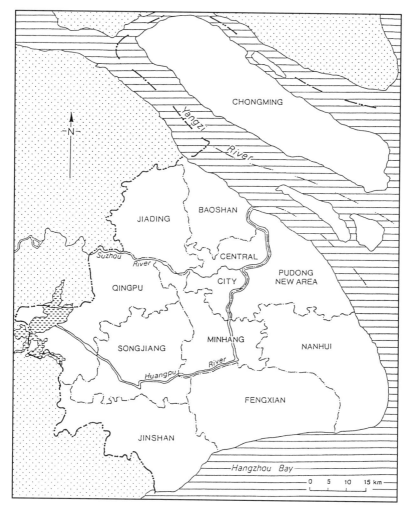

■ Figure 7.1 The Administrative Divisions of Shanghai

Kong and Shanghai display their own style of entrepreneurship, but the prognosis for Shanghai is mixed. This can be contrasted with Shanghai emigrant entrepreneurs in Hong Kong who have been highly successful and have helped launch Hong Kong's postwar transformation into the vibrant economic entity in the Asia-Pacific region that it is today (Wong, 1988). Similarly, it can be argued that Shanghai's lethargy and slower development than Guangdong in the reform period since 1978

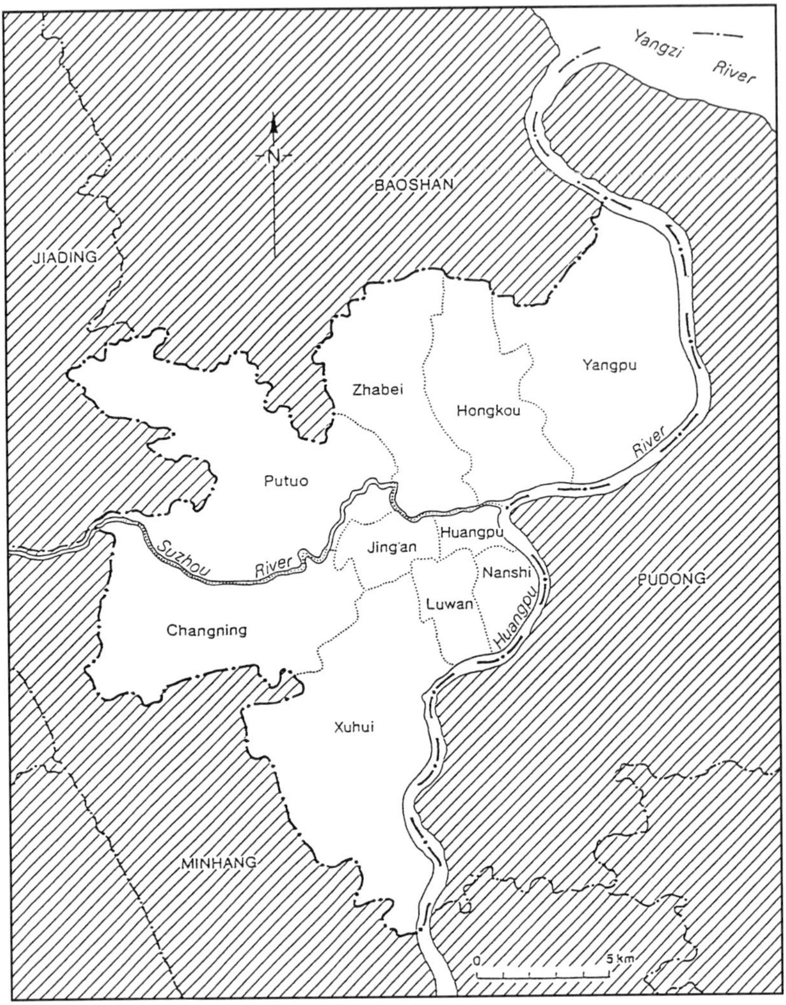

■ Figure 7.2 Urban Districts of Shanghai's Central City

owes to the absence of an entrepreneurial spirit, or at least its erosion, after decades under the command economy.

In the past, Shanghai was noted for its penchant for keeping abreast of technology and new ways of economic or social life. Lucian Pye's observation aptly drives home this point:

Historically Shanghai was quick to adopt innovations: it first encountered trains only seven years after the completion of the first transcontinental railroad in America; its first textile mills were built before any in the American South, and by 1930 it had, according to some methods of calculation, the largest mill in the world; its first cinema opened only five years after San Francisco got its first large movie house; and by the late 1930s its Commercial Press was publishing each year as many titles as the entire American publishing industry—most of which were, of course, pirated. (quoted in Howe, 1981:xv)

A recent study divides Shanghai's economic development under the PRC into three periods. The first period 1953–1978, over 26 years, was one in which Shanghai was under a command economy and in which the societal distribution of resources was a decisive factor. Economic growth averaged 8.8 percent, clearly above the national average. This was followed by the period 1979–1990, over 12 years, in which economic growth raced ahead in Guangdong and other southern areas and in which Shanghai acted as merely as a "rear guard" in economic reforms. Shanghai's manufactured products were losing ground in the domestic market, and the lack of vitality of Shanghainese enterprises was becoming evident. Annual economic growth averaged 7.5 percent, which was below the national average. The third period refers to the present phase of rapid growth since Pudong was launched in 1990 as a growth platform for Shanghai, with average double-digit annual growth. In 1994, Shanghai's GDP reached RMB197.2 billion (compared with RMB27.3 billion in 1978) and a per capita GDP of RMB15,206 (RMB2,498 in 1978) (Gao and Yu, 1994).

In the history of modern Shanghai, politics and economics have always been intertwined. The importance and meaning of political change can be set against the backdrop of economic development in the reform period. For example, the emergence of the present political leadership in Shanghai and its close links to China's president, Jiang Zemin, and premier, Zhu Rongji, who were former mayors of Shanghai, are highly critical. In any event, Xu Kuangdi, Shanghai's present mayor, and Huang Ju, the party secretary, are representatives of the new class of technocrats who tend to be better educated and professional in their orientation. Moreover, the progressive articulation of local interests in Shanghai in the 1980s by quasi-officials and intellectuals is important for its development. The vehicles were seminars, conferences, academic journals, and the local media. By the 1990s, Shanghai had effectively changed from the situation of the late 1970s, when its political leaders, as noted by a renowned China scholar, consistently failed to assert the special economic and cultural interests of their city. During that period, it was not uncommon for leaders to advocate policies and programs diametrically opposed to the interests and the welfare of the people whom they were supposed to represent (quoted in Howe, 1981:xiv).

During much of the period since 1949, a point of strained relations between Shanghai and the central government has been the allegedly unfair distribution of revenues that originated in Shanghai. Shanghai had to bear a seemingly unfair burden for decades by remitting the bulk of its revenues to the central government. Between 1949 and 1983, as much as 87 percent of Shanghai's revenue of RMB350 billion was remitted to Beijing, leaving only 13 percent for its own utilization. In contrast, the revenue for local spending in Beijing and Tianjin averaged 30 percent. In the reform period, as much as one-sixth of the revenue of the central government has been derived from Shanghai. Consequently, Shanghai is described as the "golden milk-cow" of the planned economy by the editor of a local progressive journal (White, 1987:23).

However, in 1988, Shanghai was granted the fiscal contracting system that previously was exclusively enjoyed by Guangdong and Fujian. In 1994, China adopted a "tax sharing system" whereby a uniform formula was put in place across the nation to substitute for the hitherto bilateral bargaining (Wong, 1995). Shanghai was still going through a period of difficult transition in the early 1990s, when local expenditures rapidly expanded while old responsibilities remained and the profitability of the state-owned enterprises (SOEs), traditionally a major source of revenue, was sharply reduced. As a consequence, budget deficits skyrocketed since 1985. The paid transfer of land-use rights that began only in 1988 has since greatly improved the local budget situation, especially in Pudong.

In fact, starting with fewer encumbrances, Pudong New Area has been able to pursue more effective institutional and administrative reforms since 1990. It has effected a higher degree of functional consolidation by adopting a market-oriented approach to economic development. To expedite development by foreign investors and in the interest of operational effectiveness, the hierarchical levels of government and bureaucratic red tape have been reduced.

THE QUICKENING PACE OF REFORM

Although China adopted an open policy in 1978 and Shanghai was designated one of fourteen open cities in 1984, it essentially took a backseat in the economic reforms and rapid growth that had occurred in the southern provinces. The Tiananmen incident in 1989 and its resonance in Hong Kong resulted in the choice of Shanghai as the launching pad for the next phase of rapid growth and economic reform in the 1990s. Thus, for almost every year in the 1990s, Shanghai registered a GDP growth rate in excess of 14 percent, maintaining 14.1 percent growth in 1995 (Shanghai Statistical Bureau, 1995:51). Although the recent growth rates have been impressive, Shanghai has in fact achieved comprehensive and solid progress in many sectors since 1978.

In economic development, Shanghai has experienced significant structural change, with an ever increasing emphasis on the development of the tertiary sector. Since 1978, the tertiary sector has been growing the fastest, picking up speed notably since 1990. By 1994, the value of the tertiary sector reached RMB78 billion, accounting for 39.6 percent of GDP (Shanghai Statistical Bureau, 1995:48). However, Shanghai remains a nationally eminent industrial base, with industries accounting for more than 56 percent of Shanghai's GDP in 1993 (Shanghai City, 1995:127). Industrial development is heavily concentrated in six "pillar industries," namely, steel, automobiles, petrochemicals, energy, telecommunications, and computer products, with an increasing emphasis on technological sophistication. In 1993, these industries yielded RMB31.4 billion in gross industrial output, accounting for 47 percent of Shanghai's total value. Most of these industries still focused on import substitution, with a relatively scant orientation toward exports.

Four of these pillar industries are located in Shanghai's satellite towns, whereas most of the traditional, inefficient, and small-scale factories are intermingled with residential and other land uses in the central urban area. The 1990 Population Census revealed that in Shanghai's old city with 6.39 million inhabitants, there were 4,700 industrial enterprises, averaging thirty-four plants per square kilometer. The urban area had 53.5 square kilometers, or 20.5 percent of the land, devoted to industrial use, which is much higher than the usual 15 percent for industrial use in comparable cities in Western countries (He, 1993). Thus, an extreme functional mixture and land-use fragmentation, in part a result of historical and geographic factors and of the administrative apportionment of land after 1949, has been a hindrance to urban optimization. Since 1978, the new policies have failed to produce any dramatic change in the entrenched chaotic pattern of industrial location. Various solutions to the seemingly intractable problems are being sought.

One of the daunting tasks faced by Shanghai, indeed by China as a whole, in its effort to restructure and modernize its industries is the magnitude of change required to reform SOEs. In the growth of industrial development in Shanghai in the 1980s, new institutions, such as enterprise groups, independent commodity producers, and "horizontal linkages," appeared to open up markets and renovate industries. The formation of "horizontal linkages" is one way of avoiding duplication of industrial activities by separate and administrative units. In an effort to promote flexibility and change within industrial enterprises, it has been reported that parts of some factories in Shanghai are run along quasi-capitalist lines, using a "one factory, two systems" formula (Lam, 1995).

During the 1980s, Shanghai was able to attract a total of U.S.$3.3 billion in foreign investment. Since Pudong was established as a new open area in 1990, the amount of foreign investment in 1992 alone was equivalent to the entire preceding decade. Utilized direct foreign investment reached U.S.$3.2 billion in 1994, which can be compared with U.S.$2.3 billion in 1993 (Shanghai Statistical Bureau, 1995). According to the results of a recent survey, the "hard" investment environment in Shanghai is generally satisfactory, but the "soft" environment needs improvement in specific ways (Nyaw, 1996). Consequently, multinational corporations (MNCs) are attracted to Shanghai, where they can base their operations in China. By August 1994, 146 MNCs with a total of 281 projects had invested in Shanghai. Of the world's 100 top MNCs, thirty-seven are represented in Shanghai for the most part, bringing with them high technology (Xie, 1995). Shanghai opened the first of two stock exchanges in China in September 1990 and now has at least nine commodity exchanges.

To improve Shanghai's investment environment and to enable it to carry forward its reform program, Shanghai's urban and suburban areas underwent momentous changes. To begin with, much of urban Shanghai is a historical artifact, a product of colonial rule that left a legacy of unbalanced development, incompatible infrastructure, and difficult north-south access between districts. Of special importance has been the massive investment in infrastructure development over the past five years, spurred on by the opening of Pudong. The Nanpu Bridge and the Yangpu Bridge were completed in 1991 and 1993, respectively, improving circulation between the banks of the Huangpu River. The 16-kilometer Line One of the subway system, linking north and south Puxi at a cost of U.S.$680 million, was opened in December 1994, making it the largest municipal project in Shanghai's history. The inner-ring road was opened to traffic in December 1994, linking Puxi and Pudong. During the period 1988–1993, Shanghai devoted more than RMB26.4 billion to infrastructure development, which was 1.4 times the total infrastructure expenditures for the preceding 10 years (Shanghai People's Government Reception Office, 1993:4). Many of the urban development and renewal problems stem from decades of land use dictated by politics and whim rather than logic and efficiency. Fortunately, the revenues from leased land over the past few years have put the government in a more favorable position to pursue urban change and reform.

Since 1958, an active satellite-town program, for a variety of planning goals, has been implemented in Shanghai. Seven satellite towns— Wusong, Minhang, Wujing, Anting, Songjiang, Jiading, and Jinshanwei—have undergone rapid growth since 1984. However, heavy industry has been promoted in these towns at the expense of light industry, and residential infrastructure has been neglected. As a result, the satellite towns are of relatively little interest to residents in the central city. After all, the urban bias of "better a bed in the city than an apartment in the suburbs" is pervasive (He, 1993). Pudong's development, some observers have cautioned, might jeopardize the growth of the satellite towns. Development in these towns likely could be accelerated by opening them up to foreign investment, as has already occurred in Minhang.

In light of Shanghai being China's largest city with a huge population, population control has been a prominent feature of its development since 1949. A broad interpretation of population control over the
years, linking it to labor mobility, can be applied in particular to Shanghai's export of trained manpower to other parts of China. Although
Shanghai sent, as part of the *xiafang* movement, 829,000 educated and
youthful residents to the countryside during the 1950–1964 period,
they returned en masse in the late 1970s. Between 1977 and 1982,
498,700 educated youths returned, 264,900 in 1979 alone (He, 1993).
Compounding this was the problem during the 1980s of the temporary
population. A 1988 survey of temporary migrants in large Chinese
cities revealed that Shanghai had 2.09 million such inhabitants, who
presented the city with both challenges and opportunities (Li and Hu,
1991). Thus, Shanghai's population has grown more from immigrants
than from births. Temporary migrants now account for about one-
third of the total population. Shanghai's low fertility pre-dates public
reforms, reaching birth-rate lows of 10 per 1,000 in 1972–1977, and
its life expectancy is the highest of all the provinces.

The changing population dynamics have direct implications for
some social sectors. The advances in health services during the past
four decades are remarkable. As a result of the increasing affluence of
the rural population, a shift has occurred in patient demands for health
services from rural to county and city hospitals. A growing aging population implies changing health care and social needs. In education,
changes since 1978 are equally significant. The content of education
has veered toward more vocational education and an emphasis on util-
itarianism in tertiary education. The supply of graduates from tertiary
institutions cannot meet demand. A variety of measures have been
taken to improve the quality of education. The shared goal for many in
Shanghai is "first-rate education for a first-rate city." One tangible
piece of evidence of social progress in the reform period is housing,
which has seen significant improvements on all fronts. For example, the
per capita living area almost doubled from 4.4 square meters in 1980
to 7.3 square meters in 1993. The housing system reform programs
have proceeded apace with good results. By the mid-1990s, the provision of housing was no longer confined to the government. A secondary housing market, albeit limited and small in many ways, has

emerged. To develop further in this direction, foreign developers have been allowed to construct mass housing in Shanghai, as they have in Guangzhou and Wuhan. This has attracted more than 4,000 foreign companies, including 100 large overseas corporations (Sito, 1994).

Since 1990, the biggest boost to Shanghai's development has been the policy initiatives adopted for Pudong. Pudong is widely viewed as a vehicle for Shanghai's reemergence as a world-class city. By 1994, the ten large infrastructure projects launched in 1990 were completed, and achievements were notable in every respect. After five years, Pudong has become the most important area for economic growth in Shanghai, accounting for one-third of its growth in 1994. Pudong's GDP of RMB6 billion in 1990 (constituting 8 percent of Shanghai's total) soared to RMB29.1 billion in 1994, accounting for 15 percent of Shanghai's total. In the first half of 1995, Pudong recorded a 20 percent growth rate over the same period in 1994, with its GDP totaling RMB17.3 billion. During the past five years, RMB25 billion has been invested in Pudong's infrastructure (Foo, 1995). Lujiazui is being developed as a new Chinese Wall Street, with the Shanghai Stock Exchange having moved there in the autumn of 1996. Lujiazui's status as a financial district in relation to the Bund in Puxi is yet to be clarified, as thirty-seven Western-style buildings in the latter are being leased out. Looking ahead, Pudong has been accorded eighteen new priority policies for the Ninth Five-Year Plan, covering a wide spectrum, from taxation, to finance, to foreign exchange control, and so on. Overall, it is expected that Pudong will turn Shanghai from an industrial dinosaur into an economic dynamo and will lead Shanghai into the twenty-first century as an ultramodern, externally oriented, and technologically sophisticated world city.

Notwithstanding the impressive growth that Shanghai has been able to attain during the past few years, Shanghai's relative importance in China has been reduced markedly. A comparison of Shanghai's economic position in China between 1978 and the 1990s shows dramatic declines. Mainly as a result of the rapid economic growth in many parts of coastal China, especially in South China, Shanghai no longer enjoys its preeminent position as an economic, trade, and transport center. Table 7.1 attempts to show Shanghai's changing positions in some selected indicators in the reform period. Its relative decline in national

■ Table 7.1 Shanghai's Shares in National Totals in Selected Indicators, 1978–1997

	1978			1985			1997		
	Shanghai	National	Shanghai/ National %	Shanghai	National	Shanghai/ National %	Shanghai	National	Shanghai/ National %
Population and labor force									
Year-end population (10,000)	1,098	96,259	1.14	1,217	104,532	1.16	1,305.46	123,626	1.06
Total employment (10,000)	697	39,856	1.75	764	49,873	1.53	847.25	69,600	1.22
Employment in urban state-owned units (10,000)	36	7,451	4.51	383	8,990	4.26	292.8	10,766	2.72
Economy									
GDP (RMB100 million)	312[a]	4,518[a]	6.91	467	8,964	5.21	3,360.21	74,772.4	4.49
Total investment in fixed assets (RMB100 million)	45[a]	911[a]	4.94	119	2,543	4.68	1,977.59	24,941.11	7.93
Total municipal financial revenue (RMB100 million)	190.7	1,121	17.01	264	1,866	14.15	1,070.95	8,642	12.39
Gross output value of industry (RMB100 million)	545	4,237	12.86	830	9,716	8.54	5,649.93	113,733	4.97
Per capita consumption (RMB)	410	184	222.83	961	437	219.91	6,819.94	2,936	232.29

Foreign capital and trade								
Foreign capital actually utilized (U.S.$100 million)	—	—	—	1.09	46.47	2.35	63.45	644.08	9.85
Direct foreign investment (U.S.$100 million)	—	—	—	1.07	16.61	6.44	48.08	452.57	10.62
Total value of export (U.S.$100 million)	29[a]	181.2[a]	16.00	33.6	273.5	12.29	334.51	1,827	18.31
Transport and communication								
Volume of freight traffic (100 million ton/km)	1,487[a]	12,026[a]	12.36	2,015	18,365	10.97	4,016	38,232	10.50
Cargo handled at principal ports (10,000 metric tons)	7,955	19,834	40.11	11,291	31,154	36.24	16,397	87,846	18.67

[a] 1980 figures.

Source: State Statistical Bureau (1986, 1998); Shanghai Statistical Bureau (1986, 1998).

importance is most obvious in GDP, government revenue, gross output value of industry, volume of freight traffic, and amount of cargo handled. To be sure, in all these sectors massive growth has been realized since 1978, but other parts of China have grown even faster.

THE FUTURE OF SHANGHAI

Although the open policy since 1978 has greatly transformed Shanghai in every way, especially since 1990, what fascinates Shanghainese and concerned observers most is the vision of its future. They are acutely conscious of its past achievements, and given its prevailing favorable political and economic climate in relation to the country and the Asia-Pacific region, Shanghai is building for an even grander future.

One area to which Shanghai needs to devote more attention and resources is the environment. Shanghai remains poor in environmental quality both in absolute terms and in comparison with other Chinese cities. The Huangpu River is but "a chemical cocktail composed of raw sewage, toxic urban wastes, and huge amounts of industrial discharges" (Murphey, 1988:176). As recently as 1992, only 14 percent of the domestic sewage in Shanghai was treated prior to discharge. Cleaner production technologies should be adopted, but with the rapid economic growth, the pressure on the environment will only exacerbate the problem.

As a strategic objective at the Fourteenth Party Congress held in October 1992, Shanghai was designated to develop as a "dragon head and three centers" to lead the Yangzi basin and China at large into the twenty-first century (Shanghai City, 1995:150). The three centers refer to Shanghai as an economic center, a financial center, and a trading center.

How likely is it that Shanghai will be able to perform its "dragon head" role? As an economic center, Shanghai's relative importance in the national picture is diminishing despite impressive absolute gains. For example, Guangdong has overtaken Shanghai in share of national GDP, foreign investment, and exports. Shanghai's role as an economic center in the future is well described by Urban C. Lehner (1994):

Just as Guangdong was the showcase for China's economic reforms in the 1980s, Shanghai will be the laboratory in the years ahead for an even more important set of reforms—converting loss-ridden state enterprises into profit-making businesses and making the banking system solvent.

To establish itself as a financial center, Shanghai has a long way to go. After 19 years of economic reform, China's banking system is largely unreformed. The refusal by officials in China to move the headquarters of specialized banks from Beijing to Shanghai has slowed Shanghai's aspirations to become the financial center of the country. The way ahead is fraught with difficulties if Shanghai and China as a whole are to win the confidence of foreign investors. Jesse Wong (1994) candidly projects this viewpoint:

> They see no quick way forward as long as China insists on its vision of a socialist market economy, which requires investors to accept the state sometimes as a partner, sometimes as a competitor and always as the final legal and regulatory arbiter.

In trade, as Table 7.1 shows, Shanghai's relative share in the total cargo handled at ports has dramatically declined, being halved in terms of percentage between 1978 and 1997. The future growth of Shanghai's trade must be viewed against the fact that a growing proportion of China's trade is handled by Guangdong and Hong Kong. As the Shanghai port is largely a river port, it cannot handle the fourth- and fifth-generation container ships and 10,000-ton vessels. Little hope exists that it will become a hub port in the global container network. Thus, it comes as little surprise that Shanghai handles only about one-tenth of Hong Kong's yearly container traffic (Huang, 1994). To remedy Shanghai's inadequacies in ocean transport, the central government approved, in early 1996, a 10-year project to establish Shanghai as a transport center through the construction of a 100-kilometer deep-water embankment and other facilities. This is one of several options being considered.

In planning for and speculating on Shanghai's future, the often raised question is, Will Shanghai overtake and replace Hong Kong, and, if so, when?

To begin with, one should be aware of the increasingly close and growing economic links that have been established between Shanghai and Hong Kong in recent years. In 1992, Shanghai's exports to Hong Kong amounted to U.S.$1.1 billion, whereas its imports from Hong Kong totaled U.S.$700 million (Lee, 1994). In fact, Hong Kong is the largest investor in Shanghai, with a cumulative investor stock totaling U.S.$12 billion up to 1994 and another U.S.$5 billion in the first three quarters of 1994 alone. Whereas Hong Kong has the advantage of being blessed with, among other assets, a natural and deepwater port, modern infrastructures, worldwide trading connections, and a sound legal system, Shanghai has an unrivaled geographic position in terms of Northeast Asia and the Yangzi River basin, a huge hinterland, a strong science and technology base stemming from its numerous universities and research institutes, a vast city region with a large population, and a more diversified and balanced economy. Clearly, both have strengths and weaknesses. In the course of rational decision making in China and in the spirit of the "one country, two systems" formula that has been designed for Hong Kong, the territory, as a special administrative region under China after 1997, should continue to play a critical role in the regional economy of Asia and beyond. Two contrasting positions can be summarized concerning the relative roles of Shanghai and Hong Kong in the years ahead.

In the worst scenario from Hong Kong's perspective, Shanghai's future is envisaged by Jim Rohwer (1995) as follows:

> Sometime in the first decade of the 21st century it [Shanghai] will displace Hong Kong as China's main financial-service centre and shortly after surpass Tokyo as the most sophisticated and open financial market in the East Asian time zone—and so join London and New York as one of the indispensable big three of world finance.

This is probably an overly optimistic projection of Shanghai's future. However, in 20 years' time, some of Hong Kong's functions likely will be taken over by Shanghai, which will be supported by a strong industrial base and most likely will achieve more balanced growth than Hong Kong.

On the other hand, a more realistic assessment of Shanghai's future in relation to Hong Kong might be that both cities will retain their distinctiveness in entrepreneurship, which will guide their different styles of economic development. Similarly, Hong Kong as China's foremost port and a center of foreign trade will remain for a long time to come. Shanghai likely will emerge as the domestic financial center of China, with Hong Kong remaining as a regional and international financial center. Rather than seeing one city replacing the other, a respected banker in Hong Kong perceives Shanghai and Hong Kong metaphorically to be like the eyes of a dragon that will spearhead China's huge and rapidly growing economy to greater strength and diversity (Lee, 1994).

Whatever the relative positions of Shanghai and Hong Kong in the future, Pudong is viewed as a window of opportunity to shake off the shackles of constraints and conflicts inherent in Puxi's pattern of development and to achieve a new world of miracle growth and modernity. Pudong will be one of three cross-century megaprojects in China, the other two being the Three-Gorges Dam Project and the South Water North Diversion Engineering Project. All of these are located in the Yangzi River basin, meaning all of them will have a positive reinforcing influence on the future of Shanghai.

In discussing prospects for Shanghai's future, Murphey (1953) was most perspicacious about its true worth at the tumultuous early 1950s when he maintained the following:

> Great cities do not arise by accident but they are not destroyed by whim. The geographic facts which have made Shanghai will prosper in the future once peace has been restored in East Asia. (205)

Murphey was proven right. When more peaceful conditions returned in the 1980s, Shanghai did make fundamental and favorable changes across a broad range of social and economic life. Murphey (1988) describes Shanghai of the late 1980s as follows:

> Shanghai has not come full circle. The revolution has made a permanent change, but the radical decades are over, and the city's char-

acter and function are again being shaped by circumstances, location, and [the] vital role it can perform for the new China. (181)

Although the future of Shanghai is anyone's guess, it is beyond doubt that the present circumstances are the most propitious in more than 50 years for Shanghai to reassert the advantages of its geographic location and to play a vital role leading China and the Yangzi River basin powerfully and purposefully into the twenty-first century.

Sustainable Urban Development in China and Hong Kong

INTRODUCTION

At the Thirteenth Pacific Science Congress held in Vancouver, British Columbia, Canada, in 1975, Maurice Strong declared that the environment held the key to the success or failure of the Pacific. He lamented the practices of careless, exploitative development that could destroy both the natural and the cultural environments in parts of the Pacific. He also underlined the influences of urbanization and industrialization and the introduction of the universalizing culture of consumerism, both of which had brought with them their admitted benefits, gross distortions, inequities, and a host of problems. He advocated a strategy of "ecodevelopment," which would be accompanied by a high degree of environmental security (Strong, 1976).

Despite this and other clarion calls for a comprehensive approach to planning the development of countries and regions, the world has continued to be struck by increasing numbers of environmental disasters, many of whose cataclysmic consequences still exist today. In Asia, many examples of environmental disorder in its cities can be cited to highlight the notion that the ecology of cities is extremely fragile and vulnerable to unsustainable development or to sheer human neglect. As human settlements, defined simply as organized human activity, become large, the margin of error allowed for a decision or a practice becomes smaller before catastrophe strikes. With the trend toward large cities appearing stronger than ever, as the next section shows, it is imperative that planners and decision makers in Asian cities evaluate their present development policies and evolve ecologically sound and sustainable patterns of growth. Failure to achieve these objectives will spell an uncertain future, ecologically, for Asian cities.

Taking into consideration the increasingly interdependent world in environmental terms, this chapter examines the following. The first section considers the patterns of human settlements from the standpoints of geographic and demographic trends. The second section addresses the recent concern about global warming as it affects Asian cities and the extent to which they themselves are to be blamed for contributing to this disquieting trend. The third section analyzes the pressure points in Asian cities by means of a sector-by-sector survey as it bears on sustainable development. The fourth section considers economic and institutional factors, including environmental legislation and the role of nongovernmental organizations (NGOs), with a view to their effect on human settlements. The conclusion speculates on future developments. Special attention is given to large cities rather than to smaller human settlements in Asia, simply because the former are most ecologically at stake. For consistency of illustration, examples are drawn, wherever possible, from China and Hong Kong, which represent, respectively, socialist and capitalist planning systems and greatly varied levels of economic development and modernization. Hong Kong's example of unfettered capitalism provides a sharp contrast to China's command-turned-market economy, a juxtaposition rendered all the more meaningful even after Hong Kong's return to China in 1997. From the standpoint of an urban ecosystem, Hong Kong is especially interesting, as it was one of the few cities studied intensively in the 1970s through a systematic research program (Boyden, 1977; Newcombe, 1977; Boyden et al., 1981).

THE STRENGTHENING LINKS: POPULATION, URBANIZATION, AND THE ENVIRONMENT

From 1960 to 1995, the world's urban population more than doubled from 1.19 to 2.58 billion. This unprecedented pace of urbanization occurred most rapidly in developing countries, including those in Asia.

■ Table 8.1 Selected Indicators of Urbanization in Asia

	Population (millions)	Urban population as % of total		Average annual growth rate of urban population		% of urban population in urban agglomerations of 1 million or more	
	1997	1985	1997	1980– 1995	1992– 1997	1980	1995
Bangladesh	125.6	13.4	19.4	5.6	5.3	46	47
China	1,230.4	22.5	31.9	4.2	3.9	41	35
Hong Kong	6.5	92.9	95.3	1.9	0.7	100	95
India	955.2	24.3	27.5	3.2	3.0	25	35
Indonesia	199.9	26.1	37.3	5.3	4.3	33	39
Japan	126.0	76.0	78.0	0.6	n.a.	44	48
Malaysia	21.7	45.9	55.2	4.4	3.7	16	11
Myanmar	46.4	24.0	27.1	2.1	3.4	7	9
Nepal	21.7	8.5	14.8	8.0	6.9	0	0
North Korea	23.9[a]	57.0[b]	61.0[a]	n.a.	2.4[c]	10	10
Pakistan	135.3	29.8	35.9	4.9	4.5	39	53
Philippines	73.5	43.0	56.1	5.2	4.0	33	25
Singapore	3.1	100.0	100.0	1.2	0.9	100	95
South Korea	46.0	64.9	83.2	4.0	2.6	65	64
Sri Lanka	18.6	21.1	23.1	1.2	2.4	0	0
Taiwan	21.6	50.7	57.4[a]	3.5	2.0[c]	n.a.	n.a.
Thailand	60.6	17.9	20.7	2.8	2.6	59	56

Note: n.a. = data not available.
[a] 1995 data.
[b] 1980 data.
[c] Average annual growth rate of urban population between 1990 and 1995.
Source: Asian Development Bank (1998, tables 1 and 4); World Bank (1997, 1998, table 1).

However, both the pace and the level of urbanization within Asia have been marked by intraregional disparities, reflecting fundamental differences in demographic transition, structural transformation, and incorporation into the world economy (Lo and Salih, 1987; McGee, 1988). For example, Table 8.1 reveals that in the period 1980–1995, the level of urbanization has increased to varying degrees in individual countries within the three subregions. The level of urbanization, of course, varies markedly, with the highest levels reached in East Asia (except China). The annual growth rate of urban population also differs sharply, with the highest rates recorded in South Asian countries. The table also shows a tendency for an increasingly large proportion of the urban population to be concentrated in cities of over one million inhabitants. Population projections by the United Nations have it that thirteen of the thirty largest cities in the world will be located in Asia by the year 2000.

Unlike the experience of urbanization in developed countries in the past, Asian cities have witnessed rapid growth not so much from massive rural-to-urban migration as from natural increase. From 1975 to 1980, Pakistan, Thailand, the Philippines, and Malaysia had less than 40 percent of their urban growth accounted for by migration (Lo and Salih, 1987:43). In China, migration contributed 43.2 percent to the urban growth in the period 1949–1979 (Chan, 1986). The crux of the problem is that population growth has been rapid in both rural and urban areas. Many Asian countries are caught in what Lester R. Brown (1987) has termed the "demographic trap." Most of them stagnated for decades at the stage of high fertility and low mortality without any real success in combining economic policies and family-planning programs to reduce birth rates and sustain gains in living standards. Continuing rapid population growth threatens the life-support systems and the environment, the deterioration of which in turn would lead to reduced per capita food production and income. It has been suggested that countries with populations expanding at a rate of 2 to 4 percent per year might find it almost impossible to restore tree cover, to protect their soils, and to take other steps toward a sustainable development path (Brown and Wolf, 1989:176).

Within Asia, only a handful of countries—Japan, South Korea, Singapore, Hong Kong, and most recently China—have successfully realized population fertility decline in recent decades. Since 1979, China has vigorously promoted a one-child policy so that, by the year 2000, the target population will be 1.2 billion. Thus, the total fertility rate of China dropped from 5.8 in 1970 to 2.2 in 1980 and 2.1 in 1984. The rate was reduced further in the 1990s, having reached less than

1.1 since 1995. Despite rural resistance and varying degrees of success across provinces, the one-child policy has been earnestly implemented in China with telling results (Hsu, 1985). This policy, coupled with economic reforms in agriculture, has been attributed to an increase in food output per person by almost half for China's farmers from 1976 to 1984 (Brown et al., 1989:188). In recent years, it has not been uncommon for incomes in rural China to be higher than their urban counterparts. The rapid fertility decline in China has been accompanied by a notable rise in the educational attainment of Chinese women (Freedman et al., 1988). The changing demographic structure also means that aging and the welfare of the elderly will increasingly have to be taken into account in socioeconomic planning (Yang, 1988).

Although it has attracted considerable attention because of its recent population control policy, China has also devoted attention to problems related to rural-urban population distribution, to urban growth rates, and to the relations between employment opportunities and rural and urban development (Goldstein, 1985:62). Rural-urban relations represent one dimension of the internal forces historically and nationally rooted that shape patterns of human settlements. Contributing to these forces is the widespread urban bias that favors urban development at the expense of rural areas. For example, Lester R. Brown and Jodi L. Jacobson (1987:46) have suggested that one way of restoring a nation's optimum rural-urban balance would be to let market forces play a more prominent role in economic development. Perhaps more than any Asian country, China has, since 1949, devoted much attention and resources to its rural development. However, with the adoption of more liberal economic policies since 1978, rural prosperity has been paralleled by the rapid development of coastal cities, especially the large ones, with repercussions on their environmental status.

THE NEXUS BETWEEN URBANIZATION AND GLOBAL WARMING

As urbanization proceeds apace, development policy, the energy utilization pattern, and industrialization may all go hand in hand with little regard to their effects on the environment. In addition to the effect of deforestation in the rural areas, cities, through their burning of coal and other hydrocarbons as well as through other practices, are responsible for the production of increasing amounts of carbon dioxide, methane, nitrous oxide, and chlorofluorocarbons (CFCs)—"greenhouse" gases—that have recently led to alarming warming trends in the earth's climate, with potentially disastrous and irreversible changes to the ecosystem.

Although long-term climatic change is short of being scientifically certain, the signs are becoming increasingly obvious that the world is in the midst of a momentous transition. The average global temperature rose by 0.3 degrees Centigrade from 1970 to 1980, but the five warmest years of the past century all fell in 1980s. Weather abnormalities were experienced in many Asian countries and elsewhere. In July 1988, temperatures in parts of central China reached 36 to 40 degrees Centigrade on 10 consecutive days. Serious heat waves hit such cities as Shanghai, Nanjing, and Wuhan, causing many people to suffer or die from heatstroke (Brown et al., 1989:3). While eighteen provinces in China, including the grain belt in the middle and upper reaches of the Yangzi River, were experiencing drought, torrential rains in Zhejiang were resulting in damaging floods. The global use of coal is still growing at 2 to 5 percent per year, with China, along with Russia and the United States, being the leaders. In China, coal burned every year accounts for 72.9 percent of the total energy consumption, with oil (18.7 percent), natural gas (2.6 percent), and hydroelectric power (4.8 percent) accounting for the rest. This pattern of fuel consumption leads to sulfur dioxide and particulates being the major air pollutants. In 1980, the total sulfur dioxide emission was estimated to be about five million metric tons, of which 85 percent came from coal combustion with a sulfur content varying from 0.5 to 5 percent. Ash content was also high at 20 percent (Ning et al., 1987).

The extent of the problem of air pollution is more severe in the urban areas of North China than in the south and in the winter than in the summer because of the larger amounts of coal burned during cold days. Evidence is increasingly available showing the extent to which China is suffering from its massive use of coal. In a forested section of Sichuan province, 90 percent of one local area that was once covered with pines is now bare as a result of air pollution. Urban residents in

China suffer acutely from the ill effects of air pollution, as tall smoke-stacks are seldom used and pollution control equipment is nonexistent (Brown and Flavin, 1988:14–15). Acid rain has been reported to occur extensively throughout China and in many cities to the south of the Yangzi River. In Chongqing and Guiyang, precipitation recorded an average pH value of less than 4.5 (any value less than 5.6 is considered acidic). In downtown Shanghai, the rainfall has an annual average pH value of 4.7 with a probability of 50 percent. Acid rain has been recorded everywhere in China except Beijing and Urumqi (Ning et al., 1987).

During the past few years, worldwide attention has been directed to the depletion of the ozone layer, which acts as the earth's protective shield against ultraviolet radiation from the sun. Ozone depletion has suddenly become a reality rather than a theory. Although China, together with India, was responsible for only 2 percent of the global CFC use in 1986 (thus of relatively minor importance), this might well change if the present government's intention of mass producing refrigerators for every household by the year 2000, compared with the present level of one refrigerator for every ten households, materializes (Shea, 1988a, 1989). Refrigeration is one of many industrial products that employ CFCs for specific functions, in this case as a coolant.

Hong Kong, which depends heavily on fossil fuels for energy generation, transport, and other uses, is adopting anything but a climate-sensitive energy policy. It faces serious air pollution, with concentrations of sulfur dioxide, nitrous oxide, nitrogen dioxide, ozone, and particulates exceeding acceptable levels in many parts of the territory. Sulfur dioxide pollution is serious in certain districts, with rainfall acidity measured in the period 1990–1992 in pH values at 4.3 at Kwun Tong, 4.29 at Central Western, 4.26 at Junk Bay, and 4.17 at Kwai Chung (Sequeira and Lai, 1998, table 1a). Air pollution continued to deteriorate in Hong Kong in the 1990s. During an episode in January 1996, the air pollution index rose to an average of 117 in the urban areas, 120 in the industrial areas, and 104 in some new towns in the New Territories (Ng and Ng, 1997:484). In late September 1998, the index reached a new height of 167, making Hong Kong one of the most polluted cities in Asia and comparable to the world's most polluted metropolis, Mexico City (*South China Morning Post,* September 23, 1998).

The impact of global warming on cities can be considered at different levels. Weather abnormalities in the form of heat waves, severe hurricanes, heavy rains, and floods already beset some regions of the world. In the short term, it has been suggested that in Asia a readjustment in the timing and extent of monsoons will occur. Hot weather will prevail in the middle latitudes, as indicated by China's heat waves in 1988. Rainfall will increase by 7 to 11 percent, with the largest changes affecting regions between 30 degrees north and 30 degrees south latitude. Cloudiness will also decrease generally. With the depletion of the ozone layer, skin cancers and cataracts will increase, and the human immune system will be depressed, along with reduced crop yields, depleted marine fisheries, materials damage, reduced biological diversity, and increased smog. In the long term, if ocean water levels rise with global warming and the thawing of the ice in the polar regions as predicted, the consequences will be devastating for low-lying river deltas and floodplains in Asia and many of its coastal cities. From 1890 to 1940, the mean temperature increase in the Northern Hemisphere was from 0.3 to 0.6 degrees Centigrade, and the global mean sea level rose by 45 millimeters over the same period (Bach, 1984). Studies have suggested that a temperature rise of 3 degrees Centigrade by 2050 would raise the sea level by 50 to 100 centimeters (Brown et al., 1989:10). A rise of even one meter would threaten cities in many parts of the world, including Shanghai and other Chinese cities. Furthermore, rapid global warming would disrupt a wide range of human and natural systems, making adjustment difficult and the management of economies complex. For example, irrigation works, settlement patterns, and food production would be tragically disrupted.

THE URBAN ENVIRONMENT UNDER STRESS

The severity and extent of environmental problems in Third World cities are attested to when a new journal, *Environment and Urbanization,* was launched in April 1989. The inaugural issue draws attention to the alarming range of pollution consequences in numerous Asian cities. My own (Yeung, 1991) review of the Asian urban environment from the viewpoint of basic infrastructure and its access by the poor indicates not only that the urban poor are inadequately served but also that a variety of institutional and attitudinal factors impede the improvement of the situation.

It might be observed that prior to the mid-1970s, the Chinese environment was widely believed to be a Maoist miracle and a model for developing countries (Lam, 1986:80). In stark contrast, Vaclav Smil (1984) provided the following assessment of the contemporary Chinese situation:

> The closest analogy to China's urban environment today are the growing industrial cities of nineteenth century Europe and North America: largely uncontrolled combustion of poor quality coal is releasing huge quantities of particulate matter, sulfur dioxide, and carcinogens into the air, and waste waters are dumped untreated. Also, open spaces are rare, greenery is scarce, living conditions are crowded, and the places keep growing at fast rates, promising more congestion and degradation to come. (153)

Although Chinese cities are far from being alone in Asia in the environmental ills that Smil has identified, it is instructive to review the pressures to which these cities are being subjected. Each will differ greatly in the way they affect the urban environment.

Food Supply

Food supply is one of the brighter spots of the urban environment in China and Hong Kong. Urban agriculture in Chinese cities and Hong Kong is very intensive and highly successful in different ways (Yeung, 1985). William G. Skinner (1981:215–234) reported that in the six large Chinese cities that he visited, well over 85 percent of the vegetables consumed by the urban population was produced within the bounds of the municipality. Vegetable production, highly structured spatially, has evolved as part of the traditional ecological complex tied to pig breeding and recycling of night soil and rubbish produced by the urban population for application to vegetable fields. In Guangzhou, up to nine crops per year can be grown sequentially on a single field. In Hong Kong, growing six crops of cabbage per year is not uncommon. Fish constitutes an important part of the Chinese diet, especially in South China. Aquaculture is well developed and provides almost 50 percent of the food fish in China. Also, the dyke-pond system has been practiced for untold generations, and in certain Chinese cities over 90 percent of the food fish originates from this source (Bardach, 1984). An effective ecological cycle of the dyke-pond system has been perfected in the Pearl River delta of South China, providing a steady supply of fish to the urban areas (Zhong, 1989).

Shanghai can be cited as an example of how large Chinese cities are organized in terms of food production. Large Chinese cities are almost always greatly overbounded, with the inclusion of sizable rural populations and farming areas. In Shanghai's huge city region, two factors have contributed to its recent increased food production. One is the transfer of the control of the production, distribution, and marketing of food from diverse operating units to the Shanghai municipal government. The other is the modernization of farming achieved by means of mechanization, electrification, water-conservancy work, and the large-scale provision of modern inputs. Spatially, two zones can be distinguished for the purpose of urban agriculture. The nearby suburbs *(neichiao)* refer to the inner zone immediately surrounding the built-up area devoted to year-round vegetable production and the outlying suburbs *(waichiao)* where coarse and hardy crops are grown. Thus, Shanghai is totally self-sufficient in vegetables, most grains, and significant proportions of pork, poultry, and other foods.

Unfortunately, the trend of increased food production in Chinese cities is offset by the accelerating loss of suburban farmland. For example, Beijing's vegetable land of 607,000 hectares in 1949 dwindled to 427,000 hectares in 1980, a 30 percent loss resulting from the state taking land in nearby suburbs for new housing and factories. Similarly, Shanghai lost over 650 hectares and Wuhan some 2,000 hectares of vegetable plots to construction uses in 1979 and 1980 (Smil, 1984:70).

Hong Kong, with a population of 6.5 million in 1997 on merely 1,095 square kilometers, distinguishes itself in urban agriculture by using only 2.9 percent of its total area to produce 13 percent of the fresh vegetables, 19 percent of the live pigs, and 19 percent of the live poultry consumed by its population (Hong Kong Government, 1998:127). This is even more surprising, considering the fact that 57 percent of its 7,490 hectares of agricultural land was abandoned or laid in waste in 1997 because of restriction on the conversion of agricultural land to other uses (Agricultural and Fisheries Department, 1998, appendix 3). Thus, the apparent irony in this city-state is the continual and accelerating trend of abandoned farmland along with the unmistakable move toward greater specialization, intensification, and modernization in urban agriculture. Vegetable growing and fish ponds occupied, respectively, 14.4 percent and 18.8 percent of all the agricultural land use in 1997 and constituted by far the two most important types of food commodities produced by area. Over sixty kinds of vegetables are grown by Hong Kong farmers, essentially on a year-round basis. Intensive livestock farming is indicative of the need continually to modernize the agricultural sector in Hong Kong. Thus, chicken raising transformed itself from subsistence production in 1949 to a commercial scale with a total chicken population of 7.5 million in 1997. Similarly, pig farming has become more modern and larger in scale, with a steady but definite tendency toward fewer and larger farm units, especially after the implementation of a livestock waste-control scheme. The number of locally produced pigs increased from 207,570 in 1995 to 305,600 in 1997.

Solid Waste Disposal

With economic development and population increase, solid waste disposal is becoming a growing problem in Chinese cities and Hong Kong. In 1982, 289 Chinese cities generated 73.6 million metric tons of solid wastes (or garbage) and 73 million metric tons of night soil. Only 70 percent of the solid wastes and 40 percent of the night soil were handled by urban sanitation departments. The remainder was partly transported from the cities by farmers and partly discharged into public sewage systems or rivers, thereby contributing seriously to environmental pollution. In addition, about 200 million metric tons of solid wastes and night soil have accumulated in large and medium-size cities in China (Zhang et al., 1989). The rate of increase of solid wastes in Chinese cities is far ahead of population growth at 7 to 11.5 percent per year, with Dalian increasing at 22 percent per year. If the present rates persist and remain unabated, garbage production from Chinese cities will quadruple in two decades, reaching a total of 174 million metric tons by the year 2000 (Xu, 1987). Even a more modest prediction would put the figure at 100 million metric tons by the end of the twentieth century, along with 97.5 million metric tons of night soil (Zhang et al., 1989:54).

The application of urban solid wastes to farmland has positive as well as negative effects. When mixed with night soil, solid wastes can be applied to cropland and vegetable fields to improve soil fertility and increase crop yield. However, direct application of untreated solid waste and night soil will lead to soil contamination. There are indications that the Chinese are considering incineration, source separation, waste mounds, and landfills to cope with the rapid generation of solid wastes. In fact, it has been reported that materials recovery companies under the Ministry of Commerce have sprung up all over China since the 1950s to organize solid waste recovery. Such companies employ more than 300,000 workers in more than 100,000 depots for the procurement of different kinds of waste. Recycling reusable wastes both minimizes wastes and increases nonrenewable resources (Furedy, 1989; Sun and Furedy, 1989; see also Yang, 1989).

In Hong Kong, solid wastes have increased threefold in quantity during the last 15 years, reaching a total of 20,020 metric tons per day in 1997 (Census and Statistics Department, 1998, table 16.2). The wastes in Hong Kong are collected by the government and private operators, with some kind of division of labor. The government-collected wastes, mainly of household origin, are high in plastic and putrescible waste and low in paper content and calorific value and are deposited at three large-scale landfills in the New Territories. In contrast, the wastes collected by private operators and derived from commercial and industrial sources have a generally higher calorific value and lower moisture content and are sorted at source for recycling purposes before they are transferred to landfills. Over 50 percent of recovered commercial and industrial waste is actually recovered, compared with 8 percent for the domestic sector (Planning, Environment, and Land Bureau, 1997).

Whereas both publicly and privately collected wastes have been increasing in volume at the rate of 3.3 percent per year (already much higher than population growth rates), construction wastes have been increasing exponentially since 1985, almost doubling every year. Hong Kong is highly commendable for the way in which it has disposed of food wastes from restaurants and food-processing plants. Ken Newcombe (1977:193) calculates that 130,000 metric tons of such wastes generated this way every year can be used for feeding pigs. From the viewpoint of nutrient flow and urban ecology, pig and poultry raising sustains the capacity of the existing food system to recycle food wastes back into human food.

Although the Hong Kong government commissioned studies on integrated waste management and waste reduction in 1996 and 1997, its commitment to tackle waste disposal was not matched by strong political will. Because of the government's inaction, a major local brewer dropped its long-established practice of reusing bottles in 1996. Similarly, despite the proposal in 1995 to charge for privately collected solid waste and the passing of the relevant legislation, the scheme has not been implemented because of objections by waste collectors and waste vehicle drivers (Ng and Ng, 1997).

Solid waste disposal represents only one dimension of escalating environmental deterioration. The situation has reached crisis proportions in China's largest cities, where both municipal sewage and wastewater of numerous industries are dumped largely untreated into rivers, lakes, reservoirs, and soils. The state of Chinese urban wastewater treatment speaks for itself. In 1980, only thirty-five small municipal treatment plants were available for some 200 million urban dwellers, and over 90 percent of urban wastewater was discharged untreated. In Tianjin, 1.26 million metric tons of untreated waste are dumped daily, and the Hai He River has become heavily polluted (Smil, 1984:100–102). Serious environmental pollution has gone hand in hand with industrial development. Even medium-size and historical cities in the Yangzi delta, such as Suzhou, have become much polluted (Deng, 1987), much like the fate of Guilin, a scenic city of extraordinary beauty.

In Hong Kong, environmental pollution once owed much to large-scale development of the manufacturing industry, but with the massive relocation of industries across the border to southern China since the early 1980s, pollution from manufacturing sources has markedly decreased. Nevertheless, livestock wastes, sludge from sewage treatment plants and waterworks, and clinical and chemical wastes exert considerable pressure as polluting sources for the environment.

Transport

Transport within Chinese cities and Hong Kong presents a dramatic contrast in the way in which each has applied modern technology, management methods, and planning skills in moving people and goods, often within limited space, conflicting demands, and burgeoning populations. Until recently, Chinese cities have suffered from a severe lack of significant infrastructure investments to maintain an acceptable level of basic services. Transport is one of the more visible facets of this legacy of past neglect and ill-prepares Chinese cities to embark on their modernization and development programs. A few statistics will more effectively bring home the worsening transport situation. The lack of space and an urban structure more characteristic of a nonmotorized era have not dampened the enthusiasm of urban dwellers to own motor vehicles. In the historical and medium-size city of Wuxi, the number of motor vehicles increased from 5,714 in 1981 to 13,802 in 1985. Bicycle ownership, which is positive from an environmental standpoint, also soared within the same period from 249,645 to 480,848 (Deng, 1987). However, public transport remains the mode that most people use to move about in Chinese cities.

In Beijing, about two million people go to work every day by public transport, mainly buses and trolley buses. From 1982 to 1983, bus ridership increased 4.5 percent, and subway ridership grew by 9 percent, both significantly above the city's growth in population at 1.7 percent (Chen, 1988:240). In Shanghai, road space increased only by one-half during the past 30 years, as opposed to a thirteenfold increase in motor vehicles and a ninefold increase in nonmotorized vehicles. Not surprisingly, the speed of motor vehicles dropped from 30 kilometers per hour in the 1960s to 15 kilometers per hour in the 1980s. During rush hours, every square meter of space on public buses might be crowded with ten to twelve passengers in Shanghai and other Chinese cities (Deng, 1987; Chen, 1988).

Although air pollution attributable to automobile emissions is generally within acceptable limits in Chinese cities, recent air-quality data from the Shenzhen special economic zone (SEZ) have shown that, since 1981, the levels of nitrogen oxides and ozone, both major constituents of photochemical smog, have been rising rapidly. By the year 2000, an estimated 53,000 motor vehicles will emit 36.6 metric tons of carbon monoxide, 3.1 metric tons of hydrocarbons, and 1.74 metric tons of nitrogen oxides into the air in Shenzhen (Lam, 1986:72).

In China, the impact of transport problems is borne rather evenly across the population by income group, but the weak, the young, and the elderly perhaps feel the pressure more keenly. Whereas most urban inhabitants depend on public transport for their personal mobility, the young and able-bodied have added flexibility, especially for short-distance travel, in the use of bicycles. Bicycle ownership is omnipresent and is highly applauded as a means of transport to contribute to a clean urban environment.

In sharp contrast to most Chinese cities, Hong Kong has invested massively in basic infrastructure, including transport, during the post–World War II period. Given the extremely limited road space and the rapid increase of vehicles of all types, the challenge to sound transport planning and management is ever present. Registered vehicles of all types increased from 260,000 in 1979 to 354,518 in 1989 and 500,228 in 1997, in comparison with modest increase in trafficable roads from 1,147 to 1,447 and to 1,831 kilometers in the corresponding years. Nevertheless, public transport is still depended on by most people for personal travel. In 1994, public transport carried 80 percent of the total daily person-trips (Transport Branch, 1994:6). Public transport, present in a wide variety of modes—bus, tram, peak tram, minibus, taxi, maxicab, ferry, and hydrofoil—is cheap and well patronized because it is efficiently and profitably run. The government has never hesitated to make funds available or to employ the latest technology to improve Hong Kong's transport situation.

The first cross-harbor tunnel was opened in August 1972, and the second, eastern crossing opened in October 1989. The third, western crossing was opened in April 1997. The most popular and efficient mass transit railway, opened in 1979, became in 1989 the second-largest public transport carrier after buses. It now operates three lines, totaling 38.6 kilometers, and carries two million passengers per day, distinguishing itself as one of the world's most heavily utilized mass transit systems. Not unlike other large Asian cities, traffic jams are a common occurrence in Hong Kong, especially on approach roads to the Cross Harbor Tunnel and the Lion Rock Tunnel. The situation has greatly improved since 1992, when the Tate's Cairn Tunnel was opened. Meanwhile, the government is contemplating traffic management measures, such as road pricing. In January 1990, it also released the White Paper on Transport Policy, involving an outlay of HK$55 billion in developing road and rail systems that will bring transport planning in the territory to the year 2001. It contains ambitious plans to improve the transport infrastructure, to expand public transport, and to manage the demand for road use (Yeung, 1989a; Stoner, 1990). Since the opening of Chek Lap Kok Airport and the completion of the Ten Airport Core Projects in July 1998, the transport infrastructure in Hong Kong has been notably strengthened.

Health

In terms of health indicators for their population, both China and Hong Kong have made notable progress over time and compare well with other countries. Life expectancy at birth from 1965 to 1996 soared from 56 to 71 for females and from 50 to 68 for males in China and increased from 71 to 81 for females and from 64 to 76 for males in Hong Kong. In the same period, infant mortality per 1,000 births plunged from 90 to 39 in China and from 28 to 6 in Hong Kong (World Bank, 1998, table 2). However, these commendable health indicators fail to show the health of urban dwellers, who might suffer from the ill effects of environmental pollution. In China, this is most clearly demonstrated in the deleterious consequences of air pollution on the health of residents in its larger cities. Eighty percent of all anthropogenic pollutants are accounted for by the inefficient combustion of low-quality coal in power plants, factories, ships, and millions of households. The rate of lung cancer mortality in China's largest cities has been increasing with disturbing rapidity. Lung cancer mortality in cities ranges from 17 to 31 per 100,000 inhabitants, compared with 4 to 5 per 1,000 for the country as a whole. This large difference is attributable mainly to heavy air pollution. In the northern cities, lung cancer is now the most frequent malignancy because of the more pronounced combustion of coal. In Beijing, the incidence of lung cancer grew by 30 percent from 1974 to 1978. Likewise, a recent study ascribed an annual loss of some 3.5 million workdays and over 6,000 premature deaths in Beijing, Shanghai, Wuhan, and Guangzhou to the damaging effects of air pollution (Smil, 1984:114–121).

Drinking water in the large cities also poses health problems. Shanghai's drinking water has been described as "basically chlorinated sewage." Tianjin's drinking water contains excessive concentrations of heavy metals, arsenic, and phenol, and Beijing's underground aquifers—the city's main source of drinking water—are contaminated with heavy metals, phenol, cyanide, and nitrates. Nevertheless, the greatest threat to the safety of drinking water comes from various uncontrolled industrial wastes (Smil, 1984:104).

In Hong Kong as well, some 1.5 to 2 million inhabitants are exposed to unacceptably high levels of sulfur dioxide and nitrogen oxides and about double that number to high particulate levels. The incidence of respiratory diseases has been increasing, especially among the very young and the elderly, as has that of lung cancer. Lead poisoning is another suspected adverse health effect from air pollution. The equally serious water pollution, resulting from over two million metric tons of domestic and industrial sewage being discharged into the coastal waters every day, has posed health risks from swimming at Hong Kong's otherwise lovely beaches and has led to occasional outbreaks of viral hepatitis and high levels of paralytic shellfish poisoning. In 1996, all Hong Kong waters, including Victoria Harbor, were declared water control zones. Although the government introduced a sewage charge and a trade effluent surcharge in 1995, the issue became political when politicians lobbied in 1996 for its suspension. The crux of the debate is who should pay for sewage services in Hong Kong (Ng and Ng, 1997).

Although previous studies have shown that Hong Kong people have a remarkable ability to cope with a potentially stressful high-rise, high-density living environment and are free of obvious detrimental emotional and social effects (Mitchell, 1971; Millar, 1979), recent statistics are more disquieting. Suicide deaths increased from 499 in 1984 to 741 in 1994, with the rates of increase for the age-groups above 55 especially high. The suicide death rate for people age 75 and older was the highest at 53 per 100,000 in 1994 (Yip, 1995, table 3.1). The weakening role of the family and the impact of modernization are perhaps also indicated in the persistent increase in divorces from 1,520 in 1979 to 10,492 in 1997 (Census and Statistics Department, 1998, table 1.8).

Water Supply

Water supply is literally the lifeblood of a city, and in the large over-bounded Chinese cities, the problem is enormously compounded by irrigated agriculture and politics. For example, Norton Ginsburg (1990) has shown that for the Beijing and Tianjin area, the total water consumption has nearly doubled in the last 25 to 30 years, whereas agricultural water consumption has increased by more than 500 percent. This astounding increase in rural water consumption was due to the widely held view among farmers in the North China Plain that water is primarily a "free" good and to the resultant disincentive to use water conservatively, let alone regard it as a scarce resource. Even urban residents are accustomed to paying little for water, and fines levied against industries for dumping toxic wastes in public water supplies are traditionally light or go unenforced. In Beijing, a metric ton of water costs less than a popsicle (Brown and Jacobson, 1987:37). Rationing went into effect in mid-1986, but shortages continue to plague the city. To ensure a reasonable supply of water to industries, Beijing designed a conservation plan to supply water in limited hours of the day and to rotate the supply across different sections of the city. On the other hand, in Tianjin some enterprises had to shut down temporarily for lack of water (Chen, 1988:240). In the subhumid, monsoonal environment of North China, the problem of providing water to the cities has become extremely complex. Owing to water shortages, new manufacturing industries are discouraged from locating in Beijing.

For decades, the city-state of Hong Kong struggled to explore ways of increasing the supply of water for its inhabitants. As many as fifteen major reservoirs have been built, with an elaborate system of catch waters, tunnels, and portals to collect surface runoff, and a desalinization plant for seawater has been constructed. Owing to the seasonal and sometimes highly fluctuating nature of annual rainfall, these approaches to water supply in the territory never proved adequate in meeting the demands of an ever increasing population and booming industries. In the early 1960s, water supply fell critically short of demand, leading to the imposition of severe restrictions on consumption. The worst situation was the one in which water was supplied for four hours every four days. It was realized that for any long-term solution to the problem, cooperation must be sought from the mainland across the border.

In 1963, the Chinese authorities were approached about the possibility of extracting water from the East River, some 45 miles north of the border for use in Hong Kong. After prolonged negotiation, a scheme was put in place in January 1965 that involved elaborate engineering works consisting of a series of canals, dams, and pumping stations to divert water from the East River to the Shenzhen Reservoir and on to Hong Kong by pipes (Rose, 1966). Since then, inhabitants in Hong Kong have been enjoying an around-the-clock water supply. At the same time, it has created a new kind of dependency on China. This arrangement has been renewed several times, each time raising the annual volume of water to be supplied as well as the price. An agreement was signed in December 1989 between Hong Kong's Works Branch (now Works Bureau) and the Guangdong Provincial Bureau of Water Conservancy and Hydro Power. The former provided China with advance payment to finance the expansion of the present water supply system to Hong Kong. By 1995, the quantity of water supplied to Hong Kong was 690 million cubic meters per year, rising to 840 million cubic meters per year in the year 2000. This supply will increase the dependency of Hong Kong on China from the present 2.165 billion cubic feet per year from China, or 60 to 70 percent of the total supply (Lau, 1989).

Energy Supply

In terms of energy supply, a kind of reverse dependency exists between Hong Kong and China. Chinese cities are perennially short of energy supply, a problem that Hong Kong can help China with to a degree. For example, Hong Kong's China Light and Power Company has been selling power to the Shenzhen SEZ across the border since 1979. Later, Shekou was also included. In 1988, exports to China occupied 6.4 percent of total electricity sales in Hong Kong (Chow, 1989:247). The same company also entered into a joint venture with the Chinese authorities to construct a nuclear power plant in Daya Bay about 50 kilometers northeast of Hong Kong. Construction began in August 1987 and was completed in 1994, along with the other Chinese nuclear plant at Qinshan in Zhejiang. It was reported that the third nuclear power plant, in Guangdong, was to be constructed in Yangjing by 2009, after the second plant in Lingao becomes ready in 2003 (Ehrlich, 2000). It appears that after the Chernobyl accident, whereas many developed nations have either slowed down or halted nuclear power development, China is still moving ahead. For the present, China is incurring heavy subsidies to keep fuel prices artificially low. Consumer subsidies for heavy fuel oil and crude oil equal $55.4 billion, electricity subsidies amount to $58.9 billion, and coal subsidies total $10.4 billion. Total energy subsidies reach a staggering $19.4 billion, or 7 percent of China's gross national product and 20 percent of its export earnings (Shea, 1988b:49).

Yet these fossil fuels are choking China's cities and countryside with the production of sulfur, nitrogen, hydrocarbons, and other dangerous pollutants. As China is rich in coal, and as it must meet the energy demands of a population of over one billion, it is still planning on increasing greatly its coal-fired generating capacity. Coal combustion in China is notoriously inefficient. Combustion efficiency of most household stoves is less than 15 percent, and that of most boilers in factories and offices rarely surpasses 50 percent (Smil, 1984:117). In the long run, a sustainable energy path for Chinese cities must be one that relies on renewable sources and energy efficiency. Robert Taylor (1982) has favorably observed that renewable energy technologies based on the principles of low cost, simplicity of design, and reliance on local materials and labor are being actively promoted. These technologies appear to be more applicable to the rural areas than to the cities in China.

One of the findings of the Hong Kong Human Ecology Program carried out in the 1970s was that if the city was increasingly reliant on fossil fuels for its development, so were the inhabitants for their daily lives.

The growth in energy consumption at 9 percent per year was larger than the world average. Thus, the challenge was to find ways to become low energy users (Icamina, 1980). Still, Hong Kong's insatiable demand for energy has not slowed down. In 1988, it consumed 21.01 billion kilowatt hours of electricity, giving a per capita consumption of about 3,686 kilowatt hours compared with China's 325 kilowatt hours. During the period 1979–1988, energy consumption increased at a very rapid rate of 8.8 percent per year. However, most noteworthy for the 1980s was the marked shift from oil to coal fuel in the generation of electricity in the wake of the oil crises of the previous decade. Before 1982, oil accounted for almost all the fuel for energy consumption, with coal contributing less than 1 percent. By 1988, the two local power firms generated almost all their electricity by burning coal, with the result that the fuel mix had dramatically changed in favor of coal over oil, accounting for 65 percent and 35 percent, respectively (Chow, 1989). For domestic fuel used mostly for cooking and heating water, a marked conversion has taken place from the previously popular kerosene and bottled liquefied petroleum gas (LPG) to the cleaner and easier-to-handle town gas. This shift in market preference is clearly reflected in the 17.3 percent average annual growth rate of town gas for the period 1979–1988. So pronounced was the shift that, in 1982, the government stipulated that all new buildings be supplied with town gas or piped LPG drawn from a centralized bulk storage (Chow, 1986).

Housing

Finally, as part of the urban environment, housing is one component that is under considerable stress in Chinese cities. Stories of overcrowding, delayed marriage, and family conflict stemming from the lack of adequate housing are common in most large cities in China. Despite recent investments, the housing supply is still far short of demand, as one-third of urban households were considered "house deficient" at the end of 1981. In the early 1980s, a three- or four-member household in Shanghai and four other cities in the Yangzi delta area had an average living floor space of only about 12 to 16 square meters. Most families were crowded into a single room. In 1982, 100,000 families in

Shanghai lived in conditions with living floor space per capita of only two square meters and with three generations living in one room. By 1993, Shanghai's average per capita living area rose remarkably to 7.3 square meters (Chiu, 1996:345). More than 30,000 families in Wuxi lacked dwellings of their own in 1985 (Deng, 1987). The housing shortage is increasing annually by about 10 million square meters nationwide. Many reasons can be advanced for the present critical shortage of housing in large Chinese cities, including past neglect in infrastructure investment, the prevailing attitude of treating housing as a welfare commodity from the state, and the related and absurdly low rents.

The government has correctly decided to put housing on a commercial footing, beginning as a first stage to sell completed apartments at subsidized prices in eighty large and medium-size cities across the country in 1985 (Ye, 1987). The final stage of housing reform, with the assistance of the World Bank and aimed at full cost recovery from rents and relieving the state's burden of construction and maintenance, was focused initially on Guangzhou and Shanghai. As the radical change in housing policy entailed a 25 percent urban wage increase, the scheme that was initiated in February 1988 ground to a halt because of the retraction of domestic demand and official inertia (Crothall, 1990). Consequently, in the foreseeable future, the problem of shelter will continue to be a major one for which no feasible solution is in sight and with which urban governments and their inhabitants must contend.

The housing problem in Chinese cities is one that affects everyone, but certain groups, such as young couples waiting for housing provision in order to get married, have their plight better dramatized than others. A recent study of Guangzhou shows that residential mobility is low and not a key factor in shaping social areas. In fact, the housing shortage is closely related to a housing allocation system based on the construction and allocation of housing by production/work units. Inhabitants working for large factories or powerful administrative units that have the financial resources to build dwelling units will have their own and their families' housing needs satisfied. Others working for small work units will have little or no housing, tending to rely on overburdened and overcrowded municipally owned housing (Yeh et al., 1990). Not surprisingly, the quality of housing under such a system is closely related to occupational groups with some of them better housed than others.

In sharp contrast to the situation in Chinese cities, Hong Kong has achieved outstanding success in providing housing to a large segment of its population. By the end of 1989, some 2.8 million inhabitants, representing 49 percent of the total population, were living in public housing of one type or another. Public housing has evolved from an initial emergency program to a stabilizing force in society characterized by forward planning and policy formulation. In 1988, after 35 years of direct public involvement in housing provision, the Long Term Housing Strategy was formulated to take Hong Kong's public housing development to 2001. The strategy was officially reviewed in early 1997, with objectives and targets set for 2006. The new official plan emphasizes home ownership, cooperation between the public and private sectors in their shared roles for housing provision, and identification of different types of housing needs and their satisfaction. Public housing in Hong Kong is a success of urban management, reflecting a high degree of achievement in physical planning, administrative efficiency, and financial management (Yeung, 1989b). It has benefited a large cross section of the population, and given the changing political climate and greater citizen participation, it will likely be more responsive to the housing needs of the populace in future.

THE POLITICAL ECONOMY OF A DEVELOPMENTAL URBAN ENVIRONMENT

It is clear from the foregoing review that the urban environment in Chinese cities and in Hong Kong are under considerable stress from an ecological perspective. In fact, the development policies adopted are not "developmental" in the long run; instead, they hasten the process of global climatic change that in turn will bring irreparable damage to human and natural systems and deny future generations the right to an adequate biological and physical heritage. The kind of urban development being pursued falls perilously close to what Maurice Strong (1976) described for the Pacific, in which the "main interests have been to maximize their economic return. Often minimum benefits to the people of the region have been produced, while the basis for the kind of long-term, sustained development which they need most has been destroyed" (103). Indeed, it is difficult not to agree with K. C. Lam (1989:365) when he describes Hong Kong as "a First World economy but only a Third World environment."

Under the present system, strong institutional resistance exists to any kind of initiatives seeking breakthroughs to present patterns of development, especially energy use. Christopher Flavin (1988:30) has observed that the electric power industry is probably the single most important energy institution and also the one most in need of reform. In some countries, the industry consists of either government-owned or government-regulated monopolies. They decide what kind of power plants to build and when and where to build them. Electricity prices are determined by political fiat or by regulations with little relation to costs. He goes on to suggest major institutional reforms that would permit energy efficiency research to pay dividends.

Environmental Legislation

Before energy efficiency research can make inroads into pollution problems, urban governments must introduce environmental legislation as the only vehicle for some control of the damage. In China, the problem is not simply one of legislation, for the pertinent laws on environmental protection of the natural environment, oceanic pollution, and water pollution were enacted in 1979, 1982, and 1985, respectively. Since 1979, China has approached environmental protection through legislative means and improvement in management methods (Qu, 1989). However, the regulatory framework has not been effective in curbing pollution. In Shanghai, antipollution regulations have been enacted, but wastes and garbage are still dumped. Investment funds available for water pollution control are meager. The situation is complex not because of the question of money or technology but because the urgency of the problem has not been grasped. For example, a paper and dyeing mill in Yantai has been polluting an ocean bay for years, often poisoning clams and other aquatic species.

The crux of the pollution spiral is a human one related to the Chinese management structure. Higher layers of bureaucracy cover up inferiors in their enthusiasm to maintain production targets. Such attitudes do not generate much fear of the new laws and regulations (Smil, 1984:109–110). In Shenzhen, Lam (1986) reported the adoption of an environmental strategy that is heavily reliant on modern technology. Nevertheless, stumbling blocks in the battle against pollution still exist, including the lack of rural-urban integration, the financial burden of massive waste treatment programs, the absence of a setting conducive to resource recycling, the seemingly unquenchable quest for rapid development, and the inflexible administrative setup. Thus, environmental deterioration in China is not as much a consequence of affluence as it is of industrial inefficiency and the difficulties of enforcing environmental legislation. Chinese scholars and planners are aware of the magnitude of environmental degradation and the resultant harm to their lives. Canfa Wang (1985) points to the relationship between the SEZs and the central government in environmental legislation, arguing for involving higher levels of government in the former plus greater structural and administrative flexibility. Although foreign firms might be granted concessions in economic terms, compromise must not be allowed on matters concerning environmental pollution in selecting potential investors. In a 1989 address, an influential state councillor declared war on environmental pollution and enunciated the principles of "whoever pollutes should clean up" and "whoever develops should protect" (Song, 1989).

Elsewhere, Chinese scholars also advocate alternative energy strategies and environmental protection measures to minimize pollution. Coal gasification and central heating in place of dispersed small boilers are two practical methods to abate carbon dioxide emissions from coal combustion. Unified exploitation and protection of water sources for Chinese cities are encouraged. Water reutilization should be explored, and saving should be encouraged. Construction of municipal waste water treatment should be accelerated (Qu, 1985).

Even in Hong Kong, where environmental protection was not viewed as a policy priority in the eyes of the government until the mid-1970s, the problem of enforcing environmental control is no less arduous. Since 1981, four major pieces of legislation, covering water, air, noise, and wastes, have been enacted to provide the necessary regulatory framework. The government's halfhearted intention to implement the laws without hurting the industries that are the generators of Hong Kong's wealth has been the main cause for the relative ineffectiveness of the legislation. For example, in the first water control zone covering the Tolo Harbor and Channel, 220 of the 251 discharges are exempted and thus not subject to effective control. They are required neither to keep a record of their discharge nor to provide samples of their effluent to the control authorities for analysis (Lam, 1989). In addition, the Environmental Protection Department is not staffed to the level required for enforcing the laws. Enforcement of legislative controls has been weak, but an amendment to the Waste Disposal Ordinance in 1995, covering control on the import of waste, came into effect in 1996. Implementation of the revised Livestock Waste Control Scheme in 1994 has markedly reduced pollution by livestock waste (Environmental Protection Department, 1997:18).

However, recent developments are more encouraging, for more teeth and resources are being provided by the government to protect the environment. A new Planning, Environment, and Lands Branch (now Planning, Environment and Land Bureau) within the government secretariat has been created to achieve better coordination among government departments in environmental protection. In 1989, a White Paper on Pollution in Hong Kong was released in which the government spelled out policies and set a timetable for the environmental program in the 1990s. The government now has an urgency and a confidence for tackling environmental problems that never existed before. Government spending on the environment accounted for HK$6.2 billion, or 3 percent of public spending in 1995–1996, as compared with merely 0.8 percent in 1988–1989. A sense of moving forward and purposefulness is conveyed in Hong Kong's annual environmental report (Environmental Protection Department, 1997). In the Chief Executive's third policy speech, delivered in October 1999, cleaning up Hong Kong's environment occupied a prominent position in the development agenda.

Developing the Politics

Undoubtedly, the politics of an urban developmental environment will need to be better developed at the urban, national, and international levels. Given the cumulative and overwhelming evidence of global accelerated atmospheric warming, many researchers have called for perceptual shifts of profound proportions to respond to its urgency. The occasional environmental disasters over the past several years generally effected an environmental awakening, but this is not sufficient. Energy planners, policymakers, and politicians need to be won to the new cause to halt global environmental decline.

In China, the battle waged against the urban environment is especially difficult to win because of the ambiguity of control and authority within Chinese cities. In land use and service provision, as in environmental matters, the lines of authority between the city and higher levels of government (provincial and central) are not clearly defined. It is not unusual for the latter governments to prevail over the city government when competition and conflict arise. Where the legislative instruments on environmental protection cannot be effectively enforced, as illustrated earlier, chance is high that the responsibility to protect or clean up the environment will be shirked. Thus, the local government is in need of a stronger administrative, legislative, and financial apparatus to carry out its tasks more efficiently.

The politics of ecology and the environment, termed "ecopolitics" (Wood et al., 1989), is extremely complex. It can be viewed in a hierarchical framework with five layers that represent local, subnational, national, international, and global ecopolitical scales or stages. From one level to next, the variables become more numerous and their interactions more complex. The jump from legislating national policies to negotiating international and global politics might be the most challenging of all.

Of particular importance at the local level are individual acts and people-based community efforts that, taken together, can make a real difference to the environment. These acts might include organizing local groups, teaching literacy and promoting health care, encouraging family planning, and planting trees, which collectively will make an impact on reversing global deterioration (Durning, 1989:172). Environmental NGOs engage in research, lobbying, public education, and protest activities. Their media campaigns influence public opinion and policymaking often beyond the national level. The Greenpeace movement is probably one of the largest and best-known NGOs that has been effective in championing a cleaner and safer environment. Begun in 1972 as a small Canadian group, it now has affiliates in twenty-four countries and Antarctica. Friends of the Earth, also founded in 1972, has organizations in thirty-three countries (Wood et al., 1989), including Hong Kong. To combat noise and air pollution in Hong Kong, this NGO proposed that the government consider introducing trolley buses in place of the present 3,800 franchised buses, although the probability that the proposal will be accepted is low (Wong, 1990). Along with the government's renewed commitment to a cleaner environment, grassroots interest in environmental issues in Hong Kong has notably increased lately. Green Power, another environmental NGO formed in 1987, has stepped up its activities to inculcate green ideas to the general public and political leaders (Lam, 1989:359). By contrast, NGOs are not strong in China as a social movement in general and in environmental issues in particular. Traditionally, the government has monopolized social and political groups down to the neighborhood level, leaving almost no room for other organizations to germinate.

In both China and Hong Kong, active steps have been undertaken to promote the goals of Agenda 21 arising from the Earth Summit held in Rio de Janeiro in 1992. In Hong Kong, the government commissioned a HK$41.7 million study, known as the Study on Sustainable Development for the 21st Century (SUSDEV21), to develop a framework for sustainable development pertaining to Hong Kong's unique situation. The study was almost completed in late 1999, and the crux is "whether the Hong Kong community is prepared to sacrifice an element of material prosperity for the sake of sustainable development" (Wong, 1996:386).

CONCLUSION

The examination of the case studies of China and Hong Kong from the perspective of sustainable urban development leaves one with the notion that the development policies being pursued might yield impressive economic results, but they certainly take their toll on environmental deterioration and on global warming on the widest scale. Given the trend of rapid urbanization and globalization projected for China and other parts of Asia, the potential of even greater damage to the environment is real as existing development strategies persist and economic versus ecological priorities are not reordered. Smil (1984) has assessed the Chinese situation in the starkest possible terms:

> It is not the large population per se, not the relative poverty of the nation, not its notorious political instability, but rather its staggering mistreatment of the environment that may well be the most fundamental check on China's reach toward prosperity. (199)

Indeed, this statement is food for sobering thought for Chinese planners and policymakers before striking a much-needed balance between economic development and environmental protection. So paramount are environmental concerns that some scholars would even argue that the only viable development strategy for many developing countries is one that rests on environmental criteria, one that concentrates on restoring the economy's environmental support systems. Any other, it is argued, is destined to fail (Brown et al., 1986:209).

4 Urban Futures

IMAGINE, it is the year 2006. Pearl City: one of the largest, richest urban areas in the world. Including its suburbs, it spans more than 160 kilometers from north to south. Pearl City has a population of more than 40 million. Average incomes are US$40,000 in Hong Kong and US$10,000 in the fringe suburbs of Zhongshan. Pearl City's infrastructure is the envy of the world. Mass transit rail systems and a network of highways, bridges and tunnels enable residents to travel from Stanley Market [in Hong Kong] to Guangzhou city centre in less than 90 minutes. (D. Li, 1996)

9   Planning Hong Kong for 1997 and Beyond

Pearl City is a visionary urban agglomeration, a megalopolis that connects Hong Kong to Guangzhou at either end, with a constellation of smaller but economically vibrant and culturally varied cities in between. It is one region that has benefited the most and the earliest from China's open policy. It has witnessed such rapid economic growth over the past two decades that it has earned the sobriquet of the "Fifth Dragon of Asia" (Sung et al., 1995). It would have been beyond anyone's wildest imagination prior to 1978, when China adopted its policy of economic reforms, that Hong Kong could be so intimately linked to its neighbor cities to its north. However, it is because of the phenomenal economic surges that Hong Kong and the cities in the Pearl River delta (PRD) have experienced during the past decade or so that credence is given to the opening quotation. Already, the makings of the visionary city are being unfolded. If present development trends persist, Pearl City can become a reality in a decade.

The essence of the opening quotation is that, quite evidently, Hong Kong's future is inextricably linked to the PRD. With Hong Kong's return to Chinese sovereignty on July 1, 1997, the symbiotic relation of Hong Kong to its immediate hinterland looms ever larger. Indeed, "to attempt to maintain the city-state status of Hong Kong in the 21st century flies in the face of geopolitical reality" (Laquian, 1996:18). Simply no future would exist for Hong Kong if it were to draw up blueprints of development within its own geographic confines. On the contrary, Hong Kong has already adopted development trajectories that are fully compatible with recent trends of globalization and the evolving regional and global economies.

This chapter traces how Hong Kong, in planning for its future, has, since 1984, been adjusting its goals, approach, and emphasis as rapidly changing socioeconomic circumstances warrant. The chapter is divided into three sections. The first section examines the major planning efforts as Hong Kong struggles to keep pace with the forces that tear at its urban fabric. The second section looks at how Hong Kong is preparing itself as a regional hub and world city. The third section highlights some of the key factors that impinge on Hong Kong's future.

PLANNING SINCE 1984

In an earlier paper, the author compared the urban efficiency of Hong Kong and Singapore and pointed to 1984 as being a critical year for both city-states (Yeung, 1987). That year marked the signing of the Sino-British Joint Declaration, which provided for the continuation of Hong Kong's way of life for another 50 years after 1997 under the "one country, two systems" formula. Hong Kong, with the political uncertainties out of the way, was to plan actively and purposefully for its future. The investment in infrastructure has been unprecedented in both scope and magnitude. Tertiary education underwent a breathtaking expansion. Advances have been made in representative democracy. A determined effort, with a budget to match, has been devoted toward cleaning up the environment. Greater accountability and transparency have been demanded in almost every sector of public spending. All this has been brought to bear on ensuring that the present way of life has a better chance to continue beyond 1997. This chapter seeks to concentrate mainly on urban planning and economic issues.

The period since 1984 is a most remarkable one for Hong Kong from the viewpoints of economic development and transformation of its space economy. Every development indicator underscores how rapidly Hong Kong has grown, in per capita gross domestic product (GDP), trade (especially the reemergence of Hong Kong with a vengeance as an entrepôt of China), and cross-border traffic (Table 9.1). The dynamism that has propelled Hong Kong forward has been China's openness, which began to bear fruit from the mid-1980s. Hong Kong is now in the league of the richest countries by per capita income. Yet Hong Kong spares no effort or expense to maximize its scarce land resources to better discharge its functions for the present and the future. The period under review saw Hong Kong make significant strides in adopting spatial development strategies to prepare for its future.

The year 1984 happened to be one when a Territorial Development Strategy (TDS) was adopted, after its being formulated over four years. It was designed as a new approach to rectify the hitherto deficiency in piecemeal and ameliorative planning by coordinating land use and transport development. It was a comprehensive long-term development strategy for Hong Kong from the 1990s to 2001.

In the late 1980s, several blueprints that would have momentous impacts on the shape of Hong Kong's future were acted on in quick succession. The Second Comprehensive Transport Study was released as a Green Paper for public consultation in June 1989, later adopted as a White Paper in January 1990. The White Paper provides for Hong Kong's transport demand to 2001 and covers transport infrastructure improvement, policies of expansion and improvement of public transport, and policies for managing road use. Among the recommended development programs are in the railway sector, including the Airport Railway, an extension of the Mass Transit Railway to Junk Bay and a rail link connecting the northwestern New Territories and Tsuen Wan (Yeung, 1989b; Yeh, 1993).

In April 1988, the first consultation was conducted on how the metropolitan area covering Hong Kong Island, Kowloon, New Kowloon, Tsuen Wan, Kwai Chung, and Tsing Yi were to be developed by the release of a consultative booklet *Metroplan—the Aims*. This was soon followed by the release of another document inviting public comment on the initial options. Metroplan is a long-term regional development strategy with a time horizon to 2011. It is conceived of as an approach to restructure the central city area of Hong Kong by decentralizing

■ Table 9.1 Indicators of Hong Kong's Development, 1980–1995

	1980	1985	1990	1995
GDP[a]				
GDP at current market price (HK$million)	112,981	261,070	558,859	1,105,461
GDP per capita (HK$)	22,424	47,848	97,968	179,572
External trade				
Trade volume (HK$million)				
Total	209,893	466,572	1,282,405	2,835,248
Reexport	30,072	105,270	413,999	1,112,470
	(14.3)	(22.6)	(32.3)	(39.2)
Trade with China (HK$million)				
Total	28,195	120,175	394,512	987,078
Reexport (destination)	4,642	46,023	110,908	384,043
	(16.5)	(38.3)	(28.1)	(38.9)
Workforce				
Total	2,268,700	2,540,000	2,800,000	2,905,100
Manufacturing	892,140	847,615	715,597	375,766
	(39.3)	(33.4)	(25.6)	(12.9)
Services[b]	789,454	1,082,011	1,489,245	2,104,100
	(34.8)	(42.6)	(53.2)	(72.4)
Traffic				
No. of tourists (1,000 persons)	2,301	3,657	6,581	10,200
Cross-border traffic				
Passengers via Lo Wu (in millions)	6.91	17.76	27.14	43.30
Total no. of vehicles (in millions)	0.23	1.62	4.91	8.47
Air passengers	6,200,965	8,636,518	14,832,570	21,369,958
No. of containers handled (TEUs)[c]	1,464,961	2,288,953	5,029,696	11,185,679

Note: Figures in parentheses are percentages.

[a] All figures are expenditure-based GDP.

[b] Service sector includes four categories: (1) wholesale, retail, and import/export trades; restaurants; and hotels; (2) transport, storage, and communication services; (3) financing; insurance; real estate and business services; and (4) community, social, and personal services.

[c] TEUs refers to 20-foot equivalent units (based on a standardized container size of 20 by 8 by 8 ft).

Source: Census and Statistics Department, Hong Kong Annual Digest of Statistics and Hong Kong Monthly Digest of Statistics (various years); Hong Kong Government (various years); Transport Department (1995).

population, enhancing the quality of life, and introducing new and needed facilities. It entails massive reclamation of Victoria Harbor by creating over 1,000 hectares of new land.

However, the most far-reaching in terms of its impact on Hong Kong's future development was the announcement in the governor's policy speech in October 1989 of Metroplan as well as the Port and Airport Development Strategy (PADS). The strategy is to meet the forecasted growth in Hong Kong's port and air traffic up to 2011, such that all new ports, airport, associated industrial and residential facilities, transport links, and other infrastructure will be incrementally provided for according to an integrated and cohesive plan (Hong Kong Government, 1989). The announcement was intended as a morale booster when public confidence was at an all-time low and the general outlook was pessimistic in the wake of the events at Tiananmen. A central component of PADS was the construction of a replacement airport at Chek Lap Kok in northern Lantau, largely on reclaimed land. It would necessitate comprehensive and expensive infrastructure projects to link the new airport with the urban core, some 28 kilometers away. The rationale behind the integrated development of the airport and the seaport is that new highways and other infrastructure facilities can be shared (Kwong, 1994). Although the relocation of the airport at Kai Tak would free 230 hectares of prime urban land for development, the astronomical cost of constructing the new airport at $21 billion was a constant bone of contention between the governments of China and Great Britain in the ensuing years, with the Hong Kong government and its people watching helplessly from the sidelines.

With hindsight, public officials would probably admit, perhaps only in private, that the decision to build the new airport was made in needless haste despite a consultancy report having recommended the Chek Lap Kok site as early as 1973. No prior consultation was conducted with the Chinese authorities, and this was a tactical oversight. When Chinese endorsement was required from banks that had any debt commitment in major infrastructure projects beyond 1997, the Chinese authorities did not hesitate to act decisively. This contributed to a soured political atmosphere and deepened uncertainties about Hong Kong's future. In fact, it has been argued that the planning process adopted by

PADS was outdated and ineffective, with minimum participation by the public. It was not consonant with the changed political culture in Hong Kong, in which civil society has become more vocal and demanding in terms of participation in the planning and policymaking process. The high profile that the Chinese adopted in the airport negotiations and the consequent delays, coupled with the lack of transparency in the planning of PADS, greatly eroded the legitimacy of the Hong Kong government (Ng, 1993).

The inefficacy of the planning process in the increasingly politicized climate can be best illustrated through the recent controversy surrounding the speed and scope of reclamation of Victoria Harbor. Committed and proposed reclamation amounts to a staggering 1,297 hectares, thereby dramatically narrowing the natural and scenic harbor. Opponents to the present approach of extensive creation of new land through reclamation have accused the government of favoring a lucrative but environmentally detrimental way of development rather than focusing attention on the New Territories (Chu, 1996; Ng and Cook, 1996). To be fair, it has also been pointed out that Metroplan, PADS, and other related strategies are not arbitrary decisions of single decision makers at single points of time. These proposals, which entail massive reclamations, were made through the normal government committee and interdepartmental consultation procedures. At their critical embryonic stages, when major changes and rethinking were still possible, the most vocal reclamation critics were silent (Lai, 1996:358). This caveat notwithstanding, it is not sufficient to blunt the criticism that public consultation has not been conducted in the manner of genuine dialogue between the administration and the general public and that spatial development strategies have always been predicated on the objective of facilitating economic growth (Ng, 1995:247).

The explosive economic growth that Hong Kong and the PRD had experienced since the mid-1980s was not fully accounted for in most of the previously mentioned spatial development plans. This inadequacy was soon apparent with the TDS that was adopted in 1984. In 1990, a TDS review was commissioned and public consultation was invited in 1993 with the publication of a paper presenting development options.

Two of these options provided for Hong Kong's primary economic hinterland (the PRD region) and the inner provinces of China. The inclusion of public feedback was reflected in the TDS Review of 1996 for the final round of consultation before the selected long-term development framework being decided on in early 1997.

The TDS Review attempted to remedy the weakness of not duly taking into account the rapidly accelerating integration between Hong Kong and its immediate hinterland in the PRD as well as the hub roles that Hong Kong has been performing in the regional and global economies because of globalization trends. These forces have produced surging cross-border traffic alongside air and container traffic (table 14.1 in the TDS Review). More than 20,000 vehicles per day crossed the border in 1995, up from about 18,500 per day in 1993. In addition, the number of people walking across the border at Lo Wu increased six times between 1980 and 1995, with a daily average of over 100,000 (do Rosario, 1995; Yeh, 1995). Tolo Highway, being the major artery and completed in 1985, feeds vehicular traffic across the border. It has been growing in traffic at 15 percent per year, with a daily flow in 1994 of 120,000 vehicles (Brown, 1996:199). Similarly, in the period 1986–1995, whereas aviation growth worldwide averaged 6.9 percent per year, Hong Kong grew at 10.9 percent (Becker, 1995). Container traffic also soared from 1.5 million TEUs (20-foot equivalent units) handled in 1980 to 11.2 million in 1995.

Thus, the outcome of all the spatial development plans outlined here greatly strengthened Hong Kong as a regional hub to perform its functions by 1997 and beyond. The confirmed commitment in infrastructure investment will result in a much better articulated and connected network of railways and highways, with a new airport, expansive reclaimed land, and an expanded seaport (Figure 9.1). In the five years prior to 1994, public investment in infrastructure accounted for 15 to 18 percent of public sector spending, or 2 to 3 percent of GDP. In 1993–1994, the government spent HK$26.8 billion on infrastructure, a shade above the education budget, indicating the public policy of devoting equal attention to human resources and basic facilities (Kwong, 1994:214).

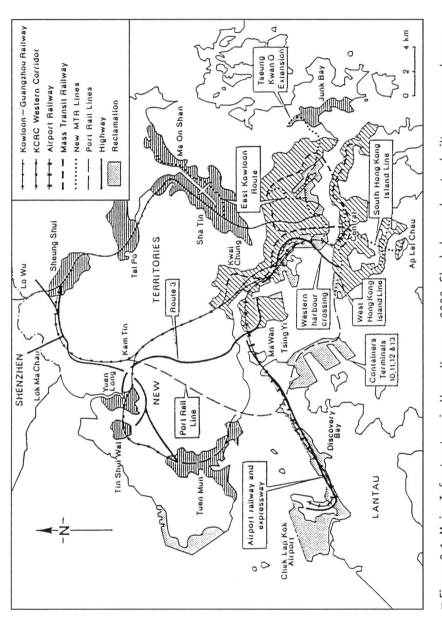

■ Figure 9.1 Major Infrastructure in Hong Kong, c. 2000. Shaded area denotes built-up area and new towns. Source: C. Y. Leung and Co.

HONG KONG AS A WORLD CITY

The first of the six objectives of the TDS Review is to enhance the role of Hong Kong as an international city and a regional center for business, finance, information, tourism, entrepôt activities, and manufacturing. Manufacturing is listed last, probably for a reason, as that sector has changed dramatically in its contribution to Hong Kong's employment and GDP over the past decade.

As shown in Table 9.1, the manufacturing workforce has declined absolutely as well as relatively since 1980, with only 12.9 percent employed in that sector by 1995. In contrast, employment in the services has grown rapidly in importance during the same period, accounting for 72.4 percent of the workforce in 1995. The service sector has been growing at an average of 14 percent over the past 15 years. Thus, Hong Kong has become mainly a service center, with services in a variety of producer activities that require a high level of technology and professional input. The precipitous decline of the role of manufacturing in the economy is the expected outcome of the large-scale relocation of manufacturing processes to the PRD, with up to 80 percent of the factories in Hong Kong having been closed for this reason. Consequently, the Hong Kong economy has had to undergo restructuring, which entailed retraining of the labor force, coping with unemployment (at a high of over 6 percent in early 1999), and readjusting its development strategies. The Hong Kong economy has undergone what has been called the "second era of industrialization." As a service center, Hong Kong will need to capture the manufacturing value chain in knowledge and information rather than in "manual" inputs (Leung, 1996).

Not unlike the other Asian newly industrialized economies (NIEs), Hong Kong has undergone economic restructuring, but the effect has been much more benign and gradual, without creating the same negative consequences of high unemployment and derelict land as in cities in North America and Europe. Instead of the "hollowing out" of the economy, Hong Kong has been able to adjust to a more heightened role in services, very much in keeping with the postulations for world cities (Lo and Yeung, 1996). Indeed, Hong Kong has taken on a stronger role as a base for research, product conception and design, prototype making and testing, marketing, and distribution, although the industries are out-processing in the PRD. Hong Kong's role can be likened to Tokyo's when the latter's manufacturing industries also moved offshore in the 1970s and 1980s. However, both cities retain the headquarters and control center functions over the manufacturing processes that operate outside their territories. By internationalizing its manufacturing through offshore locations, Tokyo has, in essence, strengthened its claim as a world city (see chapter 2). By the same token, the symbiotic relationship that Hong Kong has established with the PRD has merely extended Hong Kong's reach for favorable factors of production in the form of low land prices and cheap labor. This process of cooperation has led to the sustained high growth for both territories. Beyond the PRD, this cross-border subregional cooperative development has also drawn in Taiwan and Fujian for similar development and mutual benefit. In this extended subregional development that capitalizes on varied complementarities of the participating territories, a model of cooperative development has been perfected. The region has been popularly known as the Southern China Growth Triangle (see chapters 3 and 4), and as a mode of subregional development, the growth triangle has been emulated in the Asia-Pacific region (Thant et al., 1998).

A leading industrialist in Hong Kong has reiterated that the decline of Hong Kong's manufacturing is more apparent than real and that, from certain standpoints, the manufacturing sector is stronger than ever before. It is strong because it has remained immensely flexible and has developed a rare set of skills, enabling even small Hong Kong companies to integrate activities dispersed over a number of countries. By developing dispersed manufacturing capabilities across numerous countries, these small companies have escaped and grown beyond the limitation set by Hong Kong's small labor force and scarce land resources (Tang, 1997). These observations are compatible with the recent findings that against the background of general decline in most industries, some have become more capital intensive and larger (Yeh, 1997). To seek out ever more destinations for profitable investment, Hong Kong investors have been exporting capital to foreign countries.

According to the World Investment Report of 1996, Hong Kong was the fourth-largest exporter of capital in the world, after the United States, Great Britain, and Germany, with an outflow of $25 billion in 1995. Almost every Hong Kong company is dispersed over two and possibly three or four countries. Indications exist that the entire Asia-Pacific region is being integrated into one production unit (Hughes, 1996). Hong Kong became an exporter of foreign direct investment (FDI) of growing stature from the 1980s. Between 1984 and 1988, the average outflow of Hong Kong FDI was $2.5 billion per year, as compared with the average inflow of $1.8 billion per year. Hong Kong transnational corporations have been gearing up their operations in the Association of Southeast Asian Nations (ASEAN) region after 1985, especially in Indonesia and Thailand (Yeung, 1994).

A verification of Hong Kong's approach to new global economy is provided by an in-depth study of two leading industries—garment making and electronics—as an illustration of how Asian NIEs have been responding to changing comparative advantages. It is shown that Hong Kong's industries respond to the changing business environment by acting on an interplay of various factors at the structural, institutional, and organizational levels. Given the prevailing characteristics of the manufacturing sector, Hong Kong manufacturers have been struggling to increase their flexibility in production and to find niches for their products in the world market. This will allow them to survive by capitalizing on labor-intensive production, where outward processing comes into the picture (Lui and Chiu, 1994).

As a result of the recent migration of most of Hong Kong's labor-intensive manufacturing operations to low-labor-cost countries, notably China, labor productivity of Hong Kong's manufacturing sector increased between 1982 and 1992, on average, by about 7 percent per year, a rate higher than most other Asian NIEs. However, stagnant productivity growth in some service industries is a source of concern (Shen, 1995), as previous discussions have highlighted Hong Kong having transformed itself into a service center. It is on the quality of services that Hong Kong provides that its future will hinge.

Other scholars, educationalists, and policymakers have advocated more. Hong Kong needs to pursue high-tech industrial development.

Leaders of local universities have repeatedly called attention to the low level of spending that Hong Kong has devoted to research and development, amounting to a mere 0.04 percent of its GDP in 1989 and a long way behind the other Asian NIEs. Although the Hong Kong government has avoided direct involvement in industrial development, it has taken a markedly proactive role since the 1990s. The industrial policy has changed from one of "positive nonintervention" to one of "minimum intervention with maximum support." In 1992, an Industry and Technology Development Council was established to advise the government on industry and technology development and in formulating strategies for upgrading manufacturing industry (Yeh and Ng, 1994). Plans for developing a science park, long discussed in the community, were finally announced in late 1997. In 1999, the government announced plans to establish the Cyberport project in Pokfulam on Hong Kong Island, designed as a new push on Hong Kong's road to high-tech development. In any event, the TDS Review has included a north-south technology corridor, making provision for the location of industrial facilities and the related higher-education or research facilities.

As Hong Kong prepares for its future as a regional hub and world city, the many spatial development strategies that it has recently pursued can be conceived of as a process of world city formation. It has invested heavily so that it can discharge its functions more effectively and compete with other cities. Specifically, in land-use planning, Hong Kong has made conscious adjustments. Consequent on the recent industrial restructuring and diversification, Hong Kong has adopted a land development strategy related to office space to enhance its role as an international business and financial center. It has been recognized since 1987 that the office sector has become the most important economic sector and that special land-use needs exist for its development. Consequently, the concept of industrial/office buildings has been more flexibly applied, and the number of such development applications soared 400 percent between 1993 and 1994. Similarly, the recent increase in outward processing and subcontracting to China have led to new needs in industrial land use. The growth areas for manufacturing industries are identified along the routes between the border and the container terminals and the new airport (Yeh, 1997).

Finally, one of the problems that contemporary world cities must deal with is increased social polarization. From the latest statistics released by the government, worrying signs are being seen that polarization trends as reflected by income distribution data have been deepening. In 1971, the families in the lowest 10 percent income bracket accounted for 2.3 percent of the total income earned, and the trend in subsequent years was 1.6 percent for 1986, 1.3 percent for 1993, and 1.1 percent for 1996. On the other hand, in 1971, the families in the highest 10 percent income bracket accounted for 34.6 percent of the total income earned, and the trend in subsequent years was 35.5 percent for 1986, 37.3 percent for 1991, and 41.8 percent for 1996. The polarization between the rich and the poor has increased sharply since 1971. The income of the highest income bracket is, on average, thirty-eight times that of the lowest (Tsang, 1996; *Ming Pao*, January 9, 1997). Softening the burden of poverty in an increasingly affluent society is a challenge for the government of Hong Kong Special Administrative Region.

FACTORS AFFECTING HONG KONG'S FUTURE

Despite all the efforts and expenses that Hong Kong has invested in its future and the geopolitical climate being propitious for it to continue to play its regional and global roles, it has not gained control of the many factors that can adversely affect its future well-being. The accelerating integration of Hong Kong with China is surely a driving force for its recent economic upsurge and for its future source of growth yet at the same time can lead to uncertainties and contradictions over which the territory has little control.

In terms of infrastructure development, recent patterns of investment and decision making have demonstrated insufficient cooperation and consultation among Hong Kong and its neighbors. Within the PRD itself, cities and counties making infrastructural decisions have not been in the habit of consulting one another, and some of these decisions might not be the most rational from an economic viewpoint. The enthusiasm that many cities in the PRD have shown in constructing their own airports and deepwater seaports is an example of possible wasteful duplication. Eight airports of various sizes will exist within a radius of 60 kilometers in the PRD by the early twenty-first century, including Hong Kong's mega-airport at Chek Lap Kok, which was opened in July 1998. It has an initial capacity to handle 35 million passengers and three million metric tons of cargo per year. Whether the airports in the PRD will have enough passengers to sustain their facility is open to question, notwithstanding the projected rapid growth of civil aviation in the Asia-Pacific region and especially in China.

Two other examples will show that cooperation on new infrastructure across jurisdictions needs to be nurtured. The idea of linking Hong Kong to Zhuhai has generated as many as six proposals since the novel proposal of a Lingdingyang Bridge to span the water surface of some 40 kilometers was first suggested by Gordon Wu, who expounded in 1989 his vision of development. The debate of their relative merits dragged on. The Infrastructure Coordinating Committee (ICC), set up in December 1994 to ensure the proper coordination of infrastructural projects straddling the border, finally settled on the land point of the bridge in Hong Kong at Lan Kok Tsui (*Ming Pao*, July 19, 1996). Similarly, the controversy over the second crossing between Hong Kong and Shenzhen has not been settled. Shenzhen plans a "Western Corridor" and prefers a 6,741-meter bridge from Shekou to the vicinity of Lau Fau Shan in Hong Kong, thus enabling an efficient link to Shenzhen's Huangtian Airport and beyond. Hong Kong's preference for the second crossing is at Lok Ma Chau, with convenient linkage to Futian in Shenzhen. The two sides have apparently agreed on the Shenzhen Western Corridor with a target completion date of 2005 (Zheng, 1996; *Apple Daily*, September 27, 1999). Thus, for Hong Kong to better harmonize its infrastructural plans with its neighbors, the institutionalization of regional planning is high on the agenda of cooperative development after mid-1997 (Ng, 1995:255). The setting up of the ICC is only a necessary first step.

A second factor that is vital for Hong Kong's future is how its borders, especially that with Shenzhen, will be managed and policed. With the growing economic links between Hong Kong and the PRD, border traffic has been increasing exponentially. The present rail link at Lo Wu, run by the Kowloon-Canton Railway Corporation (KCRC), handled 55 million passengers and 1.5 million metric tons of cargo in 1997.

Hong Kong desperately needs a second rail link across the border, and KCRC has proposed the Western Corridor Railway. Designed as a Y-shaped, 52-kilometer route, it is to serve both freight and passengers. One bar of the Y would connect Hong Kong's container port at Kwai Chung to the Chinese border, and the other would serve mainly commuters in the new towns of Yuen Long and Tuen Mun (see Figure 9.1). The high costs of consultancy in the preparatory work and the construction itself have politicized the project. The government finally came to a decision to build the passenger line first at a cost of HK$49.6 billion by 2002, to be followed by the freight line (Healy and Law, 1996; Hon and Delfino, 1996). Border traffic between Hong Kong and Shenzhen is anticipated to increase at a rate of 12 percent per year, reaching a total of 120 million per year by 2000. From the Chinese viewpoint, considerable scope exists for jointly developing the border area in traffic, flood control, storage, tourism, and so on. Immigration formalities ought to be simplified further to facilitate the traffic flow, such as controlling only entry, not exit (Shengong Compatibility Research Editing Committee, 1994:142, 220). To play its role in maintaining Hong Kong's way of life, the border needs to strike a balance between being a tight one for controlling illegal immigrants and smuggling activities into Hong Kong and being a loose one for facilitating economic interaction between Hong Kong and its immediate hinterland (Yeh, 1995:283).

This leads to the third factor, which is population. Apart from the legal quota of 150 immigrants per day from China—a major source of population growth—many illegal immigrants are attracted by Hong Kong's wealth and modernity. With Hong Kong's permeable border, illegal immigration has always been a difficult problem to deal with. Planning Hong Kong's future is dependent on accurate population projection, which, experience shows, has been elusive. For example, in the TDS Review of 1993, Hong Kong's population was projected to reach 6.5 million by 2011, but it had already reached 6.3 million in 1996. The revised population projection of 7.5 million and 8.1 million made in 1996 can similarly be off target. The higher-than-expected population growth since 1993 has been due to a rapid increase of expatriate population, foreign domestic helpers, and return migrants. The Court

of Final Appeal's ruling on the right of abode in 1999 added much anx-
iety and uncertainty regarding Hong Kong's population growth. Keeping the population in stable growth is a critical factor to ensure that the
infrastructure and services built up are not subjected to unexpected
pressures.

Finally, for all the economic progress that Hong Kong has achieved
over the past decades, a heavy price in a deteriorating environment has
been paid. Until recently, an average daily 1.7 million cubic meters of
raw sewage are dumped into the harbor, along with 24 metric tons
of floating rubbish. More than 30 million cubic meters of toxic mud
from thirty ongoing land-reclamation projects must also be disposed of
(Dowell, 1994). However, the past decade has seen a determined government attempt to tackle environmental problems. In 1986, the Environmental Protection Department was established, and the landmark
policy statement in the form of a White Paper was made public in 1989.
This was a major effort to review Hong Kong's environment and to lay
out steps and targets for its improvement in the next decade. A telling
positive result is that government spending on the environment in
1995–1996 accounted for 3 percent of public spending, at HK$6.2 bil-
lion, compared with merely 0.8 percent in 1988–1989. A new air
pollution index and the related forecast system were introduced in
June 1995, as was the polluter-pays principle, in which sewage charges
were effected in April 1995. In 1996, the government commissioned an
expensive study that focused on sustainable development for Hong
Kong in the twenty-first century with the objective of developing a
framework that will keep a balance between economic and ecological
dimensions that is appropriate to Hong Kong (Wong, 1996). Thus, it
is clear that Hong Kong has lately done much to mend its environment.

CONCLUSION

The Sino-British Joint Declaration and the Basic Law are solemn, internationally recognized letters of law that form the basis of guaranteeing
Hong Kong's way of life well after 1997. Yet they have failed to allay
fears, especially after the events at Tiananmen. An extreme pessimist
even pronounced "the death of Hong Kong" (Kraar, 1995). Even a

more rational analyst would argue that, with or without the handing over of Hong Kong to China in 1997, Hong Kong would have lost out economically because of China's opening and rapid modernization. It was pointed out that Hong Kong was thrice lucky: in 1950, when China closed its doors to the world; in 1978, when those doors were opened again; and in 1987, when Taiwanese began to travel to and invest in China. Hong Kong benefited immensely from all these events, and its economic success, so it has been argued, was a historical accident (Faber, 1996).

Little did Faber realize that Hong Kong has a far-reaching and noneconomic role to play. Historically, Hong Kong has always provided a refuge for the downtrodden and the oppressed in China but more important has acted as a link between China and overseas Chinese. It has earned the sobriquet of the "capital of overseas Chinese." The numerous newspapers and magazines published in Hong Kong have provided cultural sustenance for thousands of Hong Kong emigrants in different parts of the world and for other overseas Chinese. More specifically for China, Hong Kong's modernity in its urban management, its efficiency as a business and financial center, and the drive and ingenuity of its people have profoundly influenced the thinking of planners and politicians in China. The "Hong Kong model" was touted as something to emulate for Chinese cities, especially after Deng Xiaoping's tour of the south in 1992. For example, Dalian has adopted for promotional purposes the name "Hong Kong of the North." The value of Hong Kong as a modernizing agent for socialist China should not be underestimated both in recent years and beyond 1997 (King, 1997). As an economic entity, Hong Kong has been elucidated in the previous paragraphs, and in the age of globalization, its economic development has no geographic bounds.

Without a doubt, Hong Kong faces many challenges in the years ahead. Growing competition to its economic success is being posed not only by Chinese coastal cities, notably Shanghai and Shenzhen, but also by other cities in the Asia-Pacific region. Its recent remarkable economic upsurge has taken it into the rank of the richest cities in the world in terms of per capita income. At the same time, social polarization has shown signs of intensification. Land and property prices, despite a precipitous drop after the Asian financial crisis, as well as wages, still relatively higher than those in other Asian countries, will erode Hong Kong's competitive edge should such increases not be matched by gains in productivity. Hong Kong still has been favored as one of the best places in the world to conduct business. Only the maintenance of its existing way of life will ensure that its attractiveness is sustained. With the return of Hong Kong to China, it has become the wealthiest city in China overnight. For its own sake, it must not simply be another city in China; above all, it should strive to maintain its inventive spirit, freedoms, and special character at the crossroads of geography and cultures. Governor Chris Patten (1996) was perceptive of Hong Kong's future when he eloquently stated the following:

> Hong Kong is a bridge, a vital link between East and West and, especially, between the West and China. Hong Kong represents the kind of Asia with which both West and East are comfortable. An Asia committed to open markets and open minds. An Asia committed to the rule of law and respect for human freedom. An Asia in which East and West mix so well—commercially, culturally, socially, intellectually. It offers, in that sense, a vision of the future for Asia.

Whether Hong Kong stays on that bridge or goes beyond for a larger role, the governor further observed the following:

> Hong Kong is a city in its prime. It is poised on a bridge between being a rich Chinese city—a marvellously placed gateway to China—and one of the greatest international and financial business centres. And whether it crosses that bridge, we shall see. (quoted in McGurn, 1996)

10 Globalization and Urban Futures

The foregoing chapters have revealed the interconnections between globalization and processes of urban-regional change as reflected in economic growth and social reorganizations in the Information Age. These unfolding processes have been examined in the spatial unit of the city, the nation-state, and subregional configurations. At each of these levels, globalization has been shown to be a powerful agent and process of change, so much so that since the early 1980s, Pacific Asia has forged ahead in rapid economic transition, with many planners and observers anticipating, perhaps a little prematurely, the twenty-first century to be the Pacific century. The slowly calming financial turmoil in Asia has greatly dampened the overly sanguine prognosis, but the fundamental favorable factors for sustained growth remain for the region to resume its growth dynamism once the storm has died down.

This book has focused more on China than any other country in Pacific Asia because China's trajectory of rapid growth since 1978, after adopting a historic open policy marking a sharp departure from its previous self-imposed isolation, is worthy of study and analysis in its own right. In addition, its remarkable economic transition coincided fortuitously with a period of accelerating globalization since the early 1980s. Put differently, many of the Chinese examples shown in these

pages do exemplify the outcome, dilemmas, and meanings of globalization and its interface with urban and regional development at different spatial scales of analysis. The choices of Shanghai and Guangdong are more than accidental, inasmuch as both bear historical links
to foreign investment and trade in China. Moreover, they epitomize the
fastest-growing areas of the coastal region in China, which has witnessed a momentous physical and economic transformation over the
past two decades.

This concluding chapter attempts to pull together the strands that
have surfaced in the preceding pages by anticipating urban futures in
Pacific Asia. Whereas the previous chapter highlighted how globalization has affected Hong Kong's future in its growing interaction and
integration with the Pearl River delta, bearing witness to the gathering forces of globalization, this chapter speculates on the prospect of
urban-regional change in Pacific Asia by setting itself against the same
background at the dawn of the twenty-first century.

GLOBALIZATION AND URBANIZATION

Before embarking on anticipating urban futures, it is instructive to re-
capitulate some of the salient trends related to the links between globalization and urbanization since the early 1980s. First, it is remarkable
to note how much the world has urbanized in the twentieth century. In
1900, some 15 percent of the world's population lived in urban places,
as opposed to 47.5 percent, as projected by the United Nations for
2000. In 1995, Asia and Africa were at highly comparable levels of
urbanization, with about 35 percent of their populations being classified urban. In fact, the first urban century is about to arrive, as it is certain that by the second decade of the twenty-first century, there will be,
for the first time, more people living in cities in the world. Pacific Asia
will figure prominently because its cities will continue to be engines of
growth and population concentration as they have been in the past.

Second, against the background of rapid economic transition and
urbanization, it is useful to remind ourselves that for many countries in
Pacific Asia, they have compressed an urban and economic transition
within three decades, which Western countries in their past have taken

60 years to a century to complete (McGee and Robinson, 1995:351). Such a time scale of change is also paralleled by the compression of present time and distance, made possible by recent technological advances in telecommunications and information processing. All this presents to urban planners and decision makers a range of development options as well as challenges. The urban agenda of today must reconcile a multitude of conflicting needs and constituencies. The globalized nature of some elements of contemporary life, such as media and electronic communication, crime, capital flows, and so on, reveals the palpable limits of urban governance. These activities are clearly beyond the bounds of existing urban containers.

Third, since the 1980s, the world economy has become decentralized, restructured, and consolidated, being facilitated by communications technologies, new forms of corporate organization, and new business services. Time-space compression has intensified, with the result that time horizons of both public and private decision making have decreased and the relative ease of those decisions to be spread to an ever wider space (Knox and Agnew, 1991:342). Indeed, a new world is taking shape, as Castells (1998) depicts vividly in this manner:

> The interaction between these processes [the information technology revolution, the economic crisis of both capitalism and statism, and the blooming of cultural social movements] . . . brought into being a new dominant social structure, the network society; a new economy, the informational/global economy; and a new culture, the culture of real virtuality. The logic embedded in this economy, this society, and this culture underlies social action and institutions throughout an interdependent world. (336)

Cities in the Information Age in Pacific Asia are dependent on knowledge and information trade, having moved from an economic base dependent on physical manufactured trade that was "energy intensive." Some scholars contrast European cities as having been rebuilt since 1945, with cities on the Pacific rim as having been reorganized (Blakely and Stimson, 1992:1–21).

As many are overwhelmed by the rapidity of global change over the past two decades and as we confront the commencement of a new century, it is time to pause to ponder the future, our cities, the simmering tensions, and the sustainability of our recent gains. What are the danger signals, and what can be done about them?

At the broadest level, the emerging tensions between developed and developing countries and among the regional blocs could prove to be a passing phase as the world adjusts to the shift of economic power and the new strategy economic parity among Pacific Asia, North America, and Western Europe. To help contain interregional tension, a desynchronizing of economic cycles in the three regions would be a good start. Another is the recognition of the inefficiency of the existing international economic institutions that fail to reflect new global realities. The absence of a country from Pacific Asia, with the exception of Japan, in the Great Seven (G7) process is an example (Schwab and Smadja, 1995:107).

For all the wondrous opportunities that globalization has offered to some countries and cities, many in the developing world are largely left out. They simply do not have the necessary information technology—the infrastructure of globalization—to be "plugged in." The unfortunate outcome is that they are delinked from the global economy (Svetlicic and Singer, 1996:84). Unless a start is made to bring these hapless entities into the mainstream of development, the economic and social disparities among countries and cities will be further magnified. A potential time bomb is thereby buried. In this respect, Japan and to some extent China have ventured to assist within the region, but more can be undertaken in the future.

Third, it has been suggested that the present patterns of globalization engendering economic inequities are unsustainable. A new internationalism involving social groups and aspiring for economic and gender equity, environmental sustainability, cultural autonomy, and so on is proposed. Called "globalization from below," it calls for a transformation in the North as well as in the South and in relations between the regions. Transnational activists argue that the rules and practices of globalization must be modified to increase equity between nations and regions of the world rather than allow corporate-dominated globalization to weaken democracy, labor-union strength, and environmental oversight (Hunter, 1996).

DETERMINANTS OF URBAN FUTURES [1]

At present the methodology of forecasting urban futures is developed in only a rudimentary manner, given the large number of variables involved. One method is to employ the technique of constructing exploratory scenarios by using a range of techniques to assist forecasting, such as trend extrapolation, cyclical analysis, and consensus surveys. Possible or desirable urban futures can be identified and a program designed to achieve any or all of them. It is an exercise in social engineering. Another method available to the forecaster is the use of anticipatory scenarios whose objective is to establish whether a specific normative goal or target might be achieved. The objective set for the planner might result from a national policy. Successive attempts are taken to determine alternative ways by which the objective might be achieved and which of the alternative routes should be followed (Newton and Taylor, 1985). However, neither of these methods is adopted in this chapter. What is attempted is a systematic consideration of the relevant factors that bear directly on globalization and urbanization, to be followed by speculations on urban futures in Pacific Asia.

From a global perspective, one of the most dominant concerns regarding Asian urbanization is the huge population base that exists in the region. Between 1950 and 1985, Asia's urban population increased almost fourfold to 846 million at an overall urbanization level of 29.2 percent. This figure is estimated to increase by 67 percent to 1.47 billion by the end of the twentieth century, when 37.7 percent of Asia's population will be domiciled in urban places (United Nations, 1995). This means that for Asia, hundreds of millions of new inhabitants must continually be absorbed into the present urban system, displaying the importance of the "tyranny of numbers" in any discussion on the future of urbanization in Asia. Beyond numbers alone, a tendency exists for an increasingly large proportion of urban populations to concentrate in cities of over one million inhabitants, that is, larger

---

[1] The balance of this chapter is based on a coauthored piece with T. G. McGee, duly amended and updated. See McGee and Yeung (1993).

cities. If UN population projections are accurate, by 2000, thirteen of the thirty largest cities in the world will be located in Asia, and many of them will be gargantuan urban conurbations of over eight million inhabitants each. To be exact, nine such megacities will be located in Pacific Asia, namely, Tokyo, Shanghai, Beijing, Jakarta, Tianjin, Seoul, Manila, Bangkok, and Osaka.

Already some of the giant cities of Pacific Asia are having to cope with staggering populations in terms of job and service provision. Greater Tokyo is said to contain the highest concentration of both people and wealth on earth, with 32 million people living within a 50-kilometer commuting radius and generating about 3 percent of the world's goods and services. Osaka is not too far behind, with about 20 million people living within commuting distance, forming part of Osaka-Kobe-Kyoto megalopolis (*Asiaweek,* July 6, 1990, 19). Tokyo and Osaka are not alone in having to face continuing challenges of feeding, housing, servicing, and providing effective governance for ever increasing populations, but they give a foretaste of megacities of the future for other Asian Pacific countries that undoubtedly do not command the same range and size of resources.

Especially relevant to urban growth is the concern of labor force participation. In the countries under review, the projection of labor force participation, along with overall population growth, is for modest or declining rates in Japan and the newly industrializing economies (NIEs). However, for the ASEAN-4 (Indonesia, Malaysia, Thailand, and the Philippines), both new entrants to the labor force and their rates of increase are projected to be robust until the end of the twentieth century. Between 1980 and 1995, the rate of growth of labor force formation was generally over 2 percent (World Bank, 1997, table 4). The implications for urban governments to find jobs for these new entrants to the labor force are as urgent as they are daunting. For China, the relevant figures for which are not available in the same source, the total workforce will number 717 million persons by 2000 if current participation patterns are maintained, a 26 percent increase over the 1985 employment level. The greatest increase in employment will take place in urban areas, a perfectly understood trend in view of its open policy adopted since 1978. Urban employment is projected to increase from 208 million people in 1985 to 385 million people by the end of the twentieth century. About 54 percent of all workers will live in cities and towns, compared to 36 percent at present. In China, the pressure on the cities is already being felt by a freer movement of population, one that started in 1984, resulting from the implementation of more liberal economic policies. During the Seventh Five-Year Plan (1986–1990), the planned new urban employment was set at 130 million, 100 million of which was earmarked for rural-to-urban migration and only 30 million for urban youth entering the workforce (Taylor, 1986:2). Indeed, the "floating population" in China, mainly centered on large coastal cities, reached 100 million in 1995 and might reach 200 million by 2000 (Weiss, 1995). By the mid-1990s, the annual increase in the rural labor force was about 10 million, and rural China had about 200 million surplus laborers. The ratio between the floating population, 60 percent of which originated from the countryside, and the permanent population in ten major cities in China rapidly increased from 12.6 percent in 1984 to 22.5 percent in 1987 and to 25.4 percent in 1994 (Li, 1996).

The economic health of a nation is a critical factor that shapes the character of its cities. In the post–World War II period, the rapid economic growth of Japan and the NIEs has thrust Pacific Asia into the world stage of international trade, technological innovations, and foreign investment. This group of countries continued with their impressive economic growth, as measured by gross domestic product (GDP), in the period 1985–1995. Their share of economic importance in the Pacific basin will also increase toward 2000. On the same theme, the ASEAN-4 countries as well as China are also projected to experience robust growth, with China's growth of GDP and its share in regional importance being the most notable of all Asian Pacific countries.

However, since mid-1996, signs that something had gone wrong in some regional economies were seen. For example, the Thai economy revealed a sharp slowdown in exports and economic growth, signs of a property bubble, a falling stock market, and a weakening fiscal position. These warnings were further ignored in 1997, and on July 2 of that year, Thailand plunged into a financial crisis after deciding to float the baht. The contagion swiftly spread to almost all countries in Pacific

Asia, creating an unprecedented economic crisis that at the time of this writing is still plaguing governments and people who have been accustomed for years to rapid economic growth (Y. Yeung, 1998b).

Foreign direct investment (FDI) has been a vital factor in propelling economic growth in Pacific Asia. Hand in hand with FDI is technology transfer and the changes that it will introduce into host countries for technological change/innovations and economic development. In this respect, the role played by transnational corporations (TNCs) in transferring technology to local companies and personnel is of utmost importance. The example of Singapore is salutary in illustrating the host government's realization of the process and the steps that it has taken to upgrade its technological competence. Toward the end of the 1970s, to implement Singapore's second industrialization program to restructure its economy toward high technology, high value-added, and skill-intensive industries, the government undertook a series of measures to facilitate the transition. A high-level committee was appointed to draw up plans for national computerization in 1980, followed in the next year by the establishment of the National Computer Board. The Institute of Systems Science was set up in 1981 at the National University of Singapore under a four-year partnership program with IBM. Enrollment at the university and polytechnics has also increased, providing the manpower needed by economic restructuring. Singapore is now home to 600 international manufacturing companies that operate for the mutual benefit of host/home countries. A complementary development is the implementation of a research-and-development strategy and the development of a thriving science park (Tan and Tan, 1990). By 2000, Singapore is planned to be a totally wired "intelligent island." Singapore has been investing heavily in information technology as both a user and a producer. The government's master plan, IT2000, is designed to power the developmental city-state's economic growth into the twenty-first century (*Far Eastern Economic Review*, August 27, 1998b, 40).

Rapid technological changes occurring in industrialized countries present major challenges as well as opportunities for countries in Pacific Asia. Implications exist for technological capability development, for employment, and for shifts in the structure of comparative advantage. At present, the most promising technological changes appear to be centered in microelectronics, information technology, biotechnology, and new materials technology. The first two potentially can create profound changes in the economies of the region by means of increased industrial productivity, whereas biotechnology can open up dramatic increases in agricultural productivity (United Nations, 1988:90). These changes likely will lead to spatial and organizational adjustments within cities in the region. Arthur Gilbert (1990) sums up the situation well:

> Today, global flows of digital information are being channelled to restructure industries worldwide, creating opportunities for nations with (and representing a threat for those without) strong information technology infrastructures and capabilities. (320)

Finally, energy surely is the key not only to economic growth in Pacific Asia in the 1990s but also to the shape and patterning of its cities. In terms of fuel energy requirements in the region, the forecast provides, in relative terms, for decreasing reliance on oil but an increasing relative share of nuclear power and natural gas, with coal and hydro/geothermal power remaining rather stable. Between now and 2005, the total energy demand in developing countries is expected to grow at an average rate of 4.3 percent per year. The high energy demand can be attributed to three factors: rapid growth in population and economic activity, increasing industrialization and road transportation, and diminishing availability of noncommercial sources of energy (International Energy Agency, 1988). Countries in Pacific Asia continue to depend on the Middle East for its oil. For example, Japan tried to minimize its import of Middle East oil by reducing importation from this region to 76 percent in 1979, a reduction of 9 percent since 1970. Even after the Persian Gulf War, energy supply, especially oil, will continue to be a critical factor determining the economic health and shaping urban futures in Pacific Asia.

Indeed, lately the world has become much more environmentally conscious in the light of a series of environmental disasters and the heightened concerns about global warming and the depletion of the ozone layer. The need for evolving ecologically stable cities, with an accent on resource conservation, will be recognized by more planners and policymakers (see chapter 8). Richard Meier (1976) called eloquently for resource-conserving cities in developing countries in the mid-1970s. This obviously is a relevant option for some cities of the future in Pacific Asia.

Although the questions of whether the urban revolution is an inevitable and necessary part of the process of economic development and how urban futures will stem from that development have been, and still are, heatedly contested, it does seem that certain necessary "spatial shifts" in the location of population and economic activity accompany economic and structural change. In the case of Japan, Korea, and Taiwan, this has led to the growth of one large metropolis (Tokyo, Seoul, and Taipei, respectively) as well as urbanized corridors of smaller cities that stretch between these large metropolitan centers and the next-largest city (Tokyo-Osaka, Seoul-Pusan, and Taipei-Kaohsiung, respectively). These corridors are linked by fast rail and road transportation that enable the flow of goods and people within the corridors. Today, these urban corridors (including the two centers on which they merge) play major roles in the economic activity and population distribution of these countries.

In the other parts of Pacific Asia, while these urban corridors are developing, especially in China and Malaysia, the main features of the urban pattern are a dominance of the largest urban agglomerations in the urban hierarchy and a much less developed system of secondary and intermediate cities. Some planners and policymakers have suggested that this offers the opportunity to funnel populations who are moving from rural areas away from the large metropolis to these secondary centers, thus avoiding costly investment in metropolitan infrastructure. However, given the potential volume of movement in the largest of the Asian Pacific countries (Indonesia and China), this "decentralized" pattern of urban growth is unlikely to avoid these problems completely. It should be emphasized that this prediction does not rule out the possibility of secondary centers growing in size and numbers. It is simply that they will not be able to absorb all the rural-to-urban shifts that will occur.

NEW URBAN REGIONS IN PACIFIC ASIA

Against the factors analyzed earlier, what is being hypothesized here is the emergence of great extended metropolitan regions (EMRs) in Asia that extend over many hundreds of miles. Although such regions will have many features similar to the megalopolis outlined by Gottmann in the sense of the interregional specialization and nodal characteristics, they will also have some distinctions, including a very different set of ecological preconditions and a different historical phase of incorporation into the global economy that emphasizes the role of international investment and linkages.

What are the features of these EMRs? First, and of most importance, it must be emphasized that these regions, although they have different morphologies (a corridor including several cities, one dominant city, and so on), are characterized by absorbing an increasing proportion of their countries' population and economic growth. The historical juxtaposition of port cities, which remain almost universally the center on which these regions have developed, and the high-density regions surrounding them create the necessary preconditions for global linkage and readily available surplus labor. These conditions have encouraged both national and international investors into these regions. This investment takes the form of direct investment into new industrial estates and free export zones.

Research undertaken so far on EMRs in Asian-Pacific countries shows that the proportion of national population has increased and that these regions contribute a significant component of national production. It also reinforces the arguments for the economic importance of these regions and the critical role that they play in the national economies (Ginsburg et al., 1991; McGee and Robinson, 1995).

Second, it is important to emphasize the significant role that infrastructure investment plays in these regions. Historically, many of these regions have installed well-developed systems of road and water transportation, but the acceleration of investment in ports, railway, and road construction in the colonial period and in the postindependence period has created the linkages on which the economic growth of these regions flourishes. For example, Taiwan, both in the Japanese period and in the period since the 1950s, consistently directed a major part of its public capital investment toward the transportation sector, improving the ports of Keelung and Kaohsiung and creating the new port of Taichung as well as fast electrified railways, freeways, and airports (see chapter 4). This has created a "transactional environment" that permits a collapse of time and space, eventually greatly reducing transportation costs. When world cities improve themselves physically, economically, and culturally to enable them to better discharge their functions, they are engaged in a process of world city formation. Much has been invested in these cities in Pacific Asia (see chapter 2; see also Yeung and Lo, 1998). For example, Seoul has an ambitious spatial plan that would design several megaprojects to prepare itself as a global center of the future in the Northeast Asian Natural Economic Area (Douglas, 1998).

Third, intense changes are occurring at the demographic and household levels in these regions related to declining birthrate, increasing employment of women, and growing household income from a multitude of sources. This means that an increasing number of households that formerly earned income from agriculture are now earning income from nonagricultural sources. For example, in a survey of villages in the EMR in Taiwan, up to 60 to 70 percent of household income is recorded originating from nonagricultural sources. This reflects growing opportunities for employment in manufacturing and the service sectors being offered to the inhabitants of these regions. As a result of these economic developments, the lifestyles and consumption practices of the inhabitants of these regions are changing dramatically. Data assembled for Taiwan show that in the EMR stretching from Taipei to Kaohsiung, the ownership of automobiles, televisions, radios, and so on is almost double that of the rest of Taiwan, reflecting much higher household incomes. Thus, these regions are becoming major consumption regions for both imported and domestic consumer durables. This is fostered further by international and national marketing strategies that focus on these regions. For example, the "commercial" television channels recently introduced in Kuala Lumpur and Jakarta were beamed initially to the extended metropolitan region.

Finally, the rapid growth of these regions poses many problems to national governments. The growth of industry causes environmental problems, and serious difficulties exist in delivering adequate basic services to the growing population of these regions. The problem of providing basic infrastructure services in the large cities in the region is especially acute, with the urban poor bearing the brunt of inadequacy and the resultant social and economic inequities being accentuated (Yeung, 1991).

As the previous chapters have brought to light, the EMR represents but one spatial expression of the globalization process that impinges on large cities in the region. At a general level, a recent study has emphasized the role of cities in the Pacific rim as the center of world economic and social wealth has shifted from the Atlantic to the Pacific. Many cities, such as Tianjin and Jakarta, have revitalized themselves through formulating policies to globalize their economies. They have become import-related urban centers, attracting new migrants. Information technologies have been incorporated in many of these cities to shape their economic and social environment, not unlike the automobile did in an earlier era. In short, cities in Pacific Asia are seen to have evolved a new urban form based on human resources. They are also characterized by their international environment, with common interconnections in a subregion and with an identity (Blakely and Stimson, 1992).

Economic globalization has been conducive to the formation of other urban forms that best reflect the rapid social and economic reorganization affecting the region. World cities, growth triangles, and urban corridors, which might or might not overlap with EMRs, have increasingly come to be identified with the Information Age. Looking far into the future, one possible scenario has been sketched as follows:

By the year 2040, development corridors in Southeast and East Asia should not be dissimilar to the banana-shaped, macro-economic corridor being formed in Europe, which extends across national borders from southern England to northern Italy. As the Japanese, East Asian, and Southeast Asian development corridors will attract the most investment in infrastructure and research and development, it is possible they will coalesce into a Pacific-Asia corridor running from Vladivostok to Bali. (McGee and Robinson, 1995:175)

POLICY FOR THE FUTURE OF URBAN PACIFIC ASIA

The theme that has been presented here can be regarded as quite challenging for planners and policymakers concerned with the urban future of their countries. In a very general manner, three questions can be raised about the future of Asian urbanization.

The first question relates to the type of urban system that will come to dominate the majority of Asian countries. One school of thought, represented by the Richardson hypothesis of polarization reversal, argues that the urban systems of Asia will pass through a sequence of concentration in existing urban centers, especially the largest urban center, followed by a shift in the proportion of population in the secondary centers as economic development occurs and spreads. In the Asian context, one would argue that a different pattern is emerging that indicates a continuing growth of nonagricultural population in large urban corridors or megaurban regions. As the economy of these Asian countries becomes more developed and shifts to a service economy based on finance capital (as is the case with Hong Kong and Singapore and increasingly Taipei), a growing specialization that emerges in the urban system will lead the Asian megaurban regions to move to a condition such as that described by Gottmann in *The Megalopolis* of which the best example in Pacific Asia is the Tokyo-Osaka corridor. If these arguments are valid, then from a policy point of view, it behooves the government of these countries to invest especially in the transportation and service infrastructure of these megaurban regions (see chapter 2). In the case of Japan, Taiwan, Korea, Hong Kong, and Singapore, which quite correctly are held out as the examples of the most successful economic development in Asia, it is the success in the conquest of the "space-time" relationships of their cities and countries that has been the essence of their "urban change." Whether the other countries of Asia will be able to accomplish such changes will depend on their ability to accommodate and invest capital in this sector.

Indeed, the investment in transport is being accompanied by the adoption of high-technology and communication innovations. Singapore recently hosted a Singapore 2000 exhibition, in which the Lion City was perceived as a "global technopolis" or a "communications city" well into the twenty-first century. Likewise, Hong Kong has ambitious and grandiose infrastructure investment projects, including a replacement airport at Chak Lap Kok on Lantau Island and a "Metroplan" to develop the metropolitan area at an estimated cost of $42 billion. Other large Asian Pacific cities, such as Jakarta, Kuala Lumpur, Seoul, Tokyo, Osaka, and Shanghai, have plans for the future, but the extent to which positive change can be realized will depend on resource availability and the ability to solve difficult problems. However, glimpses of future Asian cities can be appreciated in some ongoing or completed projects. In Singapore, a study is being mounted to turn 72 hectares of the downtown area into a "tropical" metropolis with plants and trees providing "vertical landscaping" on buildings. Enormous "umbrellas" would provide shade for buildings and reduce national energy consumption (*Asiaweek,* August 17, 1990, 63). A new generation of sophisticated intelligent buildings is being born, such as the Malaysia National Insurance headquarters in Johor Bahru and the Manila Stock Exchange Center completed in 1991 and 1992, respectively (*Asiaweek,* July 6, 1990, 17).

Perhaps one of the best examples of a city in Pacific Asia planning to move purposefully into the Information Age is Kuala Lumpur. Innovative and expensive plans have been made to expand the city along the southern corridor with an accent on information technology and computer networks. The showcase of this initiative is a grandiose plan to set up a Multimedia Super Corridor (MSC) at a cost of M$20 billion, stretching from the Petronas Twin Towers in the city center to the new Kuala Lumpur International Airport, about 70 kilometers from the city center. The MSC will be complemented by two virtual cities—Cyberraya and Pertrajaya (Y. Yeung, 1998d). Similar information structure is also envisaged for Johor across from Singapore. These are examples of cybercommunities as part of a digital dragon (Corey, 1997).

The second question, and one of considerable importance, is the way in which the "political economy of space" generates architectural and urban form that one would argue is related to the historical evolution of the economies of the countries and cities under discussion. It is also related to the particular phase of domination of certain types of capital (merchant, industrial, and finance). From this perspective, it is possible to argue that the NIEs and Japan are moving into a period in which finance capital is increasingly coming to dominate investment. The principal feature of the "political economy" of this form of investment is emphasis on consumption and "spectacle." Cities are placed directly in competition with one another as locales for tourism and consumption investment; credentials are established through "spectacles," such as the Olympics (Tokyo and Seoul), conferences, and expositions. For example, cities in Japan overtly compete for global attention through the hosting of international design expos (Nagoya), food festivals (Sapporo), flower expositions (Osaka), science expositions (Tsukuba), and the World Exposition (Seto, near Nagoya, in 2005)(Douglass, 1998:18). Other cities have done the same, and any mega- or world city in the region would boast of ever improving conference facilities and exhibition venues, complete with new information technologies and external networks worldwide.

To be competitive, these cities must create a built environment with an efficient transport network that is attractive to both national and foreign investment. Thus, the urban centers of these countries have been characterized by a rapid growth of housing (financed in a variety of public and private ways) that can be described as functionalist and high density, utilizing economies of scale in the provision of services. A polycentric pattern of commercial centers has developed that focuses on commercial and office development. These cities are also characterized by rapid mass transit systems as well as tourist "zones." The result of these developments is to create a built environment in which the regional identity is dominated by "international images" that mask the rich cultural traditions of the inhabitants of these countries.

At present, throughout the rest of Pacific Asia, countries and cities are still dominated by merchant capital, but with the growth of industrial and finance capital, debates continue among policymakers, architects, and planners regarding the future form and built environment of their cities. In cities such as Jakarta, Bangkok, Kuala Lumpur, Shanghai, and Beijing, elements of the "new cities of spectacle" are emerging in the form of high-rise housing, shopping, and commercial centers, but they are combined with the more traditional built environment of the city consisting of squatter and low-income housing, open markets, and small shops that still cater to the low-income populations. With the rise of the middle class in many countries, the large-scale shopping center has become a new social and economic institution across Pacific Asia (Yeung, 1998d). What one sees in this context is a kind of layering of the built environment in which the modern city is high-rise connected by "flyover" for automobile transport that passes over the "lower-order" city, reminding one of the architectural fantasies of the Buck Rogers science fiction cities of the future. Thus, a continuing battle is being waged for urban space between the two classes that inhabit the city, and if this battle is to follow the pattern of the NIEs, we will see the triumph of the city of consumption and spectacle.

One alternative to this kind of scenario is to encourage a spread-out city form linked by very fast communication of which Tokyo gives hints of possibilities. This is the EMR outlined earlier in which a much lower density environment is sustained and delivery of services (water, sewerage, and energy) is more decentralized and characterized by greater recycling and energy conservation. Given the very large number of people who will be involved in the urbanization process in Asia, few alternatives to this form of development might exist. With the rapidly expanding development of housing into the urban peripheries in the 1990s, the debate is largely settled. The reality is that a low-rise, physically expanding urban region around a number of nodal points, such as shopping malls, office complexes, and housing estates, has taken shape (McGee and Robinson, 1995:6).

This leads to the third question, which relates to the resources that are necessary to sustain the future of urban environments in Pacific Asia. These may be briefly summarized as food, energy, and finance. All these sources are closely related to the future types of cities that will emerge in Asia. If the high-density cities of "spectacle" are to become the prevailing mode, then the demands for imported food, energy and fuel, and finance to build these cities will increase. If the low-density extended city with a mode of decentralized form of energy, service provision, and collective transport comes into being, greater opportunities might exist for local food production, local service delivery, and so on as well as the persistence of some of the elements of the "traditional" built environment.

However, it might be too idealistic to imagine that the "decentralized city" will prevail, as it is extraordinarily difficult for the governments of the countries to resist global pressures for the high-density city. Certainly for China, which has been the fastest-growing country in the world during the past two decades, urban and regional transformation has been occurring at a breakneck pace. Old cities have been rebuilt, and some new ones have almost appeared from scratch. Shenzhen, just across the border from Hong Kong, has grown from a sleepy, miniscule settlement to the present metropolis of over three million in two decades. Pudong, that part of Shanghai to the east of the Huangpu River, has, since 1990, been re-created as an industrial, commercial, and financial zone in a futuristic mode and on a grand scale. These developments are symptomatic of the trends that have been the theme of this book and that seem to suggest that the future Pacific Asian city is already here.

Epilogue: Asia's Financial Crisis and Its Implications

Several of the chapters in this book have referred to the Asian financial crisis that has severely affected the economies of the region surveyed. However, the bulk of the empirical analysis was completed before the onset of the cataclysmic events since 1997. Thus, it is appropriate to dwell a little more on what the financial upheaval has meant for urban-regional change in Pacific Asia, especially in the new millennium.

To put things in perspective, it should be recalled that the last three decades of the twentieth century have witnessed, in Asia and elsewhere in the world, more fundamental and profound changes in economic growth and international connectedness than at any time in human history. Whereas the oil shocks of the 1970s introduced new elements of interdependence in the world economic order, globalization in the next two decades initiated equally revolutionary changes that touched the lives of people in every corner of the earth. People in Pacific Asia have been singularly fortunate in realizing substantial increases in income, standard of living, and personal aspirations. Growth in trade, foreign direct investment, and personal income has been so rapid since the mid-1980s that politicians and commentators were euphoric about the coming of a "Pacific century."

The financial turmoil over the past few years has highlighted the vulnerability of countries, cities, and individuals in the age of globalization. Ambitious development plans of some countries must be scaled down or postponed, whereas others are still in the throes of painful restructuring and readjustment. At the end of the twentieth century, the worst of the financial crisis appeared to have been weathered. However, some countries are still to experience negative growth in the immediate future, and real growth will return only after completion of drastic reforms and systemic changes. Notwithstanding the urban futures in the region that have been speculated on in an earlier chapter, what bodes for urban and regional change in the years ahead?

The overriding factor that will critically influence our lives in the new century is the increasing application and popularization of a new technological infrastructure. It is the advent of a new technological paradigm that is premised on information and telecommunication technology. This change is so far-reaching in our lives that it has been compared with the industrial revolution in the past. The new global economy has been called the informational economy. The process of globalizing the economy and communication has changed the way we produce, consume, manage, inform, and think (Borja and Castells, 1997:7). The demand for e-commerce, Web-based information, and telecommunication contacts will increase. In Pacific Asia outside Japan, the demand for telecommunication products and services has been increasing at an astonishing rate of 17 percent per year, with China registering the highest rates of growth (Pape, 1998:31). Many countries have plans to become an "info-society" to meet the challenges of the Information Age. In this connection, Asian countries have consciously promoted their cities as purveyors of information and knowledge, with their traditional functions in manufacturing, business, and trading being decentralized to their peripheries (Mohan, 1999). As cities compete among themselves, a differentiation of roles and importance takes place, as forces of globalization tend to be selective and to gravitate toward a smaller number of cities, world cities in particular.

Technological change provides the ambience in which economic and social transformation can be sped up. However, this must be accompanied by political stability, which is crucial for sustained and positive development. Indeed, the post–Cold War détente and the fading of communism have been the general backdrop against which rapid economic growth has been facilitated during the past two decades in Pacific Asia. What matters the most in maintaining political stability in the region, so argued many astute observers, relates to the emergence of China as a regional and global power. Its relations with the United States and Japan are of vital importance in determining Asia's political climate in the future. Taiwan, Tibet, Korea, South China Sea, and Indonesia, to name just a few, potentially can spell political instability in the region. Growth of the cities and the region will be adversely affected should this eventuality come about.

Even assuming that political stability will prevail, it cannot be "business as usual" to most governments after the financial crisis. People can no longer accept dictators or antiquated bureaucracy having lost touch with the masses. The fall of Suharto in far-flung Indonesia would not have been possible had information not been easily transmitted quickly and reliably across the archipelago. In the informational society, people demand more open governance, more active participation, and greater democratization. Whoever and wherever governs, institutions and administrations must be cognizant of the power of information and knowledge and be able to communicate effectively with his or her constituents in a fast-paced society. The need to balance global tendencies and local and regional needs and sensitivities is especially required of the new genre of political leaders. Global and local tendencies can be at once antagonistic and complementary. For example, in the global informational economy, capital is global, but labor is local. The development of policy and strategies that will allow them to dovetail their respective requirements is needed (Yeung, 1998e).

As globalization surges forward, it has been observed that economic and social polarization has occurred in both the cities and the region beyond. Urban polarization along class or caste lines is a potential destabilizing agent of change that can ruin decades of planning and industry. Equally, interregional disparity can destabilize a regime that must, through policy or administrative fiat, mitigate the uneven condition. Both examples can be found in China, which, by Deng Xiaoping's philosophy, has encouraged some people to get rich first. The new rich or urban elite are clearly visible in the urban area and are models for emulation. The rapidly growing phenomenon of temporary migrants in the range of 80 to 100 million is a manifestation of success begetting success. However, more threatening is the widening gap in economic opportunities, income, and quality of life between the coastal and the interior provinces. The central government is not unaware of the delicate situation, and it has attempted to minimize the difference through distribution and administrative measures.

Finally, a factor that bears heavily on the shape and health of the cities and the countryside in Pacific Asia is the state of the environment. The correlation of rapid economic growth and environmental degradation has been empirically corroborated. The situation is serious in many parts of Pacific Asia, but that in China warrants special mention. Over the past two decades, China has demonstrated its ability to generate economic dynamism at a rate higher than any country in the history of the global economy. Yet this has been achieved at a heavy cost to the environment. It has been submitted that in the next generation, China will emerge as the world's largest producer of greenhouse gases. The effect of acid rain on its neighbors, Japan and Korea, has been quite serious (Pape, 1998:134–135). Adopting environmentally sustainable policies is vital not only for the cities themselves but also for the country in which they are located and for neighboring countries as well. Thus, the environment will be a dimension of change in the region that must be placed high on the policy agendas of the governments in the region.

With the fallout from the financial crisis beginning to settle, this is an opportune time for governments and individuals to rethink their development agendas and for politicians and planners to rethink where they have succeeded and where they have failed. Paul Krugman's admonition of the "Asian miracle" has at last found a more responsive chord, as decision makers and students of development no longer believe in a linear pattern of economic growth. Nonetheless, many in the region still are of the firm belief that the fundamental strengths of the region—high savings rate, exemplary work ethics, strong family system, and openness to investment, trade, and technology—have not changed. As the regional economies fully recover, no reason exists to doubt that Pacific Asia will, in the early decades of the twenty-first century, rediscover its old magic of rapid economic growth. In this process, its cities and the countries at large will have a more purposeful and enhanced role to play to propel their economies forward in the increasingly globalized economy.

References

Numbers in brackets indicate chapters in which a reference is cited.

Abonyi, George, and Filologo Pante Jr. 1998. "Economic Cooperation in the Greater Mekong Subregion: The Challenges of Resource Mobilization." In *Growth Triangles in Asia*, edited by Myo Thant, Min Tang, and Hiroshi Kakazu. Hong Kong: Oxford University Press, pp. 327–372. [3]

Abu-Lughod, Janet. 1987. "The Shape of the World System in the Thirteenth Century." *Studies in Comparative International Development* 22:3–25. [1]

Agriculture and Fisheries Department. 1998. *Agriculture and Fisheries Department Annual Report 1997/98*. Hong Kong: AFD. [8]

Armstrong, Warwick, and T. G. McGee. 1985. *Theatres of Accumulation: Studies in Asian and Latin American Urbanization*. London: Methuen. [1]

Asian Development Bank. 1997. *Key Indicators of Developing Asian and Pacific Countries*. New York: Oxford University Press. [3]

———. 1998. *Key Indicators of Developing Asian and Pacific Countries*. New York: Oxford University Press. [8]

Bach, Wilfrid. 1984. *One Threatened Climate: Ways of Averting the CO_2 Problem through Rational Energy Use*. Translated by Jill Jager. Dordrecht: D. Reidel. [8]

Bairoch, Paul. 1988. *Cities and Economic Development: From the Dawn of History to the Present*. Translated by Christopher Braider. Chicago: University of Chicago Press. [2]

Bardach, Hohn E. 1984. "Fish in the Food Basket of Asian Cities." Unpublished paper, Resource Systems Institute, East-West Center, Honolulu. [8]

Batha, Emma. 1997. "Businessmen Aim to Build 37.9-Km HK-Macau Bridge." *South China Morning Post,* May 2. [6]

Becker, S. 1995. "Chinese Opera." *Far Eastern Economic Review,* April 6, 54–55. [9]

Bienefeld, Manfred. 1996. "Is a Stronger National Economy a Utopian Goal at the End of the Twentieth Century?" In *States against Markets: The Limits of Globalization,* edited by R. Boyer and Daniel Drache. London: Routledge, 415–440. [1]

Blakely, Edward J., and Robert Stimson. 1992. *New Cities of the Pacific Rim.* Monograph No. 43, Institute of Urban and Regional Development, University of California, Berkeley. [10]

Borja, Jordi, and Manuel Castells. 1997. *Local and Global: Management of Cities in the Information Age.* London: Earthscan. [epilogue]

Boyden, Stephen Vickers. 1977. "Integrated Ecological Studies of Human Settlements." *Impact of Science on Society* 27:159–169. [8]

Boyden, Stephen Vickers, S. Millar, K. Newcombe and B. O'Neill. 1981. *The Ecology of a City and Its People: The Case of Hong Kong.* Canberra: Australian National University Press. [8]

Boyer, Robert, and Daniel Drache, eds. 1996. *States against Markets: The Limits of Globalization.* London: Routledge. [1,2]

Brown, Fred N. 1996. "Roads." In *Planning Hong Kong for the 21st Century,* edited by Anthony G. O. Yeh. Hong Kong: Centre of Urban Planning and Environmental Management, University of Hong Kong, 197–210. [9]

Brown, Lester R. 1987. "Analyzing the Demographic Trap." In *State of the World 1987,* edited by Lester R. Brown et al. New York: W. W. Norton, 20–37. [8]

Brown, Lester R., et al., eds. 1986. *State of the World 1986.* New York: W. W. Norton. [8]

———. 1989. *State of the World 1989.* New York: W. W. Norton. [8]

Brown, Lester R., and Christopher Flavin. 1988. "The Earth's Vital Signs." In *State of the World 1988,* edited by Lester R. Brown et al. New York: W. W. Norton, 3–21. [8]

Brown, Lester R., and Jodi L. Jacobson. 1987. "The Future of Urbanization: Facing the Ecological and Economic Constraints." Worldwatch Paper No. 77, Washington, D.C. [8]

Brown, Lester R., and Edward C. Wolf. 1989. "Reclaiming the Future." In *State of the World 1989,* edited by Lester R. Brown et al. New York: W. W. Norton, 170–88. [8]

Burton, Sandra. 1994. "Growing by Leaps—and Triangles." *Time,* January 17, 26–28. [3]

Cai, Jiayuan. 1991. "Evaluation of the Administrative Implementation Ability in Promoting the Six-Year National Development Plan." In *Proceedings of the Seminar on Evaluating the Six-Year National Development Plan,* vol. 2, 74–81 (in Chinese). [4]

Cai, Renqun. 1992. "On Some Projects of Infrastructure Construction in the Zhujiang Delta." *Tropical Geography,* 12(3):214–220 (in Chinese). [4]

Campanella, Miriam L. 1993. "The Effects of Globalization and Turbulence on Policy-making Processes." *Government and Opposition* 28:190–205. [1]

Castells, Manuel. 1977. *The Urban Question: A Marxist Approach.* London: Edward Arnold. [2]

———. 1992. *European Cities, the Informational Society, and the Global Society.* Centre for Metropolitan Research, Amsterdam University. [2]

———. 1996. *The Rise of the Network Society.* Oxford: Blackwell. [1]

———. 1997. *The Power of Identity.* Oxford: Blackwell. [1]

———. 1998. *End of Millennium.* Oxford: Blackwell. [1,2,10]

Census and Statistics Department. Various years. *Hong Kong Annual Digest of Statistics.* Hong Kong: Government Printer. [8,9]

———. Various years. *Hong Kong Monthly Digest of Statistics.* Hong Kong: Government Printer. [9]

Chan, Kam Wing. 1986. "Rural-Urban Migration and China's Development, 1959–82." Paper presented at the Conference on Resources, Environment and Regional Development, University of Hong Kong, August 18–22. [8]

———. 1989. "Economic Growth Strategy and Urbanization Policies in China, 1949–1982." Research Paper No. 175, Centre of Urban and Community Studies, University of Toronto. [5]

———. 1994a. "Urbanization and Rural-Urban Migration since 1982: A New Baseline." *Modern China* 28(3):243–281. [5]

———. 1994b. *Cities with Invisible Walls: Reinterpreting Urbanization in Post-1949 China.* Hong Kong: Oxford University Press. [5]

Chan, Kam Wing, and Xu Xueqiang. 1985. "Urban Population Growth and Urbanization in China since 1949: Reconstructing a Baseline." *China Quarterly* 104:583–613. [5]

Chase-Dunn, Christopher. 1984. "Urbanization in the World-System: New Direction for Research." In *Cities in Transformation, Class, Capital, and the State. Urban Affairs Annual Review,* vol. 26, edited by Michael P. Smith. Beverly Hills, Calif.: Sage Publications, 111–120. [2]

Chen, Edward K. Y., and Joseph S. L. Lee. 1998. "Southern China Growth Triangle: An Overview." In *Growth Triangles in Asia,* edited by Myo Thant, Min Tang, and Hiroshi Kakazu. Hong Kong: Oxford University Press, 49–101. [3]

Chen, Jiayuan, ed. 1991. *Economic Geography of Fujian.* Beijing: New China Press (in Chinese). [4]

Chen, Mingjin, Chen Chunhua, and Su Huahong. 1995. "The Eighth Five-

Year Period: Review and Contemplation of Guangdong Economy I." *Nanfang jingji* 12: 5–7 (in Chinese). [6]

Chen, Xiangming. 1988. "Giant Cities and the Urban Hierarchy in China." In *The Metropolis Era: A World of Giant Cities,* vol. 1, edited by Mattei Dogan and John D. Kasarda. Newbury Park, Calif.: Sage Publications, 225–251. [8]

———. 1991. "China's City Hierarchy, Urban Policy and Spatial Development in the 1980s." *Urban Studies* 28(3):341–367. [5]

Cheng, Elizabeth, and Michael Taylor. 1991. "Delta Force: Pearl River Cities in Partnership with Hong Kong." *Far Eastern Economic Review,* May 16, 64–66. [4,6]

Cheng, Yuan. 1990. "Problems of Urbanization under China's Traditional Economic System." In *Chinese Urban Reform: What Model Now?,* edited by R. Yin-wang Kwok et al. New York: M. E. Sharpe, 65–77. [5]

Chiu, Rebecca. 1992. "Trends of Public Housing Development in Asia: The Cases of Singapore, Hong Kong and China." Paper presented at the Conference on Hong Kong Public Administration in Transition, Hong Kong, December 10–12. [4]

———. 1996. "Housing." In *Shanghai,* edited by Y. M. Yeung and Sung Yun-wing. Hong Kong: Chinese University Press, 341–374. [8]

Chiu, Stephen W. K., K. C. Ho, and Tai-lok Lui. 1997. *City-States in the Global Economy: Industrial Restructuring in Hong Kong and Singapore.* Boulder, Colo.: Westview Press. [1]

Choe, Sang-chuel. 1992. "Towards the 21st Century: Evolving Urban System in Northeast Asia." Paper presented at the Workshop on the Asian Pacific Urban System, Hong Kong, February 11–13. [2]

———. 1996. "The Evolving Urban System in Northeast Asia." In *Emerging World Cities in Pacific Asia,* edited by Fu-chen Lo and Yue-man Yeung. Tokyo: United Nations University Press, 498–519. [2]

Chor, Yan. 1992. "Fujian's Bullet Train Dream." *Wide Angle Monthly,* October, 86–89 (in Chinese). [4]

Chow, Larry C. H. 1986. "Urban Environment and the Consumption of Town Gas in Hong Kong." Paper presented at the Conference on Resources, Environment and Regional Development, University of Hong Kong, August 18–22. [8]

———. 1989. "Utilities." In *The Other Hong Kong Report 1989,* edited by T. L. Tsim and Bernard H. K. Luk. Hong Kong: Chinese University Press, 245–250. [8]

Chu, David K. Y. 1991. "Containerization of Hong Kong and Pearl River Delta: Opportunities and Constraints." Paper presented at the Transportation and Urban Development in Pacific Rim Conference, Vancouver, British Columbia, October 6–10. [4]

———. (1992), [4], "Transportation." In *The Other Hong Kong Report 1992,* edited by Joseph Y. S. Cheng and Paul C. K. Kwong. Hong Kong: Chinese University Press. [4]

Chu, Kennis. 1992. "Guangdong in Cash Call for Road Network Projects." *South China Morning Post,* December 27. [4]

Chu, W. K. S. 1996. "Direction of Development—Metro or New Territories." In *Planning Hong Kong for the 21st Century,* edited by Anthony G. O. Yeh. Hong Kong: Centre of Urban Planning and Environmental Management, University of Hong Kong, 291–302. [9]

Clear Thinking. 1998a. *China Infrastructure Newsletter,* March 1998. Hong Kong: Clear Thinking (H.K.), Ltd. (info@clearthinking.com). [3]

———. 1998b. *China Infrastructure Newsletter,* September 1998. Hong Kong: Clear Thinking (H.K.), Ltd. (info@clearthinking.com). [4]

Clifford, Mark, and Lincoln Kaye. 1992. "Trade and Trade-Offs: Potential Partners Weight Benefits of Cooperation." *Far Eastern Economic Review,* January 16, 18–19. [3]

Cohen, R. B. 1981. "The New International Division of Labor, Multinational Corporations and Urban Hierarchy." In *Urbanization and Urban Planning in Capitalist Society,* edited by Michael Dear and Allen J. Scott. London: Methuen, 287–315. [2]

Cooke, P., ed. 1986. *Global Restructuring, Local Response.* Redhill, Surrey: Schools Publishing. [2]

Corey, Kenneth E. 1997. "Digital Dragons and Cyber Communities: The Application of Information Technology and Telecommunications Public Policies and Private Partnerships to the Planning of Urban Areas." *International Journal of Urban Sciences* 1(2):184–96. [10]

Court, Stephen. 1993. "Where Opposites Attract." *Geographical Magazine* 65(January):24–27. [3]

Crothall, Geoffrey. 1990. "China Housing Scheme in Danger of Collapse." *South China Morning Post,* January 3. [8]

Cui, Gonghao. 1995. "On Development of Large Cities in China." *Chinese Geographical Science* 5(1):1–10. [5]

Dalgish, Brenda. 1993. "The Chinese: Will They be Capitalists?" *Maclean's,* May 10, 24–28. [6]

Deng, Shuping. 1987. "Problems in the Development and Planning of Cities in the Yangtze Delta." Paper presented at the Conference on Chinese Cities in Asian Context, Centre of Urban Studies and Urban Planning, University of Hong Kong, Hong Kong. [8]

Dicken, Peter. 1998. *Global Shift: Transforming the World Economy.* 3rd ed. London: Paul Chapman Publishing. [2,3]

Dieleman, F. M., and C. Hamnett. 1994. "Globalization, Regulation and the Urban System." *Urban Studies* 31(3):357–364. [2]

do Rosario, L. 1995. "One Country, Two Roads." *Far Eastern Economic Review,* July 6, 60–61. [9]

Douglass, Mike. 1988. "Urbanization and Urban Policies in China: A Comparative Asian Perspective." Discussion Paper No. 10, Department of Urban and Regional Planning, University of Hawaii. [5]

———. 1998. "East Asian Urbanization: Patterns, Problems, and Prospects." Discussion paper, Asia/Pacific Research Center, Stanford University. [10]

Dowell, W. 1994. "Island of Effluence." *Time,* October 31, 44. [9]

Drakakis-Smith, David, ed. 1986. *Urbanization in the Developing World.* London: Croom Helm. [2]

Dunning, John H. 1997. *Alliance Capitalism and Global Business.* London: Routledge. [1,2]

Durning, Alan B. 1989. "Mobilizing at the Grassroots." In *State of the World 1989,* edited by Lester R. Brown et al. New York: W. W. Norton, 154–173. [8]

Economic Planning Unit Malaysia and National Economic and Social Development Board Thailand. 1993. *Terms of Reference for Investigative Study of the Malaysia-Indonesia-Thailand Growth Triangle Development Project.* Discussion draft. [3]

Economist Intelligence Unit. 1996. *Economic Outlook Guangdong,* February. [6]

Edgington, David W. 1997. "The Rise of the Yen, 'Hollowing Out' and Japan's Troubled Industries." In *Asia Pacific: New Geographies of the Pacific Rim,* edited by R. F. Watters and T. G. McGee. Wellington: Victoria University Press, 170\1-89. [1]

Editorial. 1995. "Shining Shanghai," *Asiaweek,* November 24, 28. [7]

Ehrilch, Jennifer. 2000. "Anger over Plan for Third Nuclear Plant." *South China Morning Post,* January 19. [8]

El-Shakhs, Salah, and Ellen Shoshkes. 1998. "Islamic Cities in the World System." In *Globalization and the World of Large Cities,* edited by Fu-chen Lo and Yue-man Yeung. Tokyo: United Nations University Press, 228–268. [1]

Environmental Protection Department. 1997. *Environment: Hong Kong 1997.* Hong Kong: EDP. [8]

Executive Yuan. 1979. *Evaluation of the Ten Major Construction Projects.* Taipei: Council for Economic Planning and Development. [4]

Faber, M. 1996. "Dr. Doom Sees Change Will Bring Gloom." *South China Morning Post,* November 11. [9]

Far Eastern Economic Review. 1992. "Big-Budget Spending on Infrastructure." October 15, 41–42. [4]

———. 1992. "Aims Are High, Funds Are Low." November 12, 44–46. [4]

———. 1998a. *A Review of the Events of 1998.* Hong Kong: Far Eastern Economic Review. [4]

———. 1998b. "Intelligent Island." August 27, 40. [10]

Fardoust, Shahrokh, and Ashoh Dhareshwar. 1990. *A Long-Term Outlook for the World Economy: Issues and Projections for the 1990s.* Washington, D.C.: World Bank. [1]

Flavin, Christopher. 1988. "Creating a Sustainable Energy Future." In *State of the World 1988,* edited by Lester R. Brown et al. New York: W. W. Norton, 22–40. [8]

Foo Choy Peng. 1995. "Foreign Banks to Be Appointed for Pudong Trade." *South China Morning Post,* September 19. [7]

Freedman, Ronald, et al. 1988. "Education and Fertility in Two Chinese Provinces: 1967–1970 to 1979–1982." *Asia-Pacific Population Journal* 3(1): 3–30. [8]

Friedmann, John. 1986. "The World City Hypothesis." *Development and Change* 17:69–83. [2]

Friedmann, John, and Goetz Wolff. 1982. "World City Formation: An Agenda for Research and Action." *International Journal of Urban and Regional Research* 6(3):309–344. [2]

Frobel, Folker, Jurgen Heinrichs, and Otto Kreye. 1980. *The New International Division of Labour.* Cambridge: Cambridge University Press. [2]

Fujian Statistical Bureau. 1992. *Statistical Yearbook of Fujian 1992.* Yichun: Chinese Statistical Publishing Company. [4]

———. 1996. *Statistical Yearbook of Fujian 1996.* Yichun: Chinese Statistical Publishing Company. [4]

———. 1997. *Statistical Yearbook of Fujian 1997.* Yichun: Chinese Statistical Publishing Company. [3]

Fujita, K. 1991. "A World City and Flexible Specialization: Restructuring of the Tokyo Metropolis." *International Journal of Urban and Regional Research,* 15(2):269–284. [2]

Furedy, Christine. 1989. "Social Consequences in Solid Waste Management in Asian Cities." Paper presented at the Expert Group Seminar on Improving Solid Waste Management, Nagoya, United Nations Center for Regional Development. [8]

Gao Ruxi and Yu Yihong. 1994. "Shanghai's Economy: Stagnation and Re-Emergence." *Twenty-First Century,* no. 24, August, 148–157 (in Chinese). [7]

Gereffi, Gary. 1996. "The Elusive Last Lap in the Quest for Developed-Country Status." In *Globalization,* edited by James H. Mittelman. Boulder, Colo.: Lynne Rienner Publishers, 53–81. [1]

Giddens, A. 1990. *The Consequences of Modernity.* Cambridge: Polity. [1]

Gilbert, Arthur Lee. 1990. "Information Technology Transfer: The Singapore Strategy." In *Technology Transfer in the Developing Countries,* edited by Manas Chatterji, Houndmills: Macmillan, 320–334. [10]

Ginsburg, Norton. 1990. *The Urban Transition: Reflections in the American and Asian Experience.* Hong Kong: Chinese University Press. [8]

Ginsburg, Norton, Bruce Koppell, and T. G. McGee, eds. 1991. *The Extended Metropolis: Settlement Transition in Asia.* Honolulu: University of Hawaii Press. [2,10]

Goldstein, Carl. 1992a. "It's All Go in the South." *Far Eastern Economic Review,* November 12, 47. [4]

————. 1992b. "Skirting the Potholes: Hopewell Wins Chinese Vote of Confidence." *Far Eastern Economic Review,* December 3, 62–63. [4]

————. 1992c. "Ties That Bind: Hongkong Firms Seek Closer China Links." *Far Eastern Economic Review,* July 30, 61–62. [6]

Goldstein, Sidney. 1985. "Urbanization in China: New Insights from the 1982 Census." Papers of the East-West Population Institute, No. 93, Honolulu. [8]

Gondolf, Edward W., Irwin M. Marcus, and James P. Dougherry, eds. 1986. *The Global Economy: Divergent Perspectives on Economic Change.* Boulder, Colo.: Westview Press. [2]

Grunwald, Joseph, and Kenneth Flamm. 1985. *The Global Factory: Foreign Assembly in International Trade.* Washington, D.C.: Brookings Institution. [2]

Guangdong Statistical Bureau. 1991. *Statistical Yearbook of Guangdong 1991.* Yichun: Chinese Statistical Publishing Company. [4]

————. 1992. *Statistical Yearbook of Guangdong 1992.* Yichun: Chinese Statistical Publishing Company. [4]

————. 1996. *Statistical Yearbook of Guangdong 1996.* Yichun: Chinese Statistical Publishing Company. [4]

————. 1997. *Statistical Yearbook of Guangdong 1997.* Yichun: Chinese Statistical Publishing Company. [3]

————. 1998. *Statistical Yearbook of Guangdong 1998.* Yichun: Chinese Statistical Publishing Company. [4]

Guangdong Yearbook Committee. *Guangdong Yearbook 1991, 1995, 1998.* Guangzhou: Guangdong Yearbook Committee, 1991, 1995, 1998 (in Chinese). [4,6]

Guo, Zuoyi, and Chen Jianhua. 1992. "Local Government-Led Economy." *Asia-Pacific Economic News,* July 12 (in Chinese). [4]

Hamilton, F. E. Ian. 1991. "Global Economic Change." In *Global Change and Challenge: Geography for the 1990s,* edited by Robert Bennett and Robert Estall. London: Routledge, 80–102. [2]

Han, Sun Sheng, and Wong Shue Tuck. 1994. "The Influence of Chinese Reform and Pre-Reform Policies on Urban Growth in the 1980s." *Urban Geography* 15(6):537–564. [5]

Harvey, David. 1973. *Social Justice and the City.* London: Edward Arnold. [2]

He Xinggang. 1993. "Development of Pudong and Optimization of Urban Area Structure in Shanghai." *Chinese Environment and Development,* 4(3):68–88. [7]

Healy, T., and S. L. Law. 1996. "Pressure at the Border." *Asiaweek,* July 12, 21. [9]

Heenan, David A. 1977. "Global Cities of Tomorrow." *Harvard Business Review,* May–June, 79–92. [2]

Henderson, Jeffrey, and Manuel Castells, eds. 1987. *Global Restructuring and Territorial Development.* London: Sage Publications. [2]

Hirst, Paul. 1998. "Globalisation and the Changing Capacities of the Nation State: Military, Economic and Cultural Power." Paper presented at the 30th Anniversary Conference of the Institute of Southeast Asian Studies, Singapore, July 30–August 1. [1]

Hon, M. S. M., and B. Delfino. 1996. "Cargo Line Delay Cuts $6 Billion off Link Cost." *South China Morning Post,* December 12. [9]

Hong Kong Government. 1989. *Gateway to New Opportunities: Hong Kong's Port and Airport Development Strategy.* Hong Kong: Government Printer. [9]

———. Various years. *Hong Kong.* Hong Kong: Government Printer. [8,9]

Hong, Sung Woong. 1996. "Seoul: A Global City in a Nation of Rapid Growth." In *Emerging World Cities in Pacific Asia,* edited by Fu-chen Lo and Yue-man Yeung. Tokyo: United Nations University Press, 144–178. [2]

Howe, Christopher, ed. 1981. *Shanghai: Revolution and Development in an Asian Metropolis.* Cambridge: Cambridge University Press. [7]

Hsu, Mei-ling. 1985. "Growth and Control of Population in China: The Urban-Rural Contrast." *Annals of the Association of American Geographers* 75(2):241–257. [8]

Huang Renwei. 1994. "Strategic Plan for 21st Century 'Eastern Big Port.'" *Hui qiao ribao,* December 20 (in Chinese). [7]

Hughes, D. 1996. "Economies Move to Integrate." *South China Morning Post,* September 9. [9]

Hunter, Allen. 1996. "Globalization from Below? Promises and Perils of the New Internationalism." *Social Policy* 25:6–13. [10]

Huus, Karl. 1994. "Gridlock, Anyone?" *Far Eastern Economic Review,* November 10, 56–62. [5]

Icamina, Paul. 1980. "The Things That Keep Hong Kong Ticking." *The Straits Times,* January 25. [8]

International Energy Agency. 1988. *Energy Policies and Programmes of IEA Countries: 1988 Review.* Paris: IEA. [10]

Jao, Y. C. 1993. "Hong Kong as an International Financial Centre: Evolution and Prospects." In *The Asian NIEs: Success and Challenge,* edited by Tzong-biau Lin and Chyau Tuan. Hong Kong: Lo Fund Learned Society, 39–82. [2]

Ka, Yu. 1992. "Competing for 'Sphere of Influence' by Hong Kong Entrepreneurs in China." *Contemporary Monthly,* September 15, 70–71 (in Chinese). [4]

Kakazu, Hiroshi. 1998. "Northeast Asian Regional Economic Cooperation." In *Growth Triangles in Asia,* edited by Myo Thant, Min Tang, and Hiroshi Kakazu. Hong Kong: Oxford University Press, 257–296. [3]

Kao, Charles, and Joseph S. Lee. 1991. *The Taiwan Experience: 1949–1989.* Taipei: Commonwealth Publishing (in Chinese). [4]

Kennedy, Paul. 1996. "Forecast: Global Gales Ahead." *New Statesman and Society,* May 31, 28–29. [1]

Kim, Euikon. 1992. "Political Economy of the Tumen River Basin Development: Problems and Prospects." *Journal of Northeast Asian Studies* 11(2): 35–48. [3]

Kim, Karl, and Chung-tong Wu. 1998. "Regional Planning's Last Harrah: The Political Economy of the Tumen River Regional Development Plan." *Geo-Journal* 44(3):239–247. [3]

Kim, Won Bae. 1991. "The Role and Structure of Metropolises in China's Urban Economy." *Third World Planning Review* 13(20):155–177. [5]

Kim, Won Bae, Mike Douglass, Sang-Chuel Choe, and Kong Chong Ho, eds. 1997. *Culture and the City in East Asia.* Oxford: Clarendon Press. [2]

King, Ambrose. 1997. "Hong Kong and Chinese Culture in the 21st Century." *Ming Pao Monthly,* January, 18–22 (in Chinese). [9]

King, Anthony D. 1990. *Global Cities: Post Imperialism and the Internationalization of London.* London: Routledge. [2]

Kirkby, Richard J. R. 1985. *Urbanisation in China: Town and Country in a Developing Economy 1949–2000 AD.* London: Croom Helm. [5]

———. 1994. "Dilemmas of Urbanization: Review and Prospects." In *China: The Next Decades,* edited by Denis Dwyer. London: Longman, 128–155. [5]

Knight, Richard V., and Gary Gappert, eds. 1989. *Cities in a Global Society.* Vol. 35 of *Urban Affairs Annual Review.* Newbury Park, Calif.: Sage Publications. [2]

Knox, Paul, and John Agnew. 1991. *The Geography of the World-Economy.* London: Edward Arnold. [1,10]

Knox, Paul L., and Peter J. Taylor, eds. 1995. *World Cities in a World System.* Cambridge: Cambridge University Press. [2]

Kojima, Reeitsu. 1987. "Urbanization and Urban Problems in China." I.D.E. Occasional Papers Series No. 22. Tokyo: Institute of Developing Studies. [5]

Kolko, Joyce. 1988. *Restructuring the World Economy.* New York: Pantheon Books. [2]

Korff, Ruediger. 1987. "The World City Hypothesis: A Critique." *Development and Change,* 18:483–495. [2]

Kraar, L. 1995. "The Death of Hong Kong." *Fortune,* 131(2):40–52. [9]

Krugman, Paul, and Anthony J. Venables. 1995. "Globalization and the In-equity of Nations." *Quarterly Journal of Economics* 110(4):857–880. [1]

Kumar, Krishna, ed. 1980. *Transnational Enterprises: Their Impact on Third World Societies and Cultures.* Boulder, Colo.: Westview Press. [2]

Kwan, C. H. 1998. "A Japanese Perspective of Asia's Currency Crisis." Un-published paper, Nomura Research Institute, Tokyo. [1]

Kwan, Daniel. 1996. "$13.4b Earmarked for Anti-Pollution Drive." *South China Morning Post,* August 6. [6]

Kwong, Kai-sun. 1994. "Infrastructure." In *The Other Hong Kong Report 1994,* edited by Donald H. McMillen and Si-wai Man. Hong Kong: The Chinese University Press, 209–222. [9]

Lai, Lawrence W. C. 1996. "The Harbour Reclamation Debate 1995/96." In *The Other Hong Kong Report 1996,* edited by Mee-kau Nyaw and Si-ming Li. Hong Kong: The Chinese University Press, 349–366. [9]

Lam, K. C. 1986. "Environmental Protection in the Shenzhen Special Eco-nomic Zone: Achievements, Problems and Implications." In *China's Special Economic Zones: Policies, Problems and Prospects,* edited by Y. C. Jao and K. C. Leung. Hong Kong: Oxford University Press, 65–83. [8]

———. 1989. "The Environment." In *The Other Hong Kong Report 1989,* ed-ited by T. L. Tsim and Bernard H. K. Luk. Hong Kong: Chinese University Press, 333–367. [8]

Lam, Willy Wo-Lap. 1995. "All Eyes on Shanghai." *South China Morning Post,* November 2. [7]

Laquian, A. A. 1996. "Pearl River Delta Development in the World Perspec-tive." In *Planning Hong Kong for the 21st Century,* edited by Anthony G. O. Yeh. Hong Kong: Centre of Urban Planning and Environmental Man-agement, University of Hong Kong, 11–38. [9]

Lau, Muriel. 1989. "Cost of Water to Rise under New Expansion Plans." *South China Morning Post,* December 22. [8]

Le Heron, Richard, and Sam Ock Park, eds. 1995. *The Asian Pacific Rim and Globalization.* Aldershot: Avebury. [1]

Le Zeng. 1994. "The Rise of Modern Shanghai and the Decline of Guang-zhou." *Twenty-First Century,* no. 24, August, 29–38 (in Chinese). [5]

Lee, Quo-wei. 1994. "Shanghai and Hong Kong: Glowing Eyes of the Dragon." *South China Morning Post,* October 6. [7]

Lee, Tsao Yuan, ed. 1991. *Growth Triangle: The Johor-Singapore-Riau Expe-rience.* Singapore: Institute of Southeast Asian Studies. [3]

Lehner, Urban C. 1994. "As Goes Shanghai, so Goes China." *The Asian Wall Street Journal,* November 22, S-9. [7]

Lei, Qiang, and Chen Li. 1990. "Strengthening the Cooperative Development of Infrastructure Provisions in Guangdong, Hong Kong and Macau." *Hong Kong and Macau Economic Digest,* no. 5, 9–12. [4]

Leung, E. 1996. "Hong Kong and China Economic Relationship beyond 1997." Paper presented at the Conference on Planning in Hong Kong 1997 and Beyond, November 27–28, Hong Kong. [9]

Li, Cheng. 1996. "Surplus Rural Laborers and Internal Migration in China: Current Status and Future Prospects." *Asian Survey*, 11:1122–1145. [5,10]

Li, David. 1996. "Pearl City Here We Come." *South China Morning Post*, July 6. [9]

Li, Haibo. 1992. "Tumen River Delta: Far East's Future Rotterdam." *Beijing Review*, April 20–26, 5–6. [3]

Li Mengbai and Hu Xin et al., eds. 1991. *Temporary Population and Its Impact and Implications for Development in Large Cities*. Beijing: Economic Daily Press (in Chinese). [5,6,7]

Lim, Lan Yuan, and Belinda Yuen. 1998. "Urban Transportation Development and Management in Singapore." UMP-Asia Occasional Paper No. 38, Asian Institute of Technology, Bangkok. [2]

Liu, Pak-wai, Wong Yue-chim, Sung Yun-wing, and Lau Pui-king. 1992. "China's Economic Reforms and Development Strategy of Pearl River Delta." Research report, Nanyang Commercial Bank Ltd. [4]

Lo, C. P. 1994. "Economic Reforms and Socialist City Structure: A Case Study of Guangzhou, China." *Urban Geography* 15(2):128–149. [5]

Lo, Fu-chen, and Kamal Salih. 1987. "Structural Change and Spatial Transformation: Review of Urbanization in Asia, 1960–80." In *Urbanization and Urban Policies in Pacific Asia,* edited by Roland J. Fuchs, Gavin W. Jones, and Ernesto M. Pernia. Boulder, Colo.: Westview Press, 38–64. [8]

Lo, Fu-chen, and Yue-man Yeung, eds. 1996. *Emerging World Cities in Pacific Asia*. Tokyo: United Nations University Press. [1,2,9]

———. 1998. *Globalization and the World of Large Cities*. Tokyo: United Nations University Press. [1]

Lui, T. L., and S. Chiu. 1994. "A Tale of Two Industries: The Restructuring of Hong Kong's Garment-Making and Electronics Industries." *Environment and Planning A* 26:53–70. [9]

Ma, Lawrence, and Cui Gonghao. 1987. "Administrative Changes and Urban Population in China." *Annals of the Association of American Geographers* 77(3):373–395. [5]

Machimura, Takashi. 1992. "The Urban Restructuring Process in Tokyo in the 1980s: Transforming Tokyo into a World City." *International Journal of Urban and Regional Research* 16(1):114–128. [2]

MacPherson, K. L. 1996. "The Shanghai Model in Historical Perspective." In *Shanghai: Transformation and Modernization under China's Open Policy,* edited by Y. M. Yeung and Yun-wing Sung. Hong Kong: Chinese University Press, 493–527. [7]

Manuel, Gren. 1992. "US$750 Power Deal for Hopewell." *South China Morning Post*, December 19. [4]

Markusen, Ann R., and V. Gwiasda. 1994. "Multipolarity and Layering of Functions in World Cities: New York City's Struggle to Stay on Top." *International Journal of Urban and Regional Research* 18(2):167–193. [2]

Marriage, Paul, and Kennis Chu. 1992. "Wu Plans to Transform Pearl Delta." *South China Morning Post,* June 28. [4]

Martinez, Elena. 1993. "The Tumen River Area Development Programme: Implications as a 'Growth Triangle.'" Statement presented at the Workshop on Growth Triangles in Asia held at the Asian Development Bank, Manila, February 24–26. [3]

Masai, Y. 1989. "Greater Tokyo as a Global City." In *Cities in a Global Society,* edited by Richard V. Knight and Gary Gappert. Newbury Park, Calif.: Sage Publications, 153–163. [2]

McGee, T. G. 1988. "Metropolitan Governments, Urban Planning, and the Urban Poor in Asia: Lessons from the Past and Present." *Regional Development Dialogue* 9(4):1–16. [8]

McGee, T. G., and Ira M. Robinson, eds. 1995. *The Mega Urban Regions of Southeast Asia.* Vancouver: University of British Columbia Press. [10]

McGee, T. G., and Yue-man Yeung. 1993. "Urban Futures for Pacific Asia: Towards the 21st Century." In *Pacific Asia in the 21st Century,* edited by Yue-man Yeung. Hong Kong: Chinese University Press, 47–67. [10]

McGurn, W. 1996. "Diminishing Returns." *Far Eastern Economic Review,* June 13. [9]

McMichael, Philip. 1996. "Globalization: Myths and Realities." *Rural Sociology* 61(1):25–55. [1]

Meier, Richard L. 1976. "A Stable Urban Ecosystem: Its Evolution with Densely Populated Societies." *Science* 192(2334):962–968. [10]

Meyer, David R. 1986. "The World System of Cities: Relations between International Financial Metropolises and South American Cities" *Social Forces* 64(3):553–581. [2]

———. 1991. "Change in the World System of Metropolises: The Role of Business Intermediaries." *Urban Geography* 12(5):393–416. [2]

———. 1998. "World Cities as Financial Centres." In *Globalization and the World of Large Cities,* edited by Fu-chen Lo and Yue-man Yeung. Tokyo: United Nations University Press, 410–432. [2]

Millar, Sheelagh. 1979. *The Hong Kong Ecology Programme: The Biosocial Survey in Hong Kong.* Canberra: Centre for Resource and Environmental Studies, Australian National University. [8]

Mitchell, Robert, E. 1971. "Some Social Implications of High Density Housing." *American Sociological Review* 36:18–29. [8]

Mittelman, James H. 1996. *Globalization: Critical Reflections.* Boulder, Colo.: Lynne Rienner Publishers. [1]

Mohan, Rakesh. 1999. "Bright Lights, Big Problems." *Far Eastern Economic Review,* February 18 51. [epilogue]

Murphey, Rhoads. 1953. *Shanghai: Key to Modern China.* Cambridge, Mass.: Harvard University Press. [7]

———. 1988. "Shanghai." In *The Metropolis Era: Mega-Cities,* vol. 2, edited by Mattei Doggan and John D. Kasarda. Newbury Park, Calif.: Sage Publications, 157–183. [7]

Naidu, G. 1998. "Johor-Singapore-Riau Growth Triangle: Progress and Prospects." In *Growth Triangles in Asia,* edited by Myo Thant, Min Tang, and Hiroshi Kakazu. Hong Kong: Oxford University Press, 231–255. [3]

Nakakita, Toru. 1988. "The Globalization of Japanese Firms and Its Influence on Japan's Trade with Developing Countries." *The Development Economies* 26(4):306–322. [2]

Nakashima, Hirayuki. 1998. "Japan's Outward Foreign Direct Investment for Fiscal Year 1991 to 1995." *EXIM Review* 17(2):71–113. [1]

Newcombe, Ken. 1977. "Nutrient Flow in a Major Urban Settlement: Hong Kong." *Human Ecology* 5(3):179–208. [8]

Newton, P., and Taylor, M. 1985. "Probable Urban Futures." In *The Future of Urban Form: The Impact of New Technology,* edited by John Brotchie, P. Newton, P. Hall, and P. Nijkamp. London: Croom Helm, 313–336. [10]

Ng, Cho-nam, and Ng Ting-leung. 1997. "The Environment." In *The Other Hong Kong Report 1997,* edited by Joseph Y. S. Cheng. Hong Kong: Chinese University Press, 483–504. [8]

Ng, Mee-kam. 1993. "Port and Airport Development Strategy in Hong Kong." Case Studies No. 7, American Institute of Certified Planners. [9]

———. 1995. "Urban and Regional Planning." In *From Colony to SAR: Hong Kong's Challenges Ahead,* edited by Joseph Y. S. Cheng and Sonny S. H. Lo. Hong Kong: The Chinese University Press. [9]

Ng, Mee-kam, and Alison Cook. 1996. "Are There Feasible Alternatives to the Reclamation-Led Urban Development Strategy in Hong Kong?" Occasional Paper No. 132, Department of Geography, Chinese University of Hong Kong. [9]

Ning, D., Joseph B. Whitney, and David Yap. 1987. "Urban Air Pollution and Atmospheric Diffusion Research in China." *Environmental Management* 11(6):721–728. [8]

Nyaw, Mee-kau. 1996. "Investment Environment: Perceptions of Overseas Investors of Foreign-Funded Industrial Firms." In *Shanghai: Transformation and Modernization under China's Open Policy,* edited by Y. M. Yeung and Yun-wing Sung. Hong Kong: Chinese University Press, 249–272. [7]

Ohmae, Kenichi. 1990. *The Borderless World: Power and Strategy in the Interlinked Economy.* New York: Mckinsey & Company. [1]

———. 1995a. *The Evolving Global Economy: Making Sense of the New World Order.* Cambridge, Mass.: Harvard Business Review Book. [1]

———. 1995b. *The End of the Nation State: The Rise of Regional Economies.* New York: The Free Press. [1]

Pannell, Clifton W. 1986. "Recent Increase in Chinese Urbanization." *Urban Geography* 7(4):291–310. [5]

———. 1995. "China's Urban Transition." *Journal of Geography* 94(3):394–403. [5]

Pannell, Clifton W., and Jeffrey S. Torguson. 1991. "Interpreting Spatial Patterns from the 1990 China Census." *Geographical Review* 81(3):304–317. [5]

Pape, Wolfgang, ed. 1998. *East Asia by the Year 2000 and Beyond: Shaping Factors.* Richmond, Va.: Curzon Press. [epilogue]

Parsonage, James. 1992. "Southeast Asia's 'Growth Triangle': A Subregional Response to Global Transformation." *International Journal of Urban and Regional Research* 16(2):307–317. [3]

Patten C. 1996. "Hong Kong Governor's Policy Address," Hong Kong, October 2. [9]

Peet, Richard. 1991. *Global Capitalism: Theories of Societal Development.* London: Routledge. [2]

Perkins, Dwight H. 1990. "The Influence of Economic Reforms on China's Urbanization." In *Chinese Urban Reform: What Model Now?*, edited by R. Yin-wang Kwok et al. New York: M. E. Sharpe, 78–106. [5]

Pernia, Ernesto M. 1998. "Brunei Darussalam-Indonesia-Malaysia-Philippines East ASEAN Growth Area." In *Growth Triangles in Asia,* edited by Myo Thant, Min Tang, and Hiroshi Kakazu. Hong Kong: Oxford University Press, 373–411. [3]

Perry, Martin. 1991. "The Singapore Growth Triangle: State, Capital and Labour at a New Frontier in the World Economy." *Singapore Journal of Tropical Geography* 12(2):138–151. [3]

Perry, Martin, Lily Kong, and Brenda Yeoh. 1997. *Singapore: A Developmental City State.* Chichester: John Wiley & Sons. [3]

Planning, Environment, and Land Bureau. 1997. *Draft Waste Reduction Plan.* Hong Kong: PEL Branch. [8]

Prud'homme, R. 1989. "New Trends in the Cities of the World." In *Cities in a Global Society,* edited by Richard V. Knight and Gary Gappert. Newbury Park, Calif.: Sage Publications, 44–57. [2]

Pryor, E. G. 1991. "The Role of Hong Kong's Infrastructural Development in the Modernization of Southern China with Particular Reference to the Pearl River Delta." *Planning and Development* 7(1):2–10. [4]

Qu, Geping. 1985. "Strengthen Environmental Protection in Cities and Promote Their Modernization." Paper presented at the Polmet 85 Conference, Hong Kong, December 2–6. [8]

———. 1989. "Environmental Protection in China: A Brief History." *Chinese Geography and Environment* 2(3):3–29. [8]

Qureshi, Zia. 1996. "Globalization: New Opportunities, Tough Challenges." *Finance and Development* 33:30–33. [1]

Rimmer, Peter J. 1986. "Japan's World Cities: Tokyo, Osaka, Nagoya or Tokaido Megalopolis?" *Development and Change* 17:121–157. [2]

———. 1997. "Japan's Foreign Direct Investment in the Pacific Rim, 1985–1993." In *Asia Pacific: New Geographies of the Pacific Rim,* edited by R. F. Watters and T. G. McGee. Wellington: Victoria University Press, 113–132. [1]

Robertson, R. 1989. "Globality, Global Culture and Images of World Order." In *Social Change and Modernity,* edited by H. Haverkamp and H. Smelser. Berkeley and Los Angeles: University of California Press. [2]

Rohwer, Jim. 1995. "In the Region of Asian Greatness." *South China Morning Post,* December 1. [7]

Rose, John. 1966. "Hong Kong's Water-Supply Problem and China's Contribution to Its Solution." *Geographical Review* 56(3):432–437. [8]

Sassen, Saskia. 1991. *The Global City: New York, London, Tokyo.* Princeton, N.J.: Princeton University Press. [2]

———. 1994a. *Cities in a World Economy.* Thousand Oaks, Calif.: Pine Forge Press. [1]

———. 1994b. "The Urban Complex in a World Economy." *International Social Science Journal* 139:43–62. [2]

———. 1996. "Cities and Communities in the Global Economy." *American Behavioral Scientist* 39(5):629–639. [1]

Sassen-Koob, Saskia. 1989. "New York City's Informal Economy." In *The Informal Economy: Studies in Advanced and Less Developed Countries,* edited by Alejandro Portes, Manuel Castells, and Lauren A. Benton. Baltimore: Johns Hopkins University Press, 60–77. [2]

Savitch, H. V. 1996. "Cities in a Global Era: A New Paradigm for the Next Millennium." In *Preparing for the Urban Future,* edited by Michael A. Cohen et al. Washington, D.C.: Woodrow Wilson Center Press, 39–65. [1]

Scalapino, Robert. 1998. "Southeast Asian Politics in the Age of Globalization." Paper presented at the 30th Anniversary Conference of the Institute of Southeast Asian Studies, Singapore, July 30–August 1. [1]

Schwab, Klaus, and Claude Smadja. 1995. "Power and Policy: The New Economic World Order." In *The Evolving Global Economy,* edited by Kenichi Ohmae. Cambridge, Mass.: Harvard Business Review, 99–111. [1,10]

Sequeira, R., and C. C. Lai. 1998. "Small-Scale Spatial Variability in the Representative Ionic Composition of Rainwater within Urban Hong Kong." *Atmospheric Environment* 32(2):133–144. [8]

Shanghai City. 1995. *Shanghai: Striding towards the 21st Century.* Shanghai: Shanghai People's Press (in Chinese). [7]

Shanghai People's Government Reception Office. 1993. *Shanghai: Emerging International Mega-City.* Shanghai: Scientific Press (in Chinese). [7]

Shanghai Statistical Bureau. 1986. *Statistical Yearbook of Shanghai 1986.* Beijing: Chinese Statistical Press (in Chinese). [7]

———. 1995. *Statistical Yearbook of Shanghai 1995*. Beijing: Chinese Statistical Press (in Chinese). [7]

———. 1998. *Statistical Yearbook of Shanghai 1998*. Beijing: Chinese Statistical Press (in Chinese). [7]

Shea, Cynthia Pollock. 1988a. "Protecting Life on Earth: Steps to Save the Ozone Layer." Worldwatch Paper No. 87, Washington, D.C. [8]

———. 1988b. "Renewable Energy: Today's Contribution, Tomorrow's Promise." Worldwatch Paper No. 81, Washington, D.C. [8]

———. 1989. "Protecting the Ozone Layer." In *State of the World 1989*, edited by Lester R. Brown et al. New York: W. W. Norton, 77–96. [8]

Shen G. 1995. "A Challenging Decade for the Business Community: A Productivity Perspective." In *Hong Kong's Transition: A Decade after the Deal*, edited by Gungwa Wang and Siu-lun Wong. Hong Kong: Oxford University Press. [9]

Shengong Compatibility Research Editing Committee. 1994. *Compatibility Research Related to Shenzhen and Hong Kong in 1997*. Guangzhou: Guangzhou Publishing House (in Chinese). [9]

Shiode, Hirakazu. 1998. "Tumen River Development Programme: North Korea and Multilateral Cooperation." In *Growth Triangles in Asia*, edited by Myo Thant, Min Tang, and Hiroshi Kakazu. Hong Kong: Oxford University Press, 297–326. [3]

Sito, Peggy. 1994. "Waiver Raises Keen Interest in Shanghai." *South China Morning Post*, September 7. [7]

Skinner, G. William. 1981. "Vegetable Supply and Marketing in Chinese Cities." In *Vegetable Farming Systems in China*, edited by D. L. Plucknett and H. L. Beemer Jr. Boulder, Colo.: Westview Press, 215–280. [8]

Smil, Vaclav. 1984. *The Bad Earth: Environmental Degradation in China*. New York: M. E. Sharpe. [5,8]

Song, Jian. 1989. "Declaring War on Environmental Pollution—Opening Address at the Third National Congress on Environmental Protection." *Huanjing baohu* 7:2–7 (in Chinese). [8]

State Statistical Bureau, ed. 1986. *Statistical Yearbook of China 1986*. China: China Statistical Press (in Chinese). [7]

———. 1992. *Statistical Yearbook of China 1992*. China: China Statistical Press (in Chinese). [5]

———. 1997. *Statistical Yearbook of China 1997*. China: China Statistical Press (in Chinese). [5,8]

———. 1998. *Statistical Yearbook of China 1998*. China: China Statistical Press (in Chinese). [5,7]

———. Various years. *Urban Statistical Yearbook of China*. China: China Statistical Press (in Chinese). [5]

Stoner, Tad. 1990. "$30b Scheme for Three New Rail Lines Unveiled." *South China Morning Post*, January 18. [8]

Strong, Maurice F. 1976. "Environment and Man's Future in the Pacific." In *Mankind's Future in the Pacific,* edited by R. F. Scagel. Vancouver: University of British Columbia Press, 99–111. [8]

Stubbs, Richard. 1995. "Asia-Pacific Regionalization and the Global Economy." *Asian Survey* 35:785–797. [1]

Sun, Hong-chang, and Christine Furedy. 1989. "Resource Recovery in Chinese Cities." *Resource Recycling,* March/April, 30–32. [8]

Sung, Yun-wing. 1995. "The Implications of China's Admission to the WTO for Greater China." Paper presented at the Conference on Sino-American Economic Relations, Hong Kong, June 21–23. [4]

———. 1996. " 'Dragon Head' of China's Economy?" In *Shanghai: Transformation and Modernization under China's Open Policy,* edited by Y. M. Yeung and Yun-wing Sung. Hong Kong: Chinese University Press, 171–198. [6]

Sung, Yun-wing, et al. 1995. *The Fifth Dragon: The Emergence of the Pearl River Delta.* Singapore: Addison-Wesley. [6,9]

Svetlicic, Marjan, and H. W. Singer, eds. 1996.*The World Economy: Challenges of Globalization and Regionalization.* London: Macmillan. [1,10]

Szeto, Wai-fun. 1992. "New Blueprint of Cooperation between Hong Kong and Guangdong." *Wide Angle Monthly,* March, 54–57. [4]

Tan, Thiam Soon, and Tan Chwee Huat. 1990. "Role of Transnational Corporations in Transfer of Technology to Singapore." In *Technology Transfer in the Developing Countries,* edited by Manas Chatterji, Houndmills: Macmillan, 335–344. [10]

Tang, H. Y. Y. 1997. "Merged Forces to Create Economic 'Dream Team.' " *South China Morning Post,* January 13. [9]

Tang, Min, and Myo Thant. 1998. "Growth Triangles: Conceptual Issues and Operational Problems." In *Growth Triangles in Asia,* edited by Myo Thant, Min Tang, and Hiroshi Kakazu. Hong Kong: Oxford University Press, 23–48. [3]

Taylor, Jeffrey R. 1986. *Employment Outlook for China to the Year 2000.* Washington, D.C.: Center for International Research, U.S. Bureau of the Census. [10]

Taylor, Michael, and Elizabeth Cheng. 1991. "The Way Ahead: Guangdong Plan Puts Emphasis on Transport Links." *Far Eastern Economic Review,* May 16, 68. [4]

Taylor, Robert P. 1982. *Decentralized Renewable Energy Development in China: The State of the Art.* World Bank Staff Working Papers No. 535, Washington, D.C. [8]

Thant, Myo. 1998. "The Indonesia-Malaysia-Thailand Growth Triangle." In *Growth Triangles in Asia,* edited by Myo Thant, Min Tang, and Hiroshi Kakazu. Hong Kong: Oxford University Press, 413–448. [3]

Thant, Myo, Min Tang, and Hiroshi Kakazu, eds. 1998. *Growth Triangles in Asia.* 2nd ed. Hong Kong: Oxford University Press. [3,9]

Thrift, Nigel J. 1986. "The Internationalization of Producer Services and the Integration of the Pacific Basin Property Market." In *Multinationals and the Restructuring of the World-Economy,* edited by M. J. Taylor and N. J. Thrift. London: Croom Helm. [2]

Timberlake, Michael, ed. 1985. *Urbanization in the World-Economy.* Orlando: Academic Press. [2]

To, Eva. 1992. "Dreams of Power." *South China Morning Post,* March 8. [4]

Tolley, George S. 1991. "Urban Housing Reform in China." World Bank Discussion Paper No. 123. Washington, D.C.: World Bank. [5]

Transport Branch. 1994. *Report of the Working Party on Measures to Address Traffic Congestion.* Hong Kong: Government Printer. [8]

Transport Department. 1995. *Traffic and Transport Digest 1995.* Hong Kong: Government Printer. [9]

Tsai, H. H. 1996. "Globalization and the Urban System in Taiwan." In *Emerging World Cities in Pacific Asia,* edited by Fu-chen Lo and Yue-man Yeung. Tokyo: United Nations University Press, pp. 179–218. [4]

Tsang, S. K. 1996. "Hong Kong's Poverty Questions as Viewed from Economic Development." *Ming Pao,* February 13. [9]

Tyler, Gus. 1993. "The Nation-State vs. the Global Economy." *Challenge* 36:26–32. [1]

Tyson, Laura. 1992. "Lippo and Fuzhou in $1b Deal." *South China Morning Post,* November 25. [4]

United Nations. 1988. *Economic and Social Survey of Asia and the Pacific 1988.* Bangkok: Economic and Social Commission for Asia and the Pacific. [1,10]

———. 1995. *World Urbanization Prospects: The 1994 Revision.* New York: UN Department of International Economic and Social Affairs. [10]

Vatikiotis, Michael, 1993a. "Chip off the Block: Doubts Plague Singapore-Centred 'Growth Triangle.'" *Far Eastern Economic Review,* January 7, 54. [3]

———. 1993b. "Three's Company: Malaysia, Thailand, Indonesia Forge Development Zone." *Far Eastern Economic Review,* August 5, 7–8. [3]

Vogel, Ezra F. 1989. *One Step ahead in China: Guangdong under Reform.* Cambridge, Mass.: Harvard University Press. [6]

Wallace, Charles P. 1991. "New Economic Hubs Are Emerging in Asia." *Los Angeles Times,* August 31. [2]

Wallerstein, Immanuel. 1974. *The Modern World-System.* New York: Academic Press. [2]

———. 1976. "Political Economy of World Urban Systems: Directions for Comparative Research." In *The City in Comparative Perspective,* edited by

John Walton and Louis H. Masoti. New York: John Wiley & Sons, 301–313. [2]

Wallis, Keith. 1997. "Expressways Uniting with Motherland." *South China Morning Post,* April 27. [6]

Walsh, James. 1992. "Shanghai." *Time,* October 5, 19. [7]

Wang, Canfa. 1985. "How to Correctly Handle Several Factors Relating to Environmental Protection in Special Economic Zones?" *Zhongguo huanjing guanli* 20 (in Chinese). [8]

Wang, Yukun. 1992. *China: Urban Development at the Turn of the Century.* Shenyang: Liaoning People's Press (in Chinese). [5]

———. 1993. "China: Urban Development towards the Year 2000." Occasional Paper No. 19, Hong Kong Institute of Asia-Pacific Studies, The Chinese University of Hong Kong. [5]

Waters, Malcolm. 1995. *Globalization.* London: Routledge. [1]

Wei, Betty Peh-T'i. 1987. *Shanghai: Crucible of Modern China.* Hong Kong: Oxford University Press. [7]

Weiss, Julian M. 1995. "A Floating Population: Migration and Culture Shock in China." *The World & I* 10(12):220–231. [10]

Wen, Simei, and Yue Hue Zhang. 1992. "Rural Economic Development and Social Changes in Guangdong Province." In *Guangdong: "Open Door" Economic Development Strategy,* edited by Toyojiro Maruya. ASEDP No. 19. Tokyo: Institute of Developing Economies, 49–78. [6]

White, Lynn T. III. 1987. *Shanghai Shanghaied? Uneven Taxes in Reform China.* Hong Kong: Centre of Asian Studies, University of Hong Kong. [7]

Williamson, Jeffrey G. 1996. "Globalization, Convergence, and History." *Journal of Economic History* 59(2):277–306. [1]

Wong, Christine. 1995. "Fiscal Reform in 1994." In *China Review 1995,* edited by Lo Chi-kin, Suzanne Pepper, and Tsui Kai-yuen. Hong Kong: The Chinese University Press, 201–213. [7]

Wong, Fanny. 1992. "Government Commits $78b for Capital Works Projects." *South China Morning Post,* November 17. [4]

Wong, Jesse. 1994. "Long Way to Go." *The Asian Wall Street Journal,* November 22, S-4. [7]

Wong, Joon San. 1990. "Group Pushes for Trolley Bus System." *South China Morning Post,* January 30. [8]

Wong, Koon-kwai. 1996. "The Environment: Heading towards Sustainability." In *The Other Hong Kong Report 1996,* edited by Mee-lau Nyaw and Si-ming Li. Hong Kong: Chinese University Press, 367–387. [8,9]

Wong Siu-lun. 1988. *Emigrant Entrepreneurs: Shanghai Industrialists in Hong Kong.* Hong Kong: Oxford University Press. [7]

Wood, William B., George J. Demko, and Phyllis Mofson. 1989. "Ecopolitics in the Global Greenhouse" *Environment* 31(7):12–17, 32–34. [8]

World Bank. 1991. *World Development Report 1991*. Washington, D.C.: World Bank. [2,3]

———. 1992. "China: Implementation Options for Urban Housing Reform." A World Bank Country Study. Washington, D.C.: World Bank. [5]

———. 1993. "China: Urban Land Management in an Emerging Market Economy." A World Bank Country Study. Washington, D.C.: World Bank. [5]

———. 1997. *World Development Report 1997*. Washington, D.C.: World Bank. [8,10]

———. 1998. *World Development Report 1998/99*. Washington, D.C.: World Bank. [8]

Wu, Patrick. 1997. "1997 Asia-Pacific Construction Report, Taiwan" (http://www.cifrd.org.tw/document/cifrd/news1/86v8/86v8a3.htm). [4]

Wu, Yu-wan, ed. 1986. *Economic Geography of Guangdong*. Beijing: New China Press (in Chinese). [6]

Xie Kang. 1995. "World-Class MNCs Advanced towards Shanghai." *Hua qiao ribao,* January 10 (in Chinese). [7]

Xu, Zhuang. 1987. "An Integrated Analysis of the Character and State of Pollution of China's Solid Wastes." *Huanjing kexue* 5:80–84 (in Chinese). [8]

Yang, Quanhe. 1988. "The Aging of China's Population: Perspectives and Implications." *Asia-Pacific Population Journal* 3(1):55–74. [8]

Yang, Shi. 1989. "Municipal Solid Waste Management in Beijing: Present Status and Future Tasks." *Regional Development Dialogue* 10(3):113–128. [8]

Ye, Shunzan. 1987. "Urban Policies and Urban Housing Programs in China." In *Urbanization and Urban Policies in Pacific Asia,* edited by Roland J. Fuchs, Gavin W. Jones, and Ernesto M. Pernia. Boulder, Colo.: Westview Press, 201–216. [8]

Ye, Wejun, Zhang Bingshen, and Lin Jianing, eds. 1988. *A Preliminary Study on the Course of Urbanization in China*. Beijing: Chinese Prospect Press (in Chinese). [5]

Yearbook of China Cities. 1997. Beijing: Zhongguo chengshi nianjianshe. [5]

Yeh, Anthony G. O. 1993. "Urban Development of Hong Kong in the 21st Century: Opportunities and Challenges." In *Pacific Asia in the 21st Century,* edited by Yue-man Yeung. Hong Kong: The Chinese University Press, 69–103. [4,9]

———. 1995. "Planning and Management of Hong Kong's Border." In *From Colony to SAR: Hong Kong's Challenges Ahead,* edited by Joseph Y. S. Cheng and Sonny S. H. Lo. Hong Kong: Chinese University Press, 261–291. [9]

———. 1997. "Economic Restructuring and Land Use Planning in Hong Kong." *Land Use Policy* 14(1):25–39. [9]

Yeh, Anthony G. O., Kin Che Lam, Si Ming Li, and Kwan Yiu Wong. 1989.

"Spatial Development of the Pearl River Delta: Development Issues and Research Agenda." *Asian Geographer* 8(1–2):1–9. [6]

Yeh, Anthony G. O., and Mee-kam Ng. 1994. "The Changing Role of the State in High-Tech Industrial Development: The Experience of Hong Kong." *Environment and Planning C* 12:449–472. [9]

Yeh, Anthony G. O., and Xu Xueqiang. 1990. "New Cities in City Development in China, 1953–86." *Asian Geographer* 9(1):11–38. [5]

Yeh, Anthony G. O., Xu Xueqiang, and Hu Huaying. 1990. "Social Areas of Guangzhou." Paper presented at the Annual Meeting of the Association of American Geographers, April 19–20, Toronto. [8]

Yeung, H. W. C. 1994. "Hong Kong Firms in the ASEAN Region: Transnational Corporations and Foreign Direct Investment." *Environment and Planning A* 26:1931–1956. [2,9]

———. 1998a. "Capital, State and Space: Contesting the Borderless World." *Transaction of the Institute of British Geographers* 23(3):291–309. [1]

———. 1998b. *Transnational Corporations and Business Networks: Hong Kong Firms in the ASEAN Region.* London: Routledge. [2]

Yeung, Yue-man. 1985. *Urban Agriculture in Asia: A Substantive and Policy Review.* Paris: Food-Energy Nexus Programme, United Nations University. [8]

———. 1987. "Cities That Work: Hong Kong and Singapore." In *Urbanization and Urban Policies in Pacific Asia,* edited by Roland J. Fuchs, Gavin W. Jones, and Ernesto M. Pernia. Boulder, Colo.: Westview Press. [9]

———. 1989a. "The Planning Process—Strategic Options (A Critique on the Transport Infrastructure Plans of the Green Paper on Transport Policy in Hong Kong)." Occasional Paper No. 93, Department of Geography, Chinese University of Hong Kong. [8,9]

———. 1989b. "Fifteen Years of Public Housing in Hong Kong: Retrospect and Prospect." Occasional Paper No. 97, Department of Geography, The Chinese University of Hong Kong. [8]

———. 1991. "Past Approaches and Emerging Challenges." In *The Urban Poor and Basic Infrastructure Services in Asia and the Pacific.* Seminar report, Asian Development Bank, vol. 1, 27–81. [8,10]

———. 1992. "China and Hong Kong." In *Sustainable Cities: Urbanization and the Environment in International Perspectives,* edited by Richard Stren, Rodney White, and Joseph Whitney. Boulder, Colo.: Westview Press, 259–280. [4]

———. 1993. "Urban and Regional Development in China: Towards the 21st Century." Monograph No. 14, Hong Kong Institute of Asia-Pacific Studies, The Chinese University of Hong Kong (in Chinese). [5]

———. 1995. "Globalization and Asia's Urban and Regional Responses." Paper presented at the 1995 Pacific Rim Forum held in Bangkok, November 28–December 1. [1]

———. 1996. "Hong Kong's Hub Functions." In *Planning Hong Kong for the 21st Century,* edited by Anthony Gar-on Yeh. Hong Kong: Centre of Urban Planning and Environmental Management, University of Hong Kong, 143–161. [2]

———. 1998a. "The Promise and Peril of Globalization." *Progress in Human Geography* 22(4):475–477. [1]

———. 1998b. "To the Precipice and Back: Asia's Financial Turmoil." Paper presented at the workshop on Southeast Asia under Globalization, Academic Sinica, Taipei, April. [1,10]

———, ed. 1998c. *Urban Development in Asia: Retrospect and Prospect.* Hong Kong: Hong Kong Institute of Asia-Pacific Studies, The Chinese University of Hong Kong. [2]

———. 1998d. "Globalization and Southeast Asian Urbanism." Paper presented at the 30th Anniversary Conference of the Institute of Southeast Asian Studies, Singapore, July 30–August 1. [10]

———. 1998e. "Globalization and Regional Transformation in Pacific Asia." Paper presented at the Global Forum on Regional Development Policy held at the United Nations Center for Regional Development, Nagoya, December 1–4. **[epilogue]**

Yeung, Y. M., and David K. Y. Chu, eds. 1998. *Guangdong: Survey of a Province Undergoing Rapid Change.* 2nd ed. Hong Kong: Chinese University Press. [3,6,7,9]

Yeung, Yue-man, and Fu-chen Lo. 1996. "Global Restructuring and Emerging Urban Corridors in Pacific Asia." In *Emerging World Cities in Pacific Asia,* edited by Fu-chen Lo and Yue-man Yeung. Tokyo: United Nations University Press, 17–47. [2]

———. 1998. "Globalization and World City Formation in Pacific Asia." In *Globalization and the World of Large Cities,* edited by Fu-chen Lo and Yue-man Yeung. Tokyo: United Nations University Press, 155–173. [2,10]

Yeung, Y. M., and Sung Yun-wing, eds. 1996. *Shanghai: Transformation and Modernization under China's Open Policy.* Hong Kong: Chinese University Press. [6]

Yeung, Yue-man, and Xu-wei Hu, eds. 1992. *China's Coastal Cities: Catalysts for Modernization.* Honolulu: University of Hawaii Press. [2,5]

Yip, Paul S. F. 1995. *Suicides in Hong Kong 1981–1994.* Research Report Serial No. 94, Department of Statistics, The University of Hong Kong. [8]

Yuan, Geng. 1992. "The Transport Relation between Hong Kong and the South China Region in the 1990s Revisited." *Economic Reporter,* March 30, 5–9 (in Chinese). [4]

Zhang, Fudao, et al. 1989. "Urban Solid Waste in China: Current Problems and Solutions." *Chinese Geography and Environment* 2(1):54–67. [8]

Zhang, Xiangrong. 1992. "Economic Structural Reform and the Degree of Openness." In *Guangdong: "Open Door" Economic Development Strat-*

egy, edited by Toyojiro Maruya. ASEDP No. 19. Tokyo: Institute of Developing Economies, 1–17 (in Chinese). [6]

Zhang, Xing Quan. 1991. "Urbanization in China." *Urban Studies* 28(1):41–52. [5]

Zhang, Zin Hong. 1991. "The Economic Advantage of Large Cities: A Case Study of China's Urban Centres." *Habitat International* 15(4):171–181. [5]

Zheng, Caixiong. 1992. "Guangdong Determined to be Asia's Next Dragon." *China Daily,* July 18. [4]

Zheng, T. X. 1996. "Research on the Co-Operative Development of Infrastructure in the Pearl River Delta, Hong Kong and Macau." *Pearl River Delta Economy* 1:7–13 (in Chinese). [9]

Zheng, Tianxiang, and Ni Xiyuan. 1992. "Large-Scale Infrastructure Projects in Guangdong, Hong Kong and Macau in the 1990s." Unpublished research report, Zhongshan University (in Chinese). [4]

Zhong, Gongfu. 1989. "The Structural Characteristics and Effects of the Dyke-Pond System in China." *Outlook on Agriculture* 18(3):119–123. [8]

Zhou, Yixing. 1993. "Some New Trends of Chinese Urbanization in the 1990s." In *Urban and Regional Development in China: Towards the 21st Century, edited by* Yue-man Yeung. Monograph No. 14. Hong Kong: Hong Kong Institute of Asia-Pacific Studies, The Chinese University of Hong Kong, 105–131 (in Chinese). [5]

Zong, Lin. 1988. "Development and Control of Large Cities." In *A Preliminary Study on the Course of Urbanization in China,* edited by Wejun Ye, Zhang Bingshen, and Lin Jianing. Beijing: Chinese Prospect Press, 149–208 (in Chinese). [5]

———. 1993. "Experience and Prospect of Developing and Controlling China's Large Cities." In *Urban and Regional Development in China: Towards the 21st Century,* edited by Yue-man Yeung. Monograph No. 14. Hong Kong: Hong Kong Institute of Asia-Pacific Studies, The Chinese University of Hong Kong, 155–181 (in Chinese). [5]

Zou, Deci. 1990. "Review and Prospect of China's Urban Planning from 1980s to 1990s." Working paper, Centre of Urban Studies and Urban Planning, University of Hong Kong. [5]

Index

About the Author

Yue-man Yeung is professor of Geography, director of the Hong Kong Institute of Asia-Pacific Studies, and head of Shaw College of The Chinese University of Hong Kong. He received his university education in Hong Kong, Canada, and the United States, where he obtained a Ph.D. in geography at the University of Chicago. His rich and varied career has spanned teaching, research, international development, and university administration, being divided in Singapore, Canada, and Hong Kong. His wide-ranging research interests have recently focused on China's coastal cities, South China, globalization, and Asian cities. He has to his credit 21 books and 140 articles and book chapters. His latest publications include *Urban Development in Asia, Globalization and the World of Large Cities* (with Fu-chen Lo), and *Guangdong* (with David K. Y. Chu).